Hugh Bowlby Willson

Currency

The fundamental principles of monetary science postulated, explained, and applied

Hugh Bowlby Willson

Currency
The fundamental principles of monetary science postulated, explained, and applied

ISBN/EAN: 9783337313326

Printed in Europe, USA, Canada, Australia, Japan

Cover: Foto ©Suzi / pixelio.de

More available books at **www.hansebooks.com**

OR

THE FUNDAMENTAL PRINCIPLES

OF

MONETARY SCIENCE

POSTULATED, EXPLAINED, AND APPLIED

" Et sanguis et spiritus pecunia mortalibus "

" It is absurd, in any science to follow a mere written rule. . . . We should endeavor to follow what is right, and not what is established "

" The encroachments of the rich are more dangerous to the State than those of the poor." — ARISTOTLE

BY

HUGH BOWLBY WILLSON

NEW YORK

G. P. PUTNAM'S SONS

27 AND 29 WEST 23D STREET

1882

PREFACE.

A PORTION of the postulates on which this work is founded appeared in the winter of 1875–6 in "The Anglo-American Times," a journal published in London. My object was to direct attention to the desirability of embodying in a few simple, if not self-evident propositions, the ascertained and generally accepted principles of Monetary Science. Many friends and others for whose judgment I have much respect, to whom I had sent copies of the journal containing my articles, having expressed themselves warmly in favor of this plan of treating the money question, I determined to extend its scope, and to write the work I now have the honor to submit to the candid criticism of those who make economic science a study. One of the gentlemen referred to, Professor Bonamy Price of Oxford, an able analytical writer on Banking and Currency, in his usual frank and candid manner, wrote me promptly on receipt of the number of "The American Times" as follows : —

"So many thanks for your letter in 'The American Times.' It is exceedingly good; and I rejoice over it much, especially the postulates and principles. The 21st (35th in this work) is capital. I had the thought, but not definitely expressed. The meaning jumps on the reader, and masters him; and it is most true."

When I commenced my investigations on this subject
many years ago, it was my intention to write a sort of
history and synopsis of the theories and practices of
ancient and modern nations in respect to their currencies. This I soon found would occupy much more time
than I could then devote to the subject. Again, in the
winter of 1875–6 I took up the same idea; and, though
I felt that such a work would be of much utility, I
found on an examination of the authorities in the British
Museum, that I had not the time to carry out the plan.
Hence, I turned my attention to reasoning out the principles of the science of currency, and applying them to
practical purposes, with the hope of influencing thought
towards currency reform, in those countries where the
question is undergoing constant discussion. Such are
the circumstances that have led to the writing and publication of this work.

Finding in the present systems of issuing and supplying paper money, so much that is at variance with correct scientific principles, I have devoted much space to
attacking the prejudices and ignorance which uphold
them. No sound system can be established in any country without rooting out the "vested rights" of those who
make a profit out of issuing paper money. I have,
therefore, vigorously assailed the plan of delegating the
right to issue paper money to the Bank of England and
National Banks of the United States, on securities or
otherwise. The result of my deductions has been the
evolvement of a purely automatic method of supplying
both coined and paper money, — supply and demand

being the only motive power to be used in keeping the automaton in motion.

The attention of those who are laboring in the same field is directed to the circumstance, so often pointed out by Professor Price, that the "mercantile theory," which teaches that the first consideration of economists and legislators is to pursue measures that will accumulate the largest possible stores of the precious metals in a country, is still a fundamental doctrine in some minds, and exerts a powerful influence in the action of the Bank of England as well as of a large class of protectionists in America. The plan I contend for leaves these metals free to the distribution of the natural forces of industry and trade.

In conclusion, to the plan I have adopted in the treatment of the money question will be conceded the characteristic of novelty, and is put forward with the confident hope that it will lead others to perfect it. It is desirable to eliminate erroneous dogmas and fundamental errors, in order that a really correct system may be left as the result. Much has been done since the days of Adam Smith, but much still remains to be done.

H. B. W.

New York, May, 1879.

SYNOPSIS OF THE WORK.

CHAPTER V.

HOW THE VALUE OF MONEY IS SET AND REGULATED, AND
HOW IT DIFFERENTIATES OTHER VALUES.

CHAPTER VI.

'NOMISMA," OR LEGAL TENDER, AND BI-METALISM.

CHAPTER VII.

THE ORGANIZATION OF THE BANK OF ENGLAND. — THE LAW, THE FACT, AND THE SCIENCE OF THE CASE.

CHAPTER VIII.

PROFESSOR BONAMY PRICE ON THE BANK CHARTER.

CHAPTER XI.

MONEY AND BULLION. — WRONG THEORIES RESPECTING THEM.

CHAPTER XII.

POPULAR ERRORS RESPECTING THE BALANCE OF TRADE. — THE NEW MERCANTILE THEORY.

CHAPTER XIII.

MONEY, CURRENCY, LOANS, AND CHECKS. — TRUE AND
FALSE PRINCIPLES.

CHAPTER XIV.

MONEY, CURRENCY, AND BANKING, AND THE ECONOMY OF
PAPER MONEY CONSIDERED.

CHAPTER XV.

BANKS OF ISSUE, DEPOSIT, AND DISCOUNT. — THEIR ORI-
GIN. — THE ISSUE OF PAPER MONEY NOT LEGITIMATE
BANKING. — CANNOT PROPERLY BE DELEGATED TO
BANKS.

CHAPTER XVII.

"THE PRIMARY OBJECT OF PAPER MONEY IS TO SUPPLY
A BETTER TOOL OF INDUSTRY THAN METALLIC MONEY.
— INCIDENTALLY ONLY CAN IT BE PROPERLY TREATED
AS TRADING POWER, OR RESOURCES " (POSTULATE 49).

CHAPTER XVIII.

SUGGESTIONS FOR STATE ISSUE DEPARTMENTS IN GREAT BRITAIN AND THE UNITED STATES, AND CONSIDERATIONS CONNECTED THEREWITH.

CHAPTER XIX.

SIR ROBERT PEEL'S POSITION ON THE NOTE ISSUE. — MR. GLADSTONE CLAIMS THAT IT BELONGS TO THE STATE. — WHEREIN THE ACT OF 1844 HAS FAILED.

CHAPTER XX.

BANKING AND CURRENCY IN THE UNITED STATES. — EVILS
OF A SYSTEM OF UNLIMITED ISSUE OF NOTES. — CEN-
TENNIAL ADDRESS. — ONE HUNDRED YEARS OF BANKING
IN THE UNITED STATES.

CHAPTER XXI.

THE NATIONAL BANKING SYSTEM OF THE UNITED STATES. —ITS ORIGIN. — GOOD AND BAD FEATURES, AND POSITION IN AMERICAN POLITICS.

CHAPTER XXII.

CURRENCY AND BANKING IN THE UNITED STATES MADE SUBSERVIENT TO PARTY ENDS AND INTERESTS.

CHAPTER XXIII.

CURRENCY AND BANKING IN FRANCE. — THE BANK OF FRANCE.

CHAPTER XXIV.

HOW THE VOLUME OF CURRENCY AND OTHER THINGS
AFFECT THE MARKET OR EXCHANGE VALUE OF COM-
MODITIES. — PRESENT INFLATED CONDITION OF THE
CURRENCY AND BANK DISCOUNTS IN THE UNITED STATES
(MARCH, 1879), AND WHAT IT PORTENDS. — NICHOLAS
BIDDLE ON CURRENCY.

CHAPTER XXV.

GENERAL SUMMARY OF THE ARGUMENT. — THE MONEY
PROBLEM TO BE SOLVED BY A UNIVERSAL MONETARY
SYSTEM. — PLAN FOR SUCH A SYSTEM SUGGESTED. —
GREAT BRITAIN AND AMERICA TO COMBINE WITH THE
LATIN NATIONS AS THE INITIATION OF THE SYSTEM.

CHAPTER XXVI.

THE PROPOSED UNIVERSAL MONETARY SYSTEM FURTHER CONSIDERED. — SUBSIDIARY COINS TO BE CONVERTIBLE.

CHAPTER XXVII.

CHAPTER XXVIII.

CHAPTER XXIX.

INDUSTRIAL CRISES CONTINUED. — THEIR EFFECTS AND REMEDIES.

CHAPTER XXX.

INDUSTRIAL CRISES CONTINUED. — HOW "PROTECTION TO
DOMESTIC INDUSTRY" COUNTERACTS THE NATURAL
ORDER OF THINGS, — FIRST CAUSING EXTREMELY HIGH
PRICES AND OVER-SUPPLY; THEN, BY RE-ACTION, EX-
TREMELY LOW PRICES: THUS SUPERINDUCING AND
INTENSIFYING CRISES.

CHAPTER XXXI.

INDUSTRIAL CRISES. — THEIR CAUSES AND REMEDIES FUR-
THER CONSIDERED. — THE CONCLUSION.

NOTES.

APPENDIX I.

APPENDIX II.

VIEWS OF EMINENT AMERICAN STATESMEN AND ECONOMISTS ON THE ISSUE OF PAPER CURRENCY.

MEMOIR OF THE AUTHOR.

THE author of the accompanying work was by birth a Canadian, the son of a distinguished parliamentarian.

His father, the late Hon. John Willson of Saltfleet, Ont., was born of English parentage, in the State of New Jersey, in August, 1776. There were two brothers, Hugh and John, who after the death of their father, and accompanied by their guardian, in the year 1790 removed to Canada, and took up their abode at Niagara, where they remained until the majority of John, the younger, in 1797.

They then chose the beautiful shore of Lake Ontario for a home, settling the district of Saltfleet, where they resided with their families and the friends they had gathered about them, until their deaths, the elder in 1858, the latter in 1860.

They were men of master minds, rarely fitted by nature for the life-work before them; vigorous intellects, an intense thirst for knowledge, and indefatigable perseverance, coupled with keen sense of justice, and innate refinement of character. They could not do otherwise than take prominent parts in the country they settled, becoming the champions of both civil and religious lib-

erty ; and while the elder brother toiled for the good of
the church, which was so dear to his heart, the ambition of the younger, naturally expanding with the growth
and development of the country of his adoption, drifted
into, and fought stanchly through a lifetime for, political
principles.

As early as 1808, so prominently had his superior
abilities asserted themselves, he was called to represent,
not his own borough in Parliament, but one at some
distance from his home, — the West Riding of York (or,
as it was afterwards known, Halton), and, being duly
elected, took his seat accordingly, for the fifth Parliament
of Upper Canada.   He afterwards represented his own
district for a great number of years, both in the House
of Assembly and also the Legislative Council, being
speaker for a long time, and exercising an influence
second to none in the province.

To him is Canada indebted for its common-school Act.
He was its originator, and kept it steadily before him for
a series of years, until, with untiring perseverance, he
succeeded in accomplishing the cherished work of his
life, by casting the vote through which it became a law.
He was at the time speaker : there was a tie-vote.   He
promptly placed a brother member in his chair, and
descending to the floor, so closely was the battle fought,
gave the vote which made it a success.   He warmly
supported all public improvements with the entire spirit
and energy of his noble nature, thereby greatly assisting
in the development of the resources of his country.   He
was a man so sound in principles, so pure in action, so

true in allegiance, and so upright in character, that though he lived through a rebellion, and parted with the friends of his early political life in the contest, — at one time fighting almost single handed, in the Legislative Council, the crafty Lord Sydenham in the Act for the Union of the Provinces, which, as a member of the Assembly, he had defeated seventeen years previously, and which he had *always* opposed on the grounds of difference in laws, religion, language, and institutions, — the faintest taint of political corruption *never* reached his name. He carried to his grave the boast that he was the recipient of no favor from his government that he had not earned at the hands of his fellow-countrymen at the hustings, and which had not been accorded to him by acclamation.

Rising as he did by his personal ambition and exertions to the zenith of power and place, his name can never be disassociated from his country, but must always shine out in its history through forty years of parliamentary life as that of one of the most remarkable men, as well as one of the most distinguished statesman of his age.

Of such a father was born, in the early autumn of 1813, the writer of this work, at the old homestead built in 1797 on the pleasant shores of Lake Ontario. He was the second son, and perhaps of all the numerous family the one who most nearly resembled his father in intellectual ability. At all events, the path in life selected secured to him more time for scholarly attainment, and a larger development of his natural tastes and powers, than any of his brothers.

After receiving the best education which his country afforded, he chose the law as a profession. Instead of seeking preferment through the power and influence of his father, then in the zenith of his fame, he went manfully to work, to hew out unaided, as his father had done before him, a name and a place for himself. He possessed an element of character which he did not inherit from his father, — the disposition to compare mankind, not only through the medium of books, nor within the circumscribed limits afforded his father in a life-long residence in one country, but an ambition, through travel, to widen the scope of vision, whilst enlarging and strengthening his powers of mind. He was a close observer, a deep thinker, and a logical reasoner. He used all his God-endowed gifts for the benefit of his fellow creatures.

He commenced the study of law at the Law Society of Upper Canada, Osgoode Hall, in 1836; was called to the bar at the Easter term in 1842, and began the practice of law as a barrister. But his health becoming enfeebled through a severe attack of inflammatory rheumatism, the result of exposure in a terrible storm, forced him almost in the outset of his professional life to relinquish his work, and seek for a time relief in a milder clime. He went to the West Indies, and for nearly two years lived the greater part of the time in his yacht upon the southern ocean, visiting all the islands, and amusing himself by writing descriptions of all that he saw. Those letters were given to the public through the medium of "The New York Albion," — attracting considerable attention,—and to that journal he was for many years afterwards a constant contributor.

Upon his return to his native land, he resumed his profession, taking soon a prominent position in the town of Hamilton, which place he had chosen for his residence. He became closely identified with it, and worked zealously for it, even to the close of his life. He purchased a large tract of land contiguous to the city, which was afterwards incorporated within its limits, which he laid out with great taste, and embellished with avenues of fine trees, blocks of fine dwellings, etc. He was the mainspring of all improvement, a public benefactor, giving his time, his means, and his labor without stint to the work.

He was one of the originators of the Great Western Railway of Canada, and did more than any other man to make it a success, working persistently for municipal aid, which formed the nucleus of the fund with which it was subsequently constructed. Through his instrumentality was built the first large hotel *à-la* American. Waterworks for the city were projected and public libraries. The second daily newspaper in Canada owed its life to his energy. He held unmistakably "the pen of a ready writer," and it was ever prompt in the cause of humanity. He organized in 1846 the first conservative journal west of Toronto, in the semi-weekly "Spectator" of Hamilton, edited by the late Robert R. Smiley of that city, giving him at all times his influence and aid, and, when the editor was in failing health, taking entire charge of it for some months before his death.

He was chosen by his fellow-townsmen, in conjunction

with Mr. Tiffany, a prominent lawyer of that place with whom he was associated, to proceed to Washington in the winter of 1847 and 1848, to place before Congress the Reciprocity Treaty. During that winter, through the courtesy of the English Minister, he was presented to the lady who afterwards became his wife. He was successful with his treaty, which many years afterwards, at the period of his death, he was earnestly seeking to renew, with increased advantages to his countrymen, as the letter which appeared in "The New York Herald," a few days previous to his death, will testify ; for, whilst he lay ill, his home was besieged by reporters of the various New York journals, seeking information from the dying man, who was no longer able to give them items, the matter having been placed by him in the hands of the honorable members of Congress, Fernando Wood and S. S. Cox of this city, for legislation in that body.

He placed in the English and other European markets the bonds and debentures of many of the largest undertakings, not only of Canada, but of the north-western States' railroads ; and his work unconsciously, as it were, connecting itself with great enterprises, for which his powers seemed peculiarly adapted, it came to pass unintentionally that his professional life passed unobservedly from him, being superseded by that which the exigency of the times and the development of his country required from the fine perception and indefatigable perseverance of a leader in the cause of science, advancement, and political economy.

He went frequently abroad, in fact, and resided there

often for lengthened periods, doing the work that less advanced minds would have found it impossible to accomplish, but always with a modesty and single-heartedness most remarkable.

He was appointed by the Canadian Government one of their Commissioners to the Universal Exposition of Paris in 1855. During one of his prolonged sojourns in London he published a work on the "Science of Shipbuilding," which was most favorably mentioned by the English Press, and brought him prominently into the notice of the Royal Society of Naval Architecture, from which body he received an invitation to deliver before them a series of lectures, which pleasant duty he accepted, as it was greatly in accordance with his taste, it having been with him for many years a favorite study. The ships of the well-known "White Star Line" are built largely after his models and designs, as given in those lectures to the English public.

His pen was never idle : he watched with great interest the changes taking place from time to time in his own country, and wrote extensively for "The Quebec Chronicle" and other journals on the trade of the country, among other things a series of letters on the "Military Defences of Canada," which was afterwards published in pamphlet form. Soon after the close of the American Rebellion, he made, at the request of the governor of North Carolina, a most interesting and exhaustive report on the wild lands of that State, with a view to their development, through Swiss colonization, to take the place of the old-time slave labor. For many years he

had been a member of the American Institute, and delivered from time to time before them lectures upon the
issues of the day most prominent and interesting to the
public.   The lectures and plans of one season's labor
were embodied in a work entitled "High Speed River
Steamers." Another in March, 1870, "A Plea for Uncle
Sam's Money," or "Greenbacks *versus* Bank Notes;" in
October, 1874, "Money *versus* Capital and Loans;" and
again, at the request of the Congressional Committee on
the depression in labor and business in 1879, a work
entitled "Industrial Crises, their Causes and Remedies,"
printed at governmental cost.

He was a thoroughly well-read man, an accomplished
scholar, and a genial gentleman.   He was in constant
correspondence with the prominent men of the age, not
only in America, but Europe, and through this interesting
medium kept himself thoroughly informed upon all the
great events of the times.   He was a man of feeble
health, having suffered the greater part of his life from
an organic disease of the heart; and it was only by the
greatest prudence, and carefully hoarded and judiciously
used powers of mind and body, that he was enabled to
accomplish so much.   The last year of his life was given
almost exclusively to the writing of the accompanying
work.   In home life he was most lovable, a kind, indul-
gent, affectionate Christian, having been a member of the
church of England since his early manhood.

He passed from us after an illness of five days of
pleuro-pneumonia, on the 29th of April, 1880, and in
accordance with a request, oft repeated, to be interred

near his father, was laid reverently to rest by his brother
Masons, beside his honored parent in the country church-
yard at Grimsby, Ont., near the place of his birth.

> . . . "Sustained and soothed
> By an unfaltering trust, approached the grave
> Like one who draws the drapery of his couch
> About him, and lies down to pleasant dreams."

HUGH R. WILLSON.

INTRODUCTION.

I HAVE endeavored in this work to so qualify and limit
the meaning of terms, as to prevent the possibility of misconception. The habit of using the same term "indiscriminately," as Mr. Mill deliberately does, or in several
different senses, as Mr. Bageat has done, through confusion of thought, in reference to money, greatly detracts
from the writings of a majority of received authorities.
Archbishop Whately observes on this subject, "The great
defect of Adam Smith, and our economists in general, is
the want of definiteness. . . . The terms of this science
being drawn from common discourse, and seldom carefully defined by the writers who employ them, hardly one
of them has any settled and determined meaning ; and
their ambiguities are perpetually overlooked."

Mr. Henry Dunning McLeod, whose use of expressions and bad logic I have had occasion to criticise,
after quoting the above paragraph, severely, but not too
much so, remarks, —

"Cobbett wrote an English grammar, in which all the
solecisms and blunders were drawn from the speeches of
peers, and members of Parliament : so we might undertake to write a complete treatise on logic, and every
example of logical fallacy should be drawn from the
published opinions, either spoken or written, of Mr.

Ricardo, Mr. McCulloch, Mr. John Stuart Mill, Mr. Samuel Jones Loyd (Lord Overstone), Col. Torrens, Sir Robert Peel, and Sir Archibald Allison, on the subject of currency."

It would be difficult to find so stupendous a blunder or so complete a misapplication of a term as to treat bills of exchange, or any interest-bearing security, or bankers' checks, as currency. Trading or purchasing power they are; but in no sense of the words, and by no perversion of principles, are such securities money, or currency, — the latter embracing the former. Nevertheless, Mr. McLeod and a host of others have broadly claimed for them the function of currency. Bills of exchange are simple obligations set down in writing to specify something to be paid or received; and, when "discounted," the proceeds are capital, trading or purchasing power. "Trading Power" is the term I have adopted; as that also covers money, currency, and deposits of all kinds with bankers, made available by checks. McLeod, again, after defining "price" to mean the amount agreed to be paid and accepted on a bargain for the purchase and sale of an article or quantity of articles, and "value" as the average of such bargains, continually uses the terms indiscriminately.

There is no class of writers who so continually abuse economic terms, or who beget so much confusion of thought, and do so much injury to science and legislation, as the writers of "money articles" for the press. These gentlemen invariably mix up, in the most indiscriminate manner, "currency," "money," and "loans." They persistently confound the "money market" with the "loan market," and "capital" with "money," when they speak of the rate of interest on money instead of on capital or trading power. The idea that when a man makes a loan he borrows capital, not money, never occurs to them.

The late Mr. Bageat, the banker, and proprietor of "The London Economist," Professor Price says, used the word "money" in six different senses. The word "intrinsic," as applied to value, is another prolific instance of the misconception of terms. It is continually used for market value, which is what economists have chiefly to do with. "Intrinsic" refers to quality, or the fitness of a commodity for any particular use or uses. It is what Adam Smith defines, "value in use." But this sort of value does not determine "market value." The market value of diamonds and other jewels is many times that of gold, but gold is vastly more valuable in use. The same is true of steel and iron as compared with gold. The latter is several thousand times more valuable, in the estimate of the market, than steel; but the latter is infinitely more valuable intrinsically. The one kind of value relates to quality, and is innate ; the other to the price in the markets. The intrinsic value of gold consists in its peculiar adaptation for money and jewelry.

In Chap. II. I have treated specially of some of the terms, and the principles defined by them, and hope that I have in all cases avoided the habit of using the same word to convey distinctly separate meanings, meant to be conveyed.

CURRENCY.

CHAPTER I.

PRINCIPLES AND POSTULATES OF MONETARY SCIENCE.

1. Money is any thing possessing market value, which all the members of a community, by common consent, are willing to accept in payment for their labor, goods, lands, etc.

2. All civilized nations, by such common consent, have fabricated their money, or the chief part of it, out of gold and silver, or one of these metals, because of their peculiar fitness for coinage and use.

3. Money is a commodity, and possesses a market value of its own, independent of the material of which it is made ; and, like such material, its market value is governed by its volume, or supply and demand.

4. The value of money, or of any other commodity, is in the inverse ratio of its volume (Chaps. IV., XXIV.).

5. By combining the two values, that is, the value of the material (in the case of the precious metals) in a coin, and making the coin and the bullion interconvertible, without charge for coinage, or limiting such charge to the cost of coinage, the value of the coin and the metal will always tend to equilibrium.

6. Money, by its trading or exchange value, distributes

goods from producers to consumers, and abolishes barter, or the exchange of commodities in specific quantities.

7. Money, being made legal tender for debts by the state, and universally accepted as the measure of the value of all other things, serves to differentiate the value of labor, and all other things having market value in respect to each other (Chap. XXVII.).

8. The stamp of the mint or state serves only to establish the fineness and denomination of the coins, and the legal value set on it by law, but adds nothing to its market value.

9. The denominations so stamped on the various coins, constitute a scale for measuring and differentiating the value of other things, similar in principle to the scales used in measuring length, capacity, and weight.

10. A shilling cannot be made to circulate or exchange for a sovereign or half-eagle by transferring the stamp of the mint from the latter coins to the former ; nor can a sovereign be held in circulation as a shilling by being stamped as a shilling. The "legal-tender" iron money of Sparta passed for its market value as iron.

11. Trading (usually termed purchasing) Power consists of the market value of the products of labor in course of preparation, and transmission from producers to consumers, and is utilized and dealt in, in the loan market, by means of bills of exchange, and other securities representing the value of goods, and money, which forms a part of Trading Power.

12. Paper Money, if sold for its nominal or "face value" in metallic money, to banks and the public, will never depreciate, or be in excess of the requirements of the people, so long as an adequate amount of metallic money, to be determined by experience, is held to insure its convertibility under all circumstances.

13. Inconvertible Paper Money, whether legal tender

or not, is regulated in its market value wholly by supply and demand, or by limitation of its volume (Chap. V. pars. 14, 15).

14. Inconvertible Paper Money, or Debased or Over-valued Metallic Money, when made Legal Tender, and issued in full supply of the requirements of industry, invariably drives a superior or properly valued currency out of circulation. This is known as the Gresham Law, from the fact that it was first proclaimed by Sir Thomas Gresham.

15. Whenever an inconvertible paper currency has come to fill all the channels of circulation, its Trading Power becomes unstable, and subject to fluctuations in its market value.

16. When the market value of such a currency has fallen below the standard of metallic money, its Trading Power will be in the inverse ratio of its volume.

17. By withdrawing from circulation a percentage of its volume equal to the percentage of its depreciation, the remainder will return to par.

18. A state issue and sale of notes for gold, at par, all other issues being prohibited, will prevent an over-supply, and avert depreciation (postulate 12).

19. A State Issue Department, by purchasing for coin or notes, all the bullion or metal used as a standard of value offered to it, and coining the same, will be an automatic regulator of both kinds of money, metallic and paper, under the action of supply and demand (Chaps. XVII., XVIII.).

20. When a state refuses to receive its own inconvertible notes in payment of any part of the taxes levied on the public, it discredits and lowers the value of its obligations *pro tanto* (Chap. XXI. p. 4).

21. When a superior currency has been driven out of circulation by an inferior legal-tender currency, it will

always be quoted at a premium. When the inferior currency is not legal tender, the reverse will happen, as in the case of California, where the people, by universal agreement, refused to buy or sell by the paper standard.

22. When the gap between the two currencies has not become too wide through the redundancy of paper issues, the trading power of the paper, if the volume is held stationary, will be gradually raised to par by the natural laws of industry, or the increased demand for currency, caused by the growth and development of business. This is what has recently happened in the United States.

23. When the total amount of currency actually required by the people to conduct their industries, as indicated by the natural laws, consists partly of gold coin of full weight and fineness, and partly silver coin, overvalued, and partly of inconvertible paper, held at par of gold, by limitation of issue (which condition of things has existed for some years in France), the three kinds of currency will circulate on the same level of market value, and will possess equal trading power.

24. If either the overvalued silver, or the legal-tender paper, or the two together, be so increased as to make in themselves a full supply for industrial purposes, the properly valued gold currency will be driven out of circulation in conformity with the so-called "Gresham Law," and gold coin will be dealt in as bullion. If the irredeemable paper be still further increased in volume, as in the United States in 1862, so as to overrun the demands of industry for currency, the silver coin will follow the gold, and be dealt in at its bullion value, under the action of the natural laws.

25. The first indication of an excess of irredeemable paper currency becomes apparent by a rise in the foreign exchanges and a corresponding premium in gold.

26. Theory and Practice coincide in demonstrating

that gold is the most convenient and the best known metal, suited to coinage, for the purposes of a standard measure of value (Chap. V.).

27. In like manner silver has been demonstrated to be the best metal out of which to fabricate the chief part of subsidiary coins, and copper and nickel for those of still lower values.

28. An inconvertible paper currency depends wholly on its volume for its market value, and is deficient in the most important element of a sound currency, namely, the utmost attainable stability.

29. The ratio between the market values of gold and silver, or any other two products of labor, or commodities, where there is no limitation of production, or, in the case of the precious metals, of coinage, cannot be established by law of Parliament, or of all nations; because the natural laws in the long run assert their ascendency over human laws.

30. All legislative attempts to set an arbitrary and fictitious value on money or commodities have ultimately failed in free communities, for the people cannot be compelled to part with their labor or goods without adequate value.

31. When a depreciated currency has been brought up to the par of gold by the methods of contraction mentioned in former postulates, the superior or natural currency will be drawn back to the country, and, together with new coinage, will enter into circulation along with the paper.[1]

32. The quantity of money, metallic and paper, under a well-regulated monetary system, used in conducting the

[1] The large importations of American gold coin (which was sent abroad during the late war to purchase goods and supplies) during the year 1879, amounting to over seventy millions of dollars, including bullion, notwithstanding a home production of that metal of fully thirty-five million more and an equal value of silver, proves this postulate.

industries of the people, can only be properly regulated by giving the utmost freedom to the action of the great natural law of supply and demand ; and its volume does not, in a commercial country, vary much from three to five per cent of the gross sum of trading power, of which it forms a part.

33. The money market, the stock market, the loan market, and the coin, produce, and all other markets or places where any thing is sold and bought, are separate and distinct from each other, both in practice and principle, and should always be so treated by writers and speakers (Chap. XIII. pars. 6, 7).

34. The prerogative or right to coin money and regulate its legal denominations, and to issue paper money, belongs to the state, and rests on the same authority and necessity as the right of the state to regulate measures of weight, length, and capacity (Chap. XXI.).[1]

35. Commodities in transit from producers to consumers, or ultimate purchasers, represented by bills of exchange, bills of lading, warehousemen's receipts, bank credits, checks, and other devices invented by bankers and merchants to facilitate the transfer of debts and credits or property, constitute the bulk of the floating capital, or trading power, dealt in, in the loan (improperly called the money) market.

36. Floating or trading power, other than that specified in the last postulate, consists of money and capital

[1] Daniel Webster, the eminent American statesman, in his speech on the currency delivered in the United States Senate, 28th September, 1837, postulated this proposition in the following striking words : —

" It is the constitutional duty of government to see that a proper currency, suitable to the circumstances of the times and to the wants of trade and business, as well as to the payment of the debts due to the government, be maintained and preserved, — a currency of general credit, and capable of aiding the operations of government so far as those operations may be conducted by means of the circulating medium; and that these are duties, therefore, devolving on Congress, in relation to currency, beyond the mere regulation of the gold and silver coins."

accumulated from the savings of labor, the surplus of income over expenditure, and all other sources not yet invested in more permanent things, such as lands, houses, factories, steamships, and all manner of joint-stock companies' shares, or continuing undertakings, which perpetuate themselves under prudent management, or are not destroyed in use.

37. The floating capital specified in the last postulate is commonly held by banks, loan companies, discount houses, and merchants receiving deposits, and hence forms a part of the great fund or ocean of trading power, or capital, called the loan market, and is continually seeking more permanent forms of investment; and these constitute the "safety valve" of that market, by diminishing over-speculation (note III.).

38. The true and natural regulator of the rate of interest, or price paid for capital, is the law of supply and demand.

39. All artificial or legislative methods intended to fix the rate of interest, or regulate the price of capital, or wages, or hours of labor, or its products, are violations of the natural laws of industry, and fundamentally wrong, and result from ignorance (Chap. XIII. par. 10).

40. Supply and demand in monetary science are the opposing sides of the equation between production and consumption. Supply may be stated as representing labor and capital, aided and set in motion by skill and machinery; and demand as representing consumption or investment (Chap. IV., on value).

41. There can be no selling without buying; and each party to a bargain for the exchange of things having value, is both buyer and seller.

42. The domestic trade of a country is a trade carried on between the individual, corporations, and firms of such country, amongst themselves (Chap. XII., on balance of trade).

43. Foreign trade is a trade carried on between the individuals, corporations, and firms of one country with those of other countries.

44. All trade continually tends to balance itself, or to equilibrium; hence, the so-called "balance of trade" between nations is merely a matter of account between trading firms, individuals, and corporations, which always balances itself, with the same accuracy as the two sides of a merchant's or banker's ledger. Hence, the assumption that the foreign trade of a country can be permanently in favor of, or against it, is a fundamental error and a delusion (Chap. XII.).

45. All taxes and restrictions imposed by law, or by corporations possessed of large financial power, on one or more classes of foreign commodities, for the advantage and encouragement of those engaged in their production at home, are violations of the natural laws of industry; and the laws imposing such taxes and restrictions are mere usurpations, by the crafty and powerful, of the natural and inalienable rights of man.

46. The true, fundamental, and self-evident principles of trade are to buy and borrow in the cheapest, and sell and lend in the dearest markets, domestic or foreign, — all other things, such as the character of the pay and the security, being equal. The laws of nature, like the laws of nature's God, know no boundaries.

47. All sound trade is founded on the theory of mutual and reciprocal profit and advantage to the parties concerned (Chap. XII.).

48. Every thing dealt in, in the domestic and foreign markets, exerts an influence on the price of capital, labor, and commodities (the "precious metals" included), in the exact ratios of their gross market values respectively, or, in the proportion that their respective gross market values bear to the sum total of value as estimated by the measure of money (Chap. XI.).

49. The primary object and end of paper money is to supply the people with a better and more convenient and available tool of industry than metallic money (Chap. XIII. par. 12, Chap. XV. par. 13, and Chap. XVII.).

50. Sound practice and theory demand that the profit derived from the issue of paper money shall be regarded only as *incidental* and *secondary ;* and the delegating, by the state, the right to issue paper money to corporations or individuals, without payment in full to the nation, is fundamentally wrong (Chap. XV. par. 13).

51. When the state delegates its prerogative to a class of corporations to issue paper money, or lends "national currency" to such corporations, at a price below the market price of capital, and permits such corporate bodies to regulate the volume of such issues, instead of leaving it to the natural regulator, supply and demand, it violates the most important of the natural laws, the law of equal rights (Chap. XIII. par. 11).

52. The notes of a state or bank, not issued on gold, cannot properly be made legal tender ; and no notes can properly be treated by the issuer as good cash reserve against liabilities.

53. The Issue Department of the Bank of England is, by operation of law, a state department managed by a committee of directors of that bank, on its premises ; and the bank, by a bargain made with the state a century and three-quarters ago, has all its proprietary capital invested in public securities, and is enabled to own the face value of such investment, in paper money, not covered by metal, which it is most obviously improperly allowed to issue, and which constitutes its trading "reserve" (chapters on Theory and Practice of the Bank of England).

54. The national banks of the United States have, with only a few exceptions, the whole or greater part of their

capital invested in government securities, and are enabled
to own ninety per cent of the face of such securities in
money or " national currency," which compels them to
rely on depositors, or other folks' capital, for cash reserve ; which is an absurdity, and leads to over-issues and
inflation.

55. The plan of allowing banks to issue paper money
on securities, is one whereby a man can possess himself
of a valuable investment, and at the same time have
its value in money; which is absurd, and is known as
" Lawism," after its most distinguished advocate, the
eminent Scotch financier, John Law.

56. Metallic money represents and measures value.

57. Convertible paper money represents metallic money.

58. Inconvertible legal-tender paper money represents
nothing but the necessities of the people for currency,
from which it derives its ability to circulate (*vide* Mr. J.
B. McCulloch's notes on the Wealth of Nations).

59. Bills of exchange and other like securities represent the value of labor performed, or goods and property
sold (postulate 35, Chap. III. pars. 14, 15).

60. The issuing of paper money is not a part of banking, nor is it in any manner connected with the proper
and legitimate business of a banker (Chaps. XV., XVI.,
XVII. par. 16).

61. Paper money can only safely and properly be intrusted to the issue and management of the state through
a department made independent of the treasury and of
party and business influences other than supply and
demand, and should be issued only in payment of metal
offered for coinage (Chap. XVIII. par. 9).

62. How much, if any, of the accumulation of metal,
or metallic money, received in payment of notes, may be
safely used for governmental purposes, such as the payment of the public debt, can only be determined by

observation and experience on the part of the managers (Chap. XIV. par. 13, also Chaps. XIX., XXVI.).

63. Currency is only a term used to indicate money in some form, and ought always to be limited and defined in its use or meaning; and in no case can it be properly held to cover bills of exchange or any interest-bearing security (Chap. XIII.).

64. Banks and bankers are intermediary agents, or brokers, between producers and consumers (Professor Price on Banking, and Chap. III. par. 13).

65. The principal business of a banker is to turn the market value of goods, in course of production and distribution, into trading power, by " discounting " bills and other securities founded on goods or growing out of industry; and *receiving* and *lending* the accumulated savings of past industries (Chap. III. par. 13, Chap. XIV. .par. 3, and Chap. XV.).

66. Nearly all the advantages inuring to society from banking have proceeded from banks of deposit and discount; while nearly all the evils inflicted on mankind by banks are *directly traceable* to banks of issue, and the over-issues of paper money, and excessive loans (Chap. XV. par. 3).

67. Market value is determined and governed by supply and demand; which is the resultant or combined effect of competition among productive laborers, aided by capital, skill, and machinery on the one hand, and competition among buyers for consumption on the other hand (Chap. XVI.).

68. Labor, goods, and all other things offered for sale, are continually seeking trading power, or capital; and trading power, on the other hand, is continually seeking labor, etc., for the purpose of being exchanged (Chap. XI. pars. 8–10).

69. Bullion is never used to settle, either domestic or

foreign exchange balances, so long as any other com·
modity will afford a profit. It differs in no way, in
scientific or practical effect, from other commodities, as
an article of trade (chapter on Balance of Trade).

70. In the general trade of the world, bullion, as a
rule, affords the smallest profit of any commodity to
dealers : hence comparatively few make the business a
specialty.

71. There is a most obvious distinction between currency and finance ; the one being a *tool* of industry, the
other a *method*, or process for conducting business operations of nations, states, corporations, private firms, and
individuals.   Hence, as a logical corollary, the issue of
notes should be placed beyond the influences of those
who manage finance, which aims at creating and using
resources (Chap. XXV.).

CHAPTER II.

LABOR, CAPITAL, WEALTH, SKILL, AND MACHINERY.

1. THESE terms and the conceptions they embody may
be said to form the chief staples of all works on Political Economy.   They occur in almost every page, if not
paragraph, of such treatises.   As material elements they
constitute the great forces which, by long and systematic
action, have built up the whole material, if not moral,
structure of civilized society.   The application of these
forces to this end — that is, to securing to mankind the
largest amount of material comfort and moral culture,
which are the foundation of true happiness and content-
ment — may be assumed to mark the line between civilized and uncivilized man.   The science of Political
Economy, which instructs us in the best methods of em-

ploying and governing these mighty forces, is one of the
very highest import, and ought to form a part of the system of education in all schools, public and private, high
and low, and of all students whose capacities are equal to
comprehension of such topics as it embraces.   There is,
I regret to be obliged to say, one serious obstacle in the
way of "general diffusion of knowledge" on this most
important branch of education.   It is the want of a well-
arranged and compact system, so compiled as to embody
in simple self-evident propositions, or postulates, generally accepted and demonstrated truths.   The want of
such an authoritative work still leaves us at the mercy
of numerous speculative writers and instructors, who cling
with untiring pertinacity to theories exploded and overthrown a hundred years ago by Adam Smith, in his great
work "The Wealth of Nations."   On the one hand, we
have the old "mercantile theory," which held, that the
chief aim of a nation should be to maintain by legislative enactments, controlling the private rights and industries of individuals and communities, such an industrial
system as will attract the largest possible amount of the
precious metals to its shores.   The exchanges, according
to this class of philosophers, must be so "acted upon"
by the Bank of England, or the Bank of France, or the
Treasury or National Banks, of this, that, or the other
country, as to override and control the natural laws of
trade and industry, and thus retain in or attract to their
vaults a certain quantity of gold as a tangible evidence
of wealth.   On this subject I shall have more to say
hereafter.   On the other hand, we have another set of
philosophers, who propose to cut loose from metal altogether, and have only stamped pieces of paper, having
no inherent value, to measure values generally, and circulate and distribute all the valuable commodities of the
world, — a currency, in fact, depending wholly for its
market value on its volume.

2. With these few general remarks I set out upon the consideration of the terms set at the head of this chapter, and the forces they embody, so far as they bear on the subject of monetary science, as a starting-point ; and, to mark the importance of the subject-matter of this chapter, I submit the following formula or proposition as fundamental : " The civilization of a country is always in the exact ratio of the quantity of labor, capital, and machinery employed in the production of wealth, and the degree of skill, and freedom from artificial and legislative restraints, imposed on their ' employment.' "

3. In respect to these great elements, or forces of civilization, a full and completely reasoned-out system, founded on accurate analysis, would give us just what is so much needed to perfect the labors of Adam Smith, and others who have since his time endeavored to finish what he so well began. Here let me disclaim any purpose to attempt such an undertaking. I only aim in these pages to apply certain general principles, which I have postulated for convenience of application and reference, to the present defective .monetary systems of two or three of the leading commercial nations of the world. In doing so, I shall use such powers as I possess in analyzing these systems, and pointing out remedies which seem to me to lie on the very surface, and are capable of application without disturbing the industries of any one of the communities in question, and bearing as lightly as possible on mere ignorant prejudices. I shall insist : 1st, That we must get absolutely rid of all artificial interferences with the natural law of demand and supply, whether they emanate from banks, combinations of capital of any kind, or the state. 2d, That gold is the best material out of which to fabricate our money so far as it is used as a standard of value. 3d, That the state rightfully reserves to itself the power or prerogative to supply

all the metallic money needed. 4th, That paper money, being only a more convenient tool of commerce and industry, shall, for the same reasons, be also supplied by the state, and be issued directly to the people in payment of metal for coinage. 5th, That the state shall create a department clothed with adequate powers, and supplied with abundant resources, to maintain the convertibility of all paper money thus issued to the public on presentation to such department, or its agencies, in case any of the metal received for paper shall be sold. 6th, That neither banks nor commercial houses of any kind shall be employed as agents of the state for the issue and redemption of such paper money as the public shall require. 7th, That such state department shall not be under the control or influence of the minister or secretary of finance. 8th, That the money department shall be the custodian of all taxes and loans raised by the state, which shall be paid in by the officers or agents collecting or raising the same, and shall be checked out, under authority of law, by the departments, as at present or as may be provided for. 9th, That all banks now authorized to receive and issue for their own account and advantage treasury or state notes, shall be equitably compensated, and their circulation withdrawn, and the channels of such circulation be filled, *pari passu*, with state notes supplied directly to the public in payments of metal, according to the demand for them.

4. The arguments in support of this briefly stated outline of a more perfectly constructed monetary system will form the greater part of this work. I turn now to the meaning I shall attach to the several terms used to express the industrial forces of society which head this chapter. First, unless *otherwise* limited or expressed, I shall use the term LABOR in the sense of manual labor, of which there are two grand divisions, usually termed

"skilled" and "unskilled," both of which are more or less governed by mere habitual routine. But the word has a far more extensive application. The human race, with the exception of an extremely limited number who may be called the drones, or useless members of society, labor in some form or other with their hands or their brains, their body, their mind, or both. These are unquestionably the natural and healthy conditions of both men and women, and none should envy the lot of purely idle people.

5. CAPITAL AND WEALTH, if not identical in their largest senses, are so nearly allied, or so nearly cover the same ground in the field of Political Economy, as to make it difficult to mark out separate and distinguishing boundaries between them. I speak of the terms in an abstract sense. It is easy to limit or extend the meaning of either term. I cannot undertake to collate the various definitions, for instance, applied to the word "capital" by authorities of high standing on economic science. One says, "it consists of the general surplus income over outgo;" another, that "it is the savings and accumulations of labor;" another, of trade; others again make an arbitrary distinction between capital and wealth, and insist that "only such things can be called capital as are used in producing and distributing commodities."

6. A late writer, Mr. Thomson Hankey, in his work on "Banking and Currency," at p. 44 defines capital to be "any and every kind of accumulation of useful and exchangeable property." This might be accepted by readers of his book as a very good and comprehensive definition; but Mr. Hankey himself, in the very next paragraph, spoils the sense of it by a new and totally different definition of the word, or of the sense given it in his first description of what he means. He says, "Now, it should always be borne in mind, that no fresh capital

can be obtained, excepting from the same source from which all capital is originally derived ; namely, the excess of income or production over expenditure."

According to the first definition, the gross products of labor, aided more or less, as the case may be, by capital and machinery, constitute capital ; that is, provided such products consist of an "accumulation of exchangeable property," or, as I would express it, "provided they possess market value."

7. From the latter definition or application of meaning, Mr. Hankey in another paragraph infers, that " in a primitive state of society, where the community consumes immediately or presently all the produce of its labor, there can be no such thing as capital." These extracts serve to show how easy it is to fall into inaccurate and loose methods of reasoning, by having no clear perception of the definition of even the most commonly used terms in deductive and inductive sciences. It is not true in fact, that "there can be no such thing as capital in a society where the community consumes immediately or presently all the produce of its labor," for the simple reason so well expressed by Mr. Hankey himself, that " any and every kind of accumulation of useful or exchangeable property" constitutes "capital." The truth is, capital exists, and is augmented in many ways independently of the "excess of income or production over expenditure." The property in new inventions, and the discovery of new mines of valuable minerals, such as iron, copper, gold, silver, coal, and a long list of other like things, and the enhanced market value of lands and commodities, probably furnish as large a share of capital, according to Mr. Hankey's first and most correct definition, as the average "excess of income or production over expenditure." But furthermore, capital exists independent of "accumulation," which is only needful to

make it available for the purposes of convenience or manufacturers.

8. I might cite numerous other examples of the want of accuracy in defining this and other equally important terms in constant use among writers and speakers on economic subjects ; but these will suffice to show the desirability of establishing some standard authority to guide us in reaching accurate conclusions. Capital, by long usage, has come to comprehend every thing possessing "market value," a term to which I shall devote some space hereafter. In this broad sense, the word has come to be synonymous with WEALTH in whatever form it exists, or has a market or "exchange" value. But these generalizations of terms need not stand in the way of accurate reasoning, if we only adopt and rigidly adhere to the practice of *limiting* and *qualifying* the *meaning* we propose to attach to terms in their particular application. *Wealth* may, with propriety, be left to express the market value of individual and national property of every kind, over indebtedness or liability.

9. I have stated in a former paragraph (5), that capital and wealth in their largest popular acceptations cover nearly the same ground in the field of Political Economy. This statement requires some explanation, or perhaps modification. The general acceptation of capital is any thing possessing market value or trading power. The idea attached to wealth is opulence, riches, property. Now, these terms all imply market value ; and every thing possessing such value becomes trading power or capital. In these senses wealth is capital, and capital is wealth. A man's reputation or character has a market value of great importance in commercial affairs. Hence, credit founded on these qualities may fairly be classified as trading power or capital. But all prudent men, when they accept personal obligations in payment of goods,

know or believe that the goods will be honestly disposed of to meet such obligation.   In reality, then, it must be conceded that the goods themselves constitute the capital employed in their distribution.   This important principle is clearly expressed in postulate 35, Chap. I.

10. Before considering the more restricted or limited application and uses of the term CAPITAL, I wish to speak of the great confusion of ideas prevailing among writers of so-called " money articles " on the subject of capital and money.   A knowledge of Political Economy is not, as a rule, among the qualifications of gentlemen employed by the owners and managers of newspapers.   Hence, there is all but a universal use of the term " money market " instead of LOAN MARKET.

11. Floating capital, of which I shall presently speak, or trading power, which is a better and more expressive term, is what is really dealt in.   This, though convertible into money, is not money, any more than a railway or steamship share, a house, a horse, or any thing else possessing market value, is money.   Neither government, railway, or any other loans are paid in money, except to a very small extent.   The great French indemnity paid to the Germans, except seven or eight per cent, was not paid in money, but in bills, which were settled through bankers and the clearing-houses, and ultimately will be paid by the products and savings of French industry. If the writers of such articles would hold a conference, and agree never to speak of the " money market " when they mean the loan market, nor of money when the proper word is floating capital, or, better still, " trading power," they would do an inconceivable service to the world.   It would at once dispel the monster of delusions that " money is scarce " or " abundant," as the case may be, which has on all occasions developed a vast crop of charlatan currency doctors who confound the *tool*

"money" with the *tool* "capital," which differ from each
other as much as a spade differs from a plough, or a steam-
engine from the ship it propels.   It must come to such a
compact, if ever we are to cure incipient statesmen or
rank-and-file legislators of the extraordinary delusion that
capital, or trading power, which everybody seeks to acquire, can be made "cheap," by simply manufacturing
stamped or *engraved* "denominations" *on pieces of paper,*
and designating pounds or dollars.

CHAPTER III.

CAPITAL AND "TRADING POWER" FURTHER CONSIDERED. ITS TRANSFER FROM ONE FORM TO ANOTHER.

1. FLOATING CAPITAL, TRADING CAPITAL, and FIXED CAPI-
TAL are terms in constant use among economists and merchants.   To these I have added "TRADING POWER" as
being a comprehensive and valuable expression, defining
accurately what bankers and brokers mostly deal in (see
postulates 35 and 36).   I have pointed out, in the latter
part of the last chapter, the absurdity of calling the things
dealt in, in the loan market, *money*, and of treating *money*
and *capital*, or trading power, as the same thing.   It is
very obvious, that, though money is capital, capital is not
money, except when it is invested in actual money, which
forms only an infinitesimal part of the huge sums measured by money, and which may be, though they seldom
are, converted into money.   I have defined capital generally, as signifying whatever possesses market value, or
will exchange for things possessing such value, in a ratio
measured by money.   But the various inventions of
merchants and bankers for utilizing capital render it
desirable, as well as convenient, in discussing questions

of monetary science, to define the particular forms in which capital exists, and is used in the industries of the people.

2. FLOATING CAPITAL, as stated in postulates 35 and 36, on analysis, resolves itself into the simple elements of goods in the course of production, manufacture and distribution to consumers; and the accumulated savings of industry, which exist mostly in deposits with bankers and discount houses, and are credited to the owners in the ledgers of bankers and those keeping such funds and money; or in obligations payable on demand, or at a specified time. It would not be difficult for bankers to give a very accurate statement from their books, of the proportions of the two kinds of floating capital, or trading power, held by them at any particular time, or to make up averages for specified periods. Such a statement would be pregnant with interest to the scientific economist. It would show what I have postulated; namely, that the greater part, by far, of the trading power dealt in, in the loan or discount market, consists of the goods themselves, which is turned into capital by bankers, and is thus used to produce and transfer them to consumers. This trading power, then, constitutes the chief motive power or force which propels the vast and complicated machinery of the industrial world.

3. FIXED CAPITAL comes next in order of consideration. The term obviously applies only to the things themselves, and not to the trading power used in effecting their purchase, which existed originally in the forms indicated in postulates 35 and 36. I submit, that, in a scientific sense, there exists no such thing as *fixed capital* strictly speaking, except in estates held under entail, inasmuch as the lands or other things of an imperishable nature may, like goods, be used in the loan market by means of mortgages. It seems to me, that the correct and logical method of

regarding fixed capital is to refer and rigidly confine the idea of it to such things as, in themselves, possess the essential elements of perpetuity, or power of continued existence. Under this category may be classed lands, houses, factories, mines, shares in joint-stock companies, and the tools of industry, which, though perishable, possess the elements of renewal out of profits. It is very desirable that writers on economic science should have some better general understanding in respect to the meaning of capital, so as to discriminate between the position occupied, and the force exerted by each kind.

4. CASH CAPITAL, commercially speaking, consists of money, or what can instantaneously be converted into money. No further definition of the term need be given; and it ranks as a postulate. This proposition will receive great consideration when I come to treat of the Bank of England, and its traditional policy of trading on its own share of the note issue, and treating such notes as good "cash reserve," because the Bank can get cash for them, when it ought only to get the securities they are issued on.

5. The term "cash," properly speaking, applies only to money, a certain quantity of which should always be at the command of bankers and other traders. If it is intended to give it a wider signification, care should always be taken to specify the exact limitation intended to be set upon it. When I use the word, I shall use it in the commercial sense, as defined in the last paragraph. When I use the word *money*, I mean by it the metallic money made legal tender, and the measure and standard of value; and circulating notes used as currency, I desig- as "paper money."

6. While treating of capital, I will now only remark, that, when it is invested in money of any kind, it is invested in the least profitable form. Hence, all business

men seek to part with money as soon as they can find
something that will yield a profit ; as money in the till or
in hand yields nothing. As a general rule, the importation of money, or the bullion out of which it is manufactured, is an indication of an unhealthy state of trade.
A certain quantity of the precious metals is necessary for
coinage and use as money. All beyond that represents
unemployed capital. This is fundamental, and demonstrably overthrows the specious arguments in favor of the
" mercantile theory " of trade, which held that trade must
be so controlled by the state as to force the importation
of the precious metals.

7. It comes properly enough, under the head of capital, to very fully illustrate the boundaries between money
in its character of a tool, used to measure value in whatever form it exists, and things which constitute trading
power or capital. In its denominations of pounds, shillings, pence, or dollars, or francs, it acts as the scale on
the yard, or other measure of length ; while, by its market
value, it exchanges for every thing possessing value.
These functions, though distinguishable in principle, can
no more be separated from each other than the inches or
sub-divisions of the yard-measure can be separated from
the stick or metal on which they are inscribed. We use
the money-scale to measure out capital, a good deal as
we use the peck or bushel measure to estimate certain
quantities of grain, or the quintal, when we buy or sell
by weight. In these cases we only need as many yard-
sticks, or bushel measures, or quintal weights, as will
serve the purpose. We do not invest capital in a large
supply, if a comparatively small number will serve our
purpose. Just so is it with money : people will only buy
as much of it as is needed to be used in its trading
capacity to make small purchases, pay for labor, and give
change. As a measure its presence is not needed. This

is equally true in respect to paper money. Its use is mainly limited to its convenience, and, as a saving to the state, to the extent to which the state can safely use the gold it has received in payment for such paper money as the public has purchased. This question will be very fully discussed when I come to consider the right of the state to be the only issuer of such money.

8. While treating generally of capital, it may be observed, that in wealthy and wealth-producing countries, where the surplus savings, or profits of industry and invested capital, accumulate rapidly, and tend to a plethora of trading power in the loan markets, it is most desirable that a well-regulated and prudent development of private and public enterprises at home and abroad should be fostered and encouraged, — not, however, by subsidies or bonuses, but by wise legislation, giving the utmost freedom of action and protection against fraud. The plethora of unemployed capital always tends to over-trading and speculation; and these lead by logical sequence to panics and crises, so destructive to industrial interests and capital. To prevent the accumulation of too much floating capital, it is most desirable to find profitable fields of investment of the more permanent kinds.

9. Perhaps the future development and perfecting of a wisely conceived plan of co-operative associations may lead to a more healthy adjustment of demand to supply, of capital for productive permanent undertakings, and lead to a more smoothly working industrial system. This is a question for those who devote themselves to social and political science, as well as the political economist, to consider. Society now seems to need a safety valve, or, more properly speaking, a governor, to do for it what both these do for the steam-engine ; namely, to regulate the force and the motion of the machine. For this pur-

pose, freedom of action to the natural laws is the best
thing. At present the origination and management of the
joint-stock companies, which mostly absorb the surplus,
or unemployed capital, or capital that pays scarcely any
thing to the owner, is left largely in the hands of professional jobbers, who are too often hardly better than
common swindlers. People do not, and perhaps cannot,
exercise ordinary prudence in investigating for themselves
the numerous schemes presented for the purpose of ex-
tracting large profits and commissions, rather than fostering sound commercial undertakings. Government has,
to some extent, assumed the right to exercise, through
special officials, a supervision over banks, insurance and
railway companies at home. Possibly such supervision
might be extended to foreign investments so far as to see
that fraudulent practices shall not be perpetrated with
impunity. "Prevention is better than cure" where it
can be exercised without infringing the utmost lawful
freedom of action on the part of the citizen. Where a
clear and evident intent to commit a fraud is unearthed,
the state may surely exercise its power to prevent it,
instead of waiting for the commission of the act, and
then proceeding to punish the offender, who too often
"goes unwhipped of justice."

10. Another of the evils of modern society, which existed also in ancient times, and especially in ancient
Rome, is the tendency of capital to accumulate in a
comparatively few hands or families. This, too, is a
question well worthy the careful consideration of conservative men and social-science reformers. This tendency is the chief instigation to the other extreme of
communism, which seeks the overthrow of society in
order to revel in the wreck of wealth and the accumulation of past industrial savings. Great accumulations of
wealth and capital on the one hand, and extreme pov-

erty and deficient employment on the other hand, are the
predominating evils in the chief industrial countries of
the modern world, as much or more than they were of
ancient times.

11. The application of labor to the production of the
necessaries and luxuries of life, unaided by capital, is
only to be found in the rudest condition of society.   The
happy medium, it would seem, should be when skilled
labor, aided by capital invested in houses, factories, farms,
steamships, railways, and all the numerous appliances of
modern inventions, is directed by experience and ability.
There are no natural reasons for a conflict between capital and labor.   They should always act like reciprocating
engines on each other ; and it is the main intent of the
science of political economy, or of industry, as I have
suggested as a more appropriate and expressive term, to
differentiate and clearly develop the true methods of
applying these forces to the advantage of society.   Ben-
tham's proposition of " the greatest good to the greatest
number " falls short of expressing what economic science should aim to accomplish.   That science should
aim to perfect an industrial system that shall provide
employment, and the means of comfortable subsistence
and homes, for each and all the members of society.   All
legislation designed to foster monopolies, whatever the
pretext, is an assault on the rights of labor, and certainly, in the end, tends to make " the rich richer, and
the poor poorer."   The protective legislation of the
United States has caused the most wide-spread distress
amongst the industrial and laboring classes.   The National and the States' Governments have long been subject to the corrupting influences of great capitalists, who
seek to control all the avenues to industrial independence.   Hence we see the cloven foot of communism
treading like a spectre in the rich man's tracks.   Such

a condition of things calls for careful investigation on the part of those who are tracing causes from effects.

12. But to proceed with the consideration of the principles and functions of capital. I have shown how money measures value, and how it metes out capital in the loan market. To instance, we speak of ten, a hundred, or a thousand pounds or dollars, as of so much money; when, in truth, it is only capital we wish to designate, and to transfer from buyer to seller, or from debtor to creditor. But the sum specified in the check, or carried to the credit of the borrower, actually represents, and is an equivalent in value to, so much gold or currency. It is a substantial, not a mythical value. It must also be kept in mind that things possessing market value can only be properly measured by such things as possess similar value.

13. It will now be seen, by what has been said respecting money and capital, or trading power, that the business of a banker is trading in loans of such capital, or trading power, which, to a very large extent, he has been instrumental, not exactly in creating, but in evolving out of goods in course of production and distribution. The effect of this wonderful method of utilizing the trading power of goods has given rise, during the last three-quarters of a century, to enormous creation of wealth and commercial energy and activity. Without such aid, the vast system of railways now existing in the chief commercial and industrial countries, and the numerous steam and other ships traversing every sea, lake and navigable river, and supported by the carriage of goods, which, in turn, they help to produce, could not have been brought into existence at all, or, at least, not for centuries to come (postulate 64).

14. Professor Bonamy Price, who has done so much to clear up the question of banking and what a banker does,

has shown that he is, in effect, only a broker between producers and consumers, or dealers in goods. The banker takes from the hands of a seller of an invoice of goods the bill of exchange which he (the seller) has accepted in payment, and puts it in his drawer ; and, "presto change," it becomes equal to its face in gold, less a small charge for interest, which he deducts or "discounts" for his profit. He thus becomes the broker between the buyer and seller. When a banker in one country draws on a banker in another country, the same result has been effected. The banker in one country represents or acts as broker for a seller ; and in the other country the drawee, banker, or merchant, as the case may be, becomes the broker of the buyer or consumer. This is legitimate banking, with which the issue of paper money has nothing whatever to do, and hence forms no part of sound legitimate banking. Professor Price is right when he analyzes the business of a banker, and finds him to be a broker.

15. But for the quickening power of banking and bankers, by far the greater part of the capital now in active circulation would remain dormant. Goods could not furnish the means for their reproduction and distribution, as they now do, or, at most, to a very small extent. The power-loom and spinning-jenny, the forge, the anvil, and the numerous great labor-saving inventions, would have been deprived of a large proportion of their producing powers, without the aid of the banker. His magic touch turns the products of these auxiliaries to labor into trading power, more efficacious and far less costly than gold.

16. Those who will take the trouble, and have the capacity, to master these important truths, will see how absurd the cry for "more money" is, when it is not money at all that propels the great and complex indus-

trial system, except in so limited a degree as to be almost
inappreciable in the vast ocean of trading power, or
capital. I shall go on, step by step, to apply these fundamental principles, and to show wherein the monetary
system of the world fails to meet their requirements,
especially in the matter of banks of issue, and in particular the Bank of England, and National Banks of America.

CHAPTER IV.

VALUE.

1. No term used by economic writers has given rise
to more confusion and bad logic than that of value. "Intrinsic" value and market value are continually con-
founded with each other. I have pointed out the distinction between the two terms in the introduction. It is
with market value we have to deal in monetary science ;
and I always speak of it *as* "market value," so that no
one can accuse me of using them "indiscriminately."
Then, we have the contention about "the measure of
value," and "common measure of value," which will be
attended to in due time. But the great controversies
relate to what regulates market value. Ricardo, following Adam Smith and others, says, —

"It is the cost of production that must ultimately regulate the price of commodities, and not, as has often
been said, the proportion between supply and demand."

2. A little farther on he says, "supply and demand
may for a time affect the market value of a commodity."
Then, there is another school who assert that *demand
alone* sets the market value of commodities. But I shall
cite a passage from John Stuart Mill, to show the importance of the term, and likewise the desirability of having a demonstrated scientific definition of it.

3. Mr. Mill devotes several chapters to the subject; and in his opening one he says, —

"The subject on which we are about to enter fills so important and conspicuous a position in Political Economy, that, in the apprehension of many thinkers, its boundaries confound themselves with the science itself." He further observes, that some eminent economists have even proposed "to call political economy the science of values." I would suggest "the science of industry" as more appropriate and comprehensive for the larger study, and "science of values" as quite expressive of the scope of what is usually termed "monetary science."

4. It would occupy by far too much space to attempt to cite the arguments of numerous writers, who stand nearly equally divided in numbers between the two propositions stated by Mr. Ricardo. It seems to me that those who claim that the market value of commodities is regulated *alone* by the quantity or cost of the labor expended in their production, are met at the very threshold of their argument by an unanswerable rebuttal of the claim. Labor itself must be admitted to be strictly under subordination to supply and demand. But, not to anticipate my argument, I will only here say, that it would be absurd to argue that the productions of labor should be excluded from the ruling principles of labor. If the market value of labor is regulated by supply and demand, the productions of labor necessarily are. The product must be governed by the same principles as those which govern the labor of the producer. Then, there are numerous auxiliaries to production, such as capital, skill, and machinery, to be taken into the account, which, equally with mere manual labor, are admitted on all hands to be governed by supply and demand. It must be also admitted, that labor, capital, skill, and machinery cannot set a market value for themselves.

5. I use "market value" as the *average price* at which
goods are sold in an open market at any particular time,
and price as the incident of a single bargain resulting in
a sale. Adam Smith and most other great authorities
speak of " exchange value," or, as the former has it, " exchangeable value," which latter term Mr. Mill discards
as " ungrammatical." I prefer the term " market value."
I will now let Mr. J. B. McCulloch state the case for
those who assert that the cost of production in labor and
capital alone regulates market value.

" In so far," he observes, " as the cost of commodities
is concerned, it is plain it cannot be affected by the
fluctuations in the rate of wages or in the rate of profit.
The cost of commodities depends wholly on the quantity
of labor, or the sweat and toil required for their production. But a variation in the rate of wages is not a
variation in the *quantity* of labor, but merely a variation
in the price paid for that labor." It is quite true that
the *wages* of labor, or the market value of the products
of labor, do not increase or diminish the *amount* or
quantity of labor required to produce an article. But
we are not dealing with the *quantity* of labor, but the
market value and the products of labor. No one denies
that volume, or supply and demand, sets the market
value of capital; and yet capital is only the savings of
labor, or labor and capital together; and capital contributes as much to the *cost* of an article as labor itself.
Mr. McCulloch evidently misconceives the question, and
confounds quantity of labor with *cost* of labor, or its
market value.

6. Mr. Henry Dunning McLeod is a good representative of the opposite equally unsupported theory. He
asserts dogmatically, —

" It is demand or consumption, and *not labor*, that
gives value to production." Neither of these proposi-

tions, taken by itself, is true; and yet neither is wholly
untrue, or capable of accounting for the phenomenon of
market value. Without stopping to inquire minutely into
actual *first causes* which underlie production and consumption, I will proceed to lay down the principles
which govern the market value of lands, labor, and all
things having such value.

7. Divesting our minds of all extraneous and confusing ideas, and discarding from view what is called
intrinsic value, let us think only of *market value*. Thus
approaching the subject, the following formula will, I
hope, help us to reach a satisfactory result, and clear
away the confusion of ideas surrounding it in the writings
of nearly all accepted authorities on political economy.
" Market value is determined and governed by the competition amongst producers, aided by skill, capital, and
machinery on the one hand, and competition amongst
buyers for consumption on the other hand." In other
words, " Market value is *not* established by cost of labor
in production alone, or by demand for consumption
alone, but is the resultant of the two forces, — competition in the labor market, and competition amongst buyers
in the goods and other markets. The former stimulates
production and the latter consumption; and each continually acts on the other, like reciprocating engines."
The parts played in production, by skill, capital, and
machinery, taken into the account with the means of
distribution of the products of labor and the methods
of consumption, are complex questions; and their analysis belongs to the larger science of industry, or political
economy (*vide* postulate 65).

8. The truth of this postulate seems self-evident, as
it is fundamental; and its correctness will force itself on
the mind, and lead to conviction, if we pursue the investigation into all the considerations to which deductive

and inductive reasoning and analysis may lead. There
are always two sides to a bargain and sale, or a purchase,
— put it either way. The very term "market" implies
this. One of these represents supply, and the other
demand. THE AGGREGATION OF BARGAINS, RESULTING IN
SALES OR PURCHASES, AT STIPULATED PRICES, SETS THE
MARKET VALUE OF ANY GIVEN THING, whether it be labor,
land, a commodity, or any of the long list of articles
dealt in in the various markets. Though buying and
selling are proximate causes, or the results of more remote causes, they convey to the mind the conviction
of the truth of the principles which give and regulate
market value. The primary or more remote causes must
be sought in competition, or motives for competition,
among those who produce, on the one hand, and those
who consume, on the other. The necessities, tastes, and
passions of men underlie both classes, and stimulate to
action.

9. The consideration of the forces supply and demand
leads irresistibly to the conclusion that they are equally
concerned in producing the result which we are considering, namely, *market value*. In respect to consumption,
we must not confine its meaning to actual destruction,
or annihilation, to which by far the greater part of the
products of labor are destined, but extend it and its
effects to the *withdrawal* of things purchased, from competition in the markets. When we reach the point where
we find that competition, which is the result of numbers,
whose ambitious tastes and desires prompt them to action,
we shall be carried back to original and first principles.

10. Production emanates from the necessity which
impels men to labor, as well as the desire to acquire
property and wealth ; and supply is the result. Consumption also emanates from similar motives. Hence
we have the expression of an equation of forces, termed

in economic science "the law of supply and demand," which I have before said is a proximate, or secondary, rather than a primary cause. Perhaps it would be more correct to say that the law itself, as so expressed, is in fact the last link in a chain of more remote causes, ending in the accurate adjustment of the market value of every thing having such value. Another and very expressive way of defining and postulating the effect of the law of supply and demand would be to designate it as "the natural law of adjustment of values." There is a perpetual struggle going on between the producers and consumers of commodities; and the general markets may be regarded as an immense automatic machine, or system, forever at work adjusting the market value of goods, and establishing the ratio between production and consumption, and distributing labor and its products (postulate 40).

11. Though the proposition stated by Adam Smith, that "the quantity of labor expended in production is the ultimate regulator of exchange value," has been accepted by the greater part of economic writers, there seems no more reason for accepting it as a fundamental truth than there is for accepting the opposite theory of McLeod, that "demand alone" produces the phenomenon in question. I might leave the solution of the question to stand on the ground I have reasoned out, but for the very dogmatic assumption of both parties, who have, as before remarked, really "jumped to a conclusion" by simply begging the question. Mr. McCulloch, after citing Adam Smith's doctrine, quotes M. Garnier, a French economist, in favor of its truth, and then proceeds to frame a sort of algebraical formula, to show that production is the *only* force that sets market value, as follows: "Suppose that the commodities A, B, and C exchange for each other. If A suddenly rise in value, as

compared with the others, the presumption might be,
supposing that we were ignorant of the circumstance,
that something had occurred to increase the demand for
A, or to lessen the supply of both. But these are temporary and accidental causes of variation, and must, for
the reasons stated above, speedily disappear. And hence,
if A continued to maintain its increased value, as compared with B, C, etc., it would be a conclusive proof,
either that the quantity of labor required for its production had been increased, or that the quantity required
for the production of the others had been diminished."
The inference he then draws is, that "it is labor, therefore, that is the true and only measure of the cost, or,
as it has sometimes been termed, the real value, of all
things. . . . Their exchangeable *value and cost are identical.*"

12. This method of reasoning, it seems to me, proves
nothing. It is merely setting up a man of straw in order
to knock him down again. If we consider how many
forces, which are neither "temporary nor accidental," are
being brought to bear on production and consumption,
in order to diminish or increase prices, or market value,
we shall see how worthless all such illustrations are.
Some of these may be mentioned, — such as new inventions for diminishing labor; improved processes of production and manufacture; new markets; cheapening of
transport; discoveries of mines; and, finally, changes of
fashions and tastes. These are, more or less, continuing influences on supply and demand, *which perpetually
tends to equilibrium in its action on values.*

13. Mr. McCulloch, as if distrusting his own algebraical formula, next quotes a very misty illustration,
formulated by Adam Smith, who says, "The real price
of every thing, — what every thing really costs to the man
who wants to acquire it, — is the toil and trouble of

acquiring it. What every thing is worth to the man who has acquired it, and wants to dispose of it, or exchange it for something else, is the toil and trouble which it can impose on other people." There seems to me to be some confusion of thought in this passage, such as is not often met with in the great work, "The Wealth of Nations." To talk of the "price," or "cost," of a thing to the man who only "wants to acquire it," is, by itself, devoid of meaning; and the next sentence is scarcely less obscure. The most intelligible explanation of these sentences seems to be (construing them in conformity with the doctrine set up), that the worth, or value, of a thing, to him who owns or has acquired it, is measured by the "toil and labor" he would have been compelled to expend in producing the article he desires to exchange it for, if he had himself to produce or manufacture it, but which he is now able to impose on another. Suppose the thing he owns be a horse, which he desires to sell, or exchange for a carriage : the horse is worth to him "the toil and trouble" it would occasion him to construct the carriage himself, but which the ownership of the horse enables him "to impose on other people." But how this proposition proves that the cost of rearing the horse or constructing the carriage sets the exchange or market value of either, is by no means made clear by any interpretation that can be given to the language in question.

14. The contest between the two classes of disputants over these *mere dogmas* is well exemplified by the fable of the two knights who met on opposite sides of the shield which they found placed in the highway, and quarrelled and fought about the metal, and devices inscribed thereon, because they had both neglected to examine the opposite side, — a step that would have disclosed to each the important fact that he had been in possession of only half the truth.

15. The late Professor Cairnes, in his work on political economy, seems to have had very misty ideas on the question of value, and especially as to the law of supply and demand. He treats the two sides of the equation as being one and the same thing. He argues that the supplier of goods is at the same time a demander of money or something else. Hence he argues that the terms are convertible. This is what may be called "reasoning round a circle," and is an exhibition of the fatuity of even learned professors of universities, when they feel it incumbent on their official positions to attempt to say something new, and to publish treatises on a science they have never mastered, but which they have undertaken to teach to others. The late professor's method of proving his new doctrine is exactly on a par with the logic of the Oxford student who successfully demonstrated to his proctor that they were really standing on "the other side of the river." Pointing to the opposite side of the stream, he desired the proctor to admit that that was "one side the river," which, being done, the student triumphantly cried out, "I have you now; for you must admit that this is the 'other side,' *Quod erat demonstrandum.*"

16. Nothing so clearly demonstrates the desirability of a standard work on political economy, that shall contain all the established principles of the science, as the circumstance that the world is being flooded with crude theories published by professors who feel bound to rush into print, and engage public attention. The whole subject should be condensed into a moderate-sized volume suited to colleges and schools. Whoever undertakes the task should keep in view the desirability of writing intelligibly and for popular instruction, and of having clearly defined meanings attached to terms in common use.

CHAPTER V.

HOW THE VALUE OF MONEY IS SET AND REGULATED, AND HOW IT DIFFERENTIATES OTHER VALUES.

1. Money, being a commodity, has its market value, without reference to the material it is made of, set by supply and demand; or, in other words, by the increase or diminution of its volume. When it is made of a material largely used, and acted on by this natural regulator, it will be seen the raw material and the manufactured article will continually tend to differ from each other in their market values. The only method, therefore, to maintain between the two commodities, money and bullion, a close equilibrium of market values, is easy interconvertibility. Metal only becomes money after it has undergone the process of coinage. It is, consequently, necessary to reach a clear perception of what is effected by coinage. The first result is the division of the metal into convenient pieces for handling and weighing in small or large amounts. The next is the legal verification of weight and fineness. But a main element in money is, that it is made by law legal tender for debts.

2. With regard to inconvertible paper money, we know by ample experience that its market value, or trading power, can be maintained on an equality with gold or silver, or raised above their value, by limitation of volume, or by keeping the amount in circulation below the demands of the people for currency. But experience has also amply demonstrated the impossibility of artificially regulating supply to demand, when such money has been forced on society by governments. Hence mankind instinctively, as well as from the exercise of reason, have chosen one or both of the precious metals for coin-

ing their money.   Metal, then, becomes the regulator of
the market value of money, through easy and cheap interconvertibility.

3. There is nothing in gold and silver, in respect to
measuring and differentiating the market value of commodities peculiar to those metals, except their superior
fitness and convenience for coinage and practical use.
These considerations most clearly show the unfitness of
mere engraved denominations of dollars or pounds, for
money, as proposed by a large number of American
politicians and others in other countries.   They are deficient in the great principle of a convenient governor,
as needful for money as for the steam-engine.   Coin
and metal, when interconvertible in manner before stated,
will never vary in market value more than enough to
afford a minimum profit, or motive of some kind for conversion.

4. The market value of money, it has been seen, is
governed, 1st, by the quantity of metal contained in the
coin as specified by its denominations ; and, 2d, by the
limitation of the amount of all of the various denominations of such coins issued and made legal tender.   I
have shown, that if such amount is held below the quantity of coin, or money, required for conducting the industries of the people, it will necessarily rise above the
market value of the metal ; and, if such coin is issued
in excess of such demand, the excess will be exported
as bullion, and the supply of metal for coinage will be
stopped, and an equilibrium of values will ensue.

5. The practice already very generally conforms to
principles.   Under the regulations of most of the mints
of the world, the nearest approach to free trade has been
reached.   No nation now attempts to " protect " the production, or manufacture into money, of gold, which is
now substantially the measure of value of all other com-

modities, labor, etc., in most countries. Hence the owners of gold can everywhere take their gold bullion to these money factories and exchange it for its market value in coin, or money, less a small charge, or *agio*, to cover the cost of coinage (Chap. XXVI., on Seigniorage).

6. In the working of the mints we have a very clear illustration of the advantages of free trade. The law of supply and demand rules omnipotent, and without let or hinderance. All that is needed to approximate a perfect self-regulating monetary system is to make it universal, and include the issue of paper money (Chap. XXV.). But, as such a system may be far in the future, we must consider monetary principles from our present stand-point, and each nation as a unit, looking only to present exigencies.

7. When, from any cause, there occurs such a diminution in the demand for money as to leave a profit to the bullion broker, or dealer, to resort to the melting-pot, he buys up the coined money so long as it affords him a profit. If, on the other hand, there arises such a demand for money as to leave a profit to the dealer in bullion, he takes his ingots to the mint, and has them coined, or sells them for money. I shall hereafter, in Chap. XI., point out more specifically the scientific distinction between bullion, the raw material, and money, the manufactured article.

8. Paper money issued for its full face in gold, and the coin being held for its conversion on demand, is governed by the same general principles as the metallic money into which it is so made convertible ; and, as already stated, there can be no redundancy of such money, as all issued in excess of the public demands — which will seldom occur — will return to the issuer for conversion, and the coin will be exported.

9. No principles of monetary science are better established, or more demonstrably proved by long practical experience, than that no more metallic money or paper money so issued, and payable, can be held in circulation than is actually needed for industrial purposes, for the simple reason that capital invested in money lies idle, and earns no profit, so long as it is held in that form. The old adage that "money is only useful for what it will buy, or when it is spent," holds good in practice as well as in theory.

10. In view of these great fundamental truths, how senseless is the clamor for "more money." With nearly free mintage, there will always be an adequate supply of money. The cry for more capital, or trading power, after some long-continuing depression in the industries of a country, in times of crises, brought on by over trading and speculation, or by the whole people "making haste to get rich," would be more logical; because such crises stop production, and thus diminish the supply of capital.

11. When the cry is for more of an inconvertible paper currency, instead of for more capital, which is only created by the production of goods and the slow processes of industry, it is simply idiotic, for the reason that the greater the volume of such currency put in circulation, the less becomes its trading power, or market value. It adds nothing to the actual capital of a country, but only creates "a fool's paradise" for those who fancy they are growing rich because their houses, lands, and goods are measured by a yardstick of only half the standard length.) The laboring man and mechanic are also deluded by the higher prices they receive for their labor, according to this delusive measure. But all merchants, laborers, farmers, shortly find that whatever they each and all have to buy has risen in equal proportion

to what they each and all have to sell, and none are the richer for " marking up their goods."

12. The market value of an irredeemable legal-tender paper currency is regulated *only* by the limitation set on its issue. Not having any other regulator, it is not possible for those who supply it, especially where the power and prerogative of the State have been delegated to several thousand competing banks, greedy of making profit in haste, to regulate its volume properly. Hence it is deficient in the main end and purpose of money.

13. In respect to the effect of limitation in the volume of irredeemable paper money, Mr. J. B. McCulloch has truly remarked, in one of his notes to the "Wealth of Nations," which will be again referred to, that such currency being legal tender, taken in connection with the circumstance that "the people must have a circulating medium," will always make its market value depend on the limitation set on the quantity emitted.

14. With such clear and well-defined principles, in respect to the circumstances which govern the market value of an irredeemable paper currency, as those I have postulated, and more fully explained in this and Chap. XXIV., the folly and ignorance of both British and American legislators, in "fixing days for resumption," and "making preparation," will become manifest. The so-called "Gresham Law," that "an inferior currency will drive a superior currency out of circulation," requires this slight addition : " such inferior currency being issued in excess of the demands of industry." With this amendment, the remedy of the evil, or the method for resuming specie payments, becomes too obvious to require argument. Take back the excess of supply over demand, or wait till the growth of industry shall act as a contraction, by increase of demand, and the market value of the outstanding notes will come up to par of gold, and

· gold will immediately step forward, and circulate side by side with the paper, and resumption becomes an established fact by a perfectly natural process.

15. The statesmen of France, as will hereafter be shown, understood this law better than those of Great Britain, when the latter refused to act on the Bullion Report of Mr. Homer from 1810 to 1821, or those of the United States in 1874, when they passed the law to provide for the resumption of specie payments, which, while it requires the purchase of gold in immense amounts by sale of bonds bearing interest, also provides for the indefinite increase of national bank notes. This so-called "Resumption Act" is one of the best illustrations of the wisdom of the words addressed by the Swedish Chancellor Oxenstiern to his son, when the young man was about to visit the courts of Europe : " Go, my son, and see with how little wisdom mankind is governed."

16. Science and experience combine to show, beyond controversy, that some valuable and suitable metal like gold, must be made the standard, or governor, and common measure of value, and the basis of any monetary system approximating perfection ; and also that the money fabricated out of such metal, must be supplied by the nation through a department independent alike of national or other financial operations, and free, or nearly so, of cost for coinage. Under these conditions the public will always supply the metal in exchange for coin. The same considerations prove that such a department, having no discretion of its own, but bound to act on the natural law of supply and demand, is the only safe and proper issuer of paper money, which must be paid for by banks, as it now is by the people at large, for its full face value in gold ; thus making gold and paper money, like gold and bullion, interconvertible at the pleasure of the holders thereof.

17. In the matter of taxation to support the state, and provide for the administration of justice and the education of the people, each individual should be required to contribute, *pro rata*, according to his means or income, from whatever source. Beyond this necessary interference with natural rights, the Legislature should not go. The value of labor, of lands and houses, of stocks, or shares in public and private companies, of all the products of labor, and of money, metallic and paper, should be left to the regulation of the forces embodied in or expressed by the equation of supply and demand. The observance or violation of the laws of industry and of society, which rule and govern men in their social relations, marks the distinction between right and wrong, good and evil. Hence it is the duty of the legislator, the student of divinity, of law, of medicine, and the laborer in all branches of industry, to search out and ascertain, by analysis and logical reasoning, what are the laws of nature in respect to society, which are the laws of God, and are superior in their influences and tendencies to those of man, which so often violate and contemn the superior organic laws. Let all such remember that mere dogmatic teaching will never advance the cause of truth one step.

18. "Standard of value" and "measure of value" are expressions which have distinctive meanings, though continually used as synonymous. The former relates to the kind and fineness of the metal made legal tender by the state; and the latter to the scale of denominations, such as pounds or dollars, stamped on the coins. The terms also apply, in like manner, to other corporeal things, such as relate to capacity, length, and weight. All these are proper subjects for legislative determination. The Legislature only makes *uniform scales,* but the laws of industry determine the market values of the things

measured. It is thus easy, when we have made one thing, namely, gold, a common measure of value, to find out the ratio that exists at any time between the value of one article, or class of articles, and another, or other articles or classes. The scale of denominations, indicating the quantity and fineness of metal in coined money, is both a "common measure" and a "common denominator" of the values of other things. We use this scale very much as we use the scale on the yard-stick to parcel off so much cloth, or the bushel so much grain. Both measures are indispensable, — the one to mark value, the other quantity. When we have ascertained the value of a given amount or quantity of several articles, by the common measurer, we can readily estimate how much of one must be given in exchange for such given quantity of any other.

CHAPTER VI.[1]

"NOMISMA," OR LEGAL TENDER, AND BI-METALISM.

1. THE theory that gold and silver money, or coin, by being made by the State legal tender, and both supplied without limitation of their respective volumes, can be made to circulate on the same level of value, or that the market or actual value of the two metals can be maintained in equilibrium by law of parliament, is, on the face of it, an absurdity. Nevertheless, this theory has found innumerable advocates in the present day. Even some leading bankers and economists in France, where its fallacy has been demonstrated in practice and by unanswerable logic, have lately put forth vast efforts and written volumes to maintain its practicability as well as

[1] This chapter was written two years after the rest of the work.

desirability; and, in the United States, the two Houses
of Congress have stultified themselves by passing a law,
over the President's veto, asserting an impossibility, by
providing for a fixed and permanent ratio of *market
value*, — for that is the only value governing money.   To
cap the climax of absurdity, the law made it obligatory
on the President to invite a congress of nations to make
the same universal, — the better to override the great
natural law.   The "Silver Congress" having accordingly
met at Paris, it was found that none of the delegates
but those from the United States supported the absurd
proposition; and the proceedings will ever stand as a
protest against the renewal of the proposition.

2. The advocates of this law have for a time laid aside
the agitation in favor of an inconvertible paper currency,
to be issued in such quantities as "to meet the demands
of industry," in order to pass the law "to remonetize
silver," by declaring that a dollar containing $412\frac{1}{2}$ grains
of silver shall pass and be made interchangeable with a
gold dollar, worth in the market at the time the law
passed 440, and now, January, 1879, 460, grains of silver.
Nearly all the speakers, in both branches of Congress,
in favor of this law insisted on the example of the French
currency, as affording evidence that what they proposed
was correct in theory and sustained by practice.   But
the example quoted is not founded in fact.   France has
not such a bi-metallic coin circulation as these parties
assert.   The bi-metalism of France is a very different
thing from the bi-metalism of Congress.   The theory that
inspired the authors and promoters of this measure is to
issue an overvalued silver dollar in order to make a
profit to the nation by making it take the place of the
lower and more nearly correctly valued gold dollar.   This
motive was avowed by nearly all the speakers.   The law
as passed simply proposes that the nation shall purchase

silver at its *market value*, and then (like the merchant
who conceived the idea that he might increase his wealth
"by marking up his goods") mark up the price of the
article eight or ten per cent, and invites the owners of
gold coin, labor, and goods to accept the same at par,
and without demur.

3. The facts in relation to French bi-metalism are
these : France issues no bank notes of a lower denomination than 100 francs, or £4 (say $20), and no gold
coins below 10 francs, or 8s. ($2), and hence requires
a larger amount of subsidiary silver coin than the United
States, which issues all the one-dollar notes called for
by supply and demand. The gold circulation and reserve in France may be set down at £250,000,000
(say $1,250,000,000), as estimated by Mr. Ernst Seyd,
a German actuary in London, and £50,000,000 (say
$250,000,000) of subsidiary silver coins, and £80,000,000
of Bank of France notes.

4. Now, the French Government is very careful never
to emit any larger amount of silver money than will maintain its equilibrium of value with gold, by the demand
for such coins. Seeing the tendency of silver to depreciate, during the very time the silver bill was undergoing
discussion in Congress, the French Government promptly
suspended the coinage of silver ; and the effect was immediate. The depreciation, which had only reached the
half of one per cent, ceased ; and the demand for it
began to raise its value.

5. Concurrently with the discussions in Congress, the
quantity of silver coin already issued under former Acts,
and in circulation in the United States, was in excess
of the demand for it, and was being refused by the banks
on ordinary deposit accounts ; and such coin was selling
in the New York market two per cent below greenbacks,
or legal-tender treasury notes, which were one and a

half to two per cent below gold par. Nothing short of
"a craze" could have seized on a majority of Congress,
to cause them to totally disregard these palpable indications of the action of the natural laws of industry.

6. The same thing holds good in relation to the monetary systems of England and Germany as I have shown
to prevail in France. England and Germany are both
bi-metallic countries. Both use silver as "token money,"
or for subsidiary coins; but both, like France, limit the
amounts for which such coins are made legal tender, as
well as the quantity issued, within the demand for such
coin. Only the present United States Congress is stupid
or dishonest enough to make such coin unlimited legal
tender. The limitation set on the quantity that may be
issued monthly, by the new law, no doubt will prevent an
immediate considerable depreciation.

7. It is not to be doubted that *two standards of value*
may be created by law. But the significant question
presents itself, *Cui bono?* What good will result from it?
It involves the necessity of all bargains for labor, or payments for goods, etc., being made to specify whether such
payments shall be exacted in gold or silver. Such a
monetary system would be too inconvenient to satisfy
public wants, and would lead to perpetual misunder-
standings and litigation. People would always seek to
pay debts in the over-valued metal, — the cheapest money.

8. A passage in the politics of Aristotle, the greatest
of logicians, has been seized hold of, and is often quoted,
to show that the law actually creates the market value
of money. But such writers simply pervert the meaning of the great ancient Greek philosopher. He says,
"Money has value only by law, and not by nature."
Again, he says, "In virtue of a voluntary convention,
money has become the medium of exchange. We say
'nomisma' (money), because it is not so by nature, but

by law, 'nomos,' and because it is in our power to change
it, and render it useless." The meaning of these passages is simply that the law of the Legislature makes
whatever we call money "legal tender;" and, by changing
the legal-tender quality to something else, the former
money loses its value *as money*. Aristotle never asserted
that the *market value* of a metal used as money was the
result of "law," other than the natural law. I have
already pointed out in the last chapter the scientific and
practical fact, that legal-tender money has a market value
of its own, created by supply and demand for it, as money,
distinct from that of the material out of which it is made;
and this "value" is caused by its uses as a tool of industry, and is most clearly what the Greek philosopher
meant. "*The law*" *only gives it value as money, not as
metal*. This is a substantial distinction. I beg to direct
the attention of M. Cemuschi, the French banker and
economist, to this explanation; as it is to him I am indebted for these and other valuable quotations from high
authorities which will follow. He is, I think, too good
a reasoner to allow his judgment to be warped by the
mere *opinions* of others, which he evidently has miscon-
ceived.

9. I copy the following admirable explanation of the
origin and principles of money made by Justinian from
M. Cemuschi's "brochure" on Bi-Metalism, issued in
America to influence congressional legislation on the
silver question.

The great Roman jurist and economist says, "The
origin of buying and selling began with exchange (barter). Formerly money was unknown, and there existed
no terms to differentiate merchandise and price; but
every one, according to the wants of the time, and circumstances, exchanged things which were useful: for it
happens frequently that one is in need of what another

has in excess. But as it seldom coincided that what one possessed the other wanted, and conversely, a material was ' elected,' whose legal and perpetual value remedied by its homogeneity the difficulties of barter. This material being officially (or, as Aristotle would have said, lawfully) coined, circulates and holds its power, not so much from its *substance* as its *quantity*. Since then each of the two things exchanged is no longer called merchandise, but only one ; the other is called price." I have shown that money in fact abolishes exchange altogether, by being a common measure of *value*, which *value* is set by the *price* for which goods are bargained for in the market (postulate 6).

10. This pithy explanation of the origin and function of money is worth all the long and ingenious theses that have been penned by speculative writers on the subject. Justinian evidently perceived the scientific fact that money indicated the "price" or value of the thing given in exchange. In other words, he perceived how money measures market value, just as a yardstick measures length and breadth, not, however, by mere denominations, but by the actual market value of the coin, as fully explained in last chapter. Hence all well-regulated monetary systems provide an adequate supply by interconvertibility of the metallic money used as a standard of value, to meet all demands for it by those who possess the raw material, or metal. Locke has adopted almost the same precise ideas respecting the origin and functions of money, as shown in an extract from his writings heretofore quoted, when he says that " Men do not sell their goods for mere sounds," or denominations, but for the actual metal contained in the coin, or for some material, substance, or trading power measured by such coin, the coin and the metal being readily interconvertible.

11. I wish I could give M. Cemuschi credit for equally

clear perceptions as those he has enabled me to cite.   He
says, "all gold and silver produced are money : they are
dollars coming from under ground."   This is not even
metaphorically true ; because the law, or "common consent," creates the denomination called "a dollar," and
authorizes the fabrication of the coin, and gives it the
finishing stroke by making it legal tender.

12. M. Cernuschi also quotes Newton, and evidently
misconceives his meaning when he applies his language
to support his theory, that money is nothing but the
creation of the state, or has no other value except its
legal value.   Newton says, "It appears from experience,
as well as from reason, that silver flows *from* those places
where its value (he must mean legal value) is lowest in
proportion to gold, as from Spain to all Europe, and
from all Europe to the East Indies, China, and Japan ;
and that gold is most plentiful in those places in which
its (legal) value is highest in proportion to silver, as in
Spain and England."   In other words, the overvalued
metal (overvalued by law) drives the other (rightly or
under valued metal) to countries where it is undervalued,
or where its value is set by the natural laws.

13. Newton then points out how to remedy this evil,
which is to make the legal valuation to coincide with the
natural value of the metals.   By this method, however,
only a temporary equilibrium of value can be established,
because of the influence of the natural laws, which continually cause the ratio of the market value between the
two metals to vary and fluctuate, just as in the case
of other and more perishable commodities, — silver itself
having fluctuated twenty-five per cent in half a dozen
years.

14. But why, in the name of common sense, and
monetary and industrial science, should such a system
be adopted, or, where it exists, be continued, when the

simple remedy has long ago been found, and is being carried out with perfect success in so many of the commercial countries of the world? That remedy consists in making gold the legal measure of the market value of silver and all commodities, labor, lands, etc., or, in other words, making the legal (or coin) and the natural value of gold to coincide by interconvertibility, and using silver and other less valuable metals to supply just enough subsidiary coins to meet demand. (The best method to regulate such coins will be found in Chap. XXIV.) This is the only bi-metalism admissible by demonstrated principles of science, and is in perfect accord with the practical experience of commercial nations.

15. The new law of Congress, if not repealed, cannot fail to produce infinite mischief. In the first place, by seeking to pay old debts with a depreciated or over-valued metal, it casts an ineffaceable stigma on the honor and honesty of the nation. In the next place, if the law should remain on the statute-books of the nation for a few years, the overvalued silver will do exactly what Newton says of it : it will drive gold out of circulation, and the United States will have a currency like that of India, China, and Japan, *wholly of silver*, or *paper convertible into silver*. The inconvenience of such a currency, both in conducting home trade and industry, and in settlement of foreign exchanges, cannot be readily estimated. Merchants and bankers, as well as exchange brokers, will have to keep a pair of horses and a lock-up van to transport their metal daily from their counters to places of deposit. A lady going a-shopping with five hundred dollars will require to have a porter or a footman to carry thirty pounds avoirdupois weight of silver dollars ; or, if she has only the modest sum of a hundred dollars, she will have to carry the weight of an ordinary

brick in this inconvenient metal. Then, again, think of the unfortunate traveller, who has to carry more or less cash with him ! What is he to do? Mr. McKay should rewrite his book on popular delusions, in order to chronicle and do justice to this " silver craze." It will certainly come to be recorded as one of the wildest of delusions.

16. We shall, no doubt, be told by the silver-men that the practical inconvenience of a silver standard and currency will be averted by the adoption of a greenback or legal-tender national paper currency, convertible into the new, overvalued, silver coins. But this would only partially meet the question of convenience, and not at all the evils of a metallic standard that has fluctuated twenty-five per cent in four or five years. Only that long ago an ounce of silver was worth sixty-one pence in London. In less than three years it fell to forty-seven pence per ounce, and has since then oscillated between those figures ; which shows a total variation in price, as measured by gold, the more stable metal, of over twenty-five per cent. This is much worse than the fluctuations in greenbacks during the last five years.

17. As to the question of economy in adopting a cheaper metal, that, too, is a delusion. It is a more costly metal, when its ratio of value is considered, than gold. It takes fifteen times (more or less) the quantity to make it equivalent in value to gold, and fifteen times the cost to manufacture to transport and handle ; and, of course, it is subject to fifteen times the risk and wear and tear arising from use.

18. On the question of morality, the overvaluing of silver coin is exactly on a par with the alleged practices of the Jews, during the long period of the " Middle Ages," of " sweating," " clipping," and " filing " of coins, for profit, and that of many despots, who issued coins of half their former *legal* weight, and compelled their

subjects to accept them at their *old denominational* weights. This infamy now stamps every man who voted for the silver bill in the American Congress, unless he can plead ignorance.

19. M. Cemuschi is a representative bi-metallist, who argues that the law *can* set and maintain a fixed and unchangeable ratio between the two precious metals. At pp. 27 and 28 of his published evidence before the Congressional Commission on the silver question, issued in 1877, under the title, " Nomisma, or Legal Tender," he says, "*if* the relative value of gold and silver has always been determined by the conflict of the several legislations, how can we deny, that, when the legislations shall be everywhere and forever the same, the relative value of the metals will always remain the same?" He then goes on to show, in order to avoid utter stultification, that there exists what is purely an imaginary distinction between the principles which govern the market value of imperishable and perishable commodities. He says, " to fix by law a relative value between sugar and coffee, between two perishable commodities, or a legal tender and a commodity, would be a ridiculous attempt." But " nothing," he observes, " is easier than to fix by law the relative value between two everlasting legal tenders, gold and silver." Having in view the principles I have postulated, I could not find words so well selected as those quoted from M. Cemuschi, to push his own theory to the *argumentum ad absurdum*.

20. Even if the production of both these " everlasting" metals was stopped, the *demand alone* for consumption, in all its numerous ways, would continually change and fluctuate. Taste, fashion, and the cunning of workmen, in designing new and pleasing ornaments and works of art out of these metals, would keep their market value continually fluctuating or oscillating up and

down. The laws of nature are more "unchangeable" than those of the "Medes and Persians," and do not admit of such exceptions as M. Cemuschi thus boldly proclaims. His *assertion* is a mere *brutum fulmen*, on a par with the "Pope's bull against the comet."

21. I fail to see *one single advantage* established, even if the arguments of those who favor the proposed bi-metallic currency were logical and true, that is not better attained by a gold standard of value. On the other hand, I see dishonor, disgrace, folly, and vast public and private inconvenience as certain to arise from the carrying out of the new law of Congress as that the sun will continue to rise and set.

22. The following fluctuations in the market value of silver, indicating its trading power at various periods since the discovery of the silver mines of Potosi in 1545, have kindly been furnished me by Mr. Henry Kemp of Brooklyn, a Scotch gentleman well versed in correct economic principles. "Silver fell in price," says Mr. Kemp, "after the opening of the Potosi mines, from 1545 to 1697, 29.4 per cent; then rose in value, as compared with gold, from 1697 to 1776, 5.52 per cent; then it fell in price, from 1776 to 1848, 6.9 per cent; then rose again, from 1849 to 1859, 4.25; from 1859 to July, 1876, it fell 25.5 per cent; and from July, 1876, to 8th August, 1877, it once more rose 16 per cent." I add, since then to April 1, 1879, it has fallen 10 per cent; and this is the metal that the law of Congress in a few years will substitute for gold as the American standard of value.

23. The following extract from a letter addressed by M. Cemuschi, from Paris, to his friend, Mr. B. F. Nourse of Boston, during the agitation of the silver bill in Congress, is given in justice to him, and as sustaining my statement respecting bi-metalism in France and the effect of the American law : —

" It appears that the United States Government has made some engagement with the syndicate of the 4 per cents, and possibly the President will veto a bill re-opening the mint to the free coinage of silver. But let us suppose that the Congress resists the veto, and that the old silver dollar is rehabilitated in full. What the consequences?

" All the new silver of Nevada and the old silver of Germany would be brought to the American mint for coinage, and all gold would be exported from America to Europe. Against this assertion 'The Cincinnati Commercial' quotes France, where silver and gold circulate side by side, and from where gold is not exported. That is true ; but why is gold not exported from France ? Because silver is not coined, and consequently no silver is introduced into France. Should France re-open her mint to silver, she would absorb the American and German silver, and lose her gold. But, with the United States coining silver at the ratio 16, France cannot re-open her mint for coining five-franc pieces, which are at the ratio 15½ ; and then the United States will sell at a premium all their gold dollars against silver. In fact, the United States will become a silver monometallic country, just the same as English India.

" Here it is asked, what will then be the relative value of silver and gold on the general market, especially in London ? I answer, *always fluctuating.* While America has gold to give in exchange for silver, the value of silver can be high. When the American gold shall be exhausted, the value of silver will be weak. Various foreseen and unforeseen circumstances will later determine continuous changes in the respective value of gold and silver. Without a bi-metallic law fixing the same legal ratio in the principal countries, the relative value of gold and silver cannot be more stable than the relative value of sugar and coffee."

24. One of the chief arguments urged by the bi-metallists is, that their theory, if forced into effect by the arbitrary power of a combination of national governments, regardless of the natural laws of industry, would create an artificial market for silver. According to these gentlemen, the depreciation of silver would thus be arrested. They propose to compel the people of the whole civilized world to use a tool that is not the best, and which they refuse to use if they are allowed to choose for themselves.

The public needs a moderate supply of these tools for special uses, — for change, or fractional currency, for small purchases, and car and omnibus fares. But the bi-metallist says, "You must take more. You must employ a servant or a cart to carry your money, if needful." The plan overthrows the theory of making the two kinds of metallic money interconvertible, and leaving it to the choice of the people to decide how much of each kind they will have, which is the true one, founded on natural laws.

25. All laws made to force on the people the use and consumption of commodities they do not desire is the same as laws to compel them to part with their labor and goods at prices to be arbitrarily set by the state. The true theory of bi-metalism is to let the people decide how much of each kind of coins they require. The reader will find this more fully set forth in chapters XXV., XXVI., and XXVII.; and M. Cernuschi and other bi-metallists are respectfully requested to study those chapters, and indeed the whole of this work, before attempting to answer the reasons offered in this chapter against the correctness of their theory. When they come to comprehend the excessive absurdity of making any but the fittest metal the standard and measure of value, they will perceive the equal absurdity of attempting to enhance the market value of another metal, unsuited for any but a small supply of subsidiary coins, by giving to it, by law, a fictitious value. The fallacy of the theory is so glaring, so at variance with common sense, and so mischievous in its principle and practice, that the term "silver lunatics" can hardly be regarded as too severe a characterization of its advocates.

CHAPTER VII.

THE ORGANIZATION OF THE BANK OF ENGLAND. — THE LAW, THE FACT, AND THE SCIENCE OF THE CASE.

1. THE conspicuous position which the Bank of England occupies in the monetary and financial affairs of the world, and the vast influence and prestige of the bank itself, render it indispensable to consider very fully the principles involved in the plan of its organization, and the policy of its managers, which has become traditional. This chapter will be devoted to the former, and to showing that the policy and practice are at variance with the true intent and scope of the law, and with the principles of sound banking.

2. I have examined, with great patience, many of the works that have been written on this prolix subject since the passage of the Act of 1844, known as Sir Robert Peel's Act, which gave rise to the policy ever since carried out without change, and which seems to have made of the bank a mere automaton, so far as the issue and circulation of notes are concerned. What I propose to show is, that the Bank Act of 1844 leaves to the bank a large scope of discretionary power in respect to the issue and use of notes, which it has never exercised; and that to this circumstance is mainly due the chief evils of the British monetary and financial system.

3. Let us first see what the *law* says, and next what are the *facts* in respect to its interpretation, and the practice under the law; and finally what *science* suggests as the true policy. The law says, "That from and after the thirty-first day of August, 1844, the issue of promissory notes of the Governor and Company of the Bank of England, payable on demand, shall be separated and

thenceforth kept wholly distinct from the general banking business of the said Governor and Company; and the business of and relating to such issue shall be thenceforth conducted and carried on by said Governor and Company in a separate department, to be called the Issue Department of the Bank of England, subject to the rules and regulations hereinafter contained." The Act then specifies that the "Court of Directors may, if they think fit, appoint a committee or committees of Directors, for the conduct and management of such Issue Department." The second clause provides that "there shall be transferred, apportioned, and set apart by the said Governor and Company, to the Issue Department of the Bank of England, securities of the value of fourteen million pounds, whereof the debt due by the public to the said Governor and Company shall be and be deemed a part; there shall also, at the same time, be transferred, appropriated, and set apart by the said Governor and Company, to the said Issue Department, *so much* of the gold and silver bullion then held by the Bank of England *as shall not be required by the Banking Department thereof.*" I have italicized the last words, as they will be made to explain wherein the bank has failed to meet the spirit of the law, and to demonstrate the fundamental error of the practice of the bank.

4. The Act next provides that the Issue Department *shall* deliver to the Banking Department a gross amount of notes, including those in circulation and in hand, equal to the £14,000,000 of securities which the Banking Department has handed over to the Issue side, along with "so much gold and silver bullion" as the bank did not require for its business.

5. It will be observed that the law is mandatory; the word "shall" being used in respect to the *first step* in organizing, and fixes the amount of notes and securities

at £14,000,000; and the first statement issued under it on the first day of September, 1844, sets out with the maximum. But the next provision shows, that, *after* the organization on the distinct basis specified, the bank directors, as managers of the Issue Department, were at liberty to diminish the note issue to the bank *pari passu*, with the amount of securities held or deposited with the Issue Department. The Act says of the notes so to be delivered to the Banking Department, they "shall be deemed to be issued on *securities, coin,* and *bullion,* so appropriated and set apart to said Issue Department" (that, of course, means the entire notes issued); and it further makes this important provision, which the managers have totally ignored, and treated as a dead letter. "IT SHALL BE LAWFUL FOR SAID GOVERNOR AND COMPANY TO DIMINISH THE AMOUNT OF SUCH SECURITIES, AND AGAIN TO INCREASE THE SAME TO ANY SUM NOT EXCEEDING, IN THE WHOLE, THE SUM OF FOURTEEN MILLION POUNDS, AND SO FROM TIME TO TIME AS THEY SHALL SEE OCCASION."

6. The points I propose to make may as well be stated here. They are, that by inference, if not by the express words of the law, the bank possesses full and discretionary power in respect to the amount of "gold and silver coin and bullion" to be held for the conduct of its banking business; and also might increase and diminish its note circulation within the specified limitation of £14,000,000 (now increased to £15,000,000 by the lapsing of country bank circulation provided for by the Act), and thus control the outgo and inflow of notes according to the indications of supply and demand. I shall also show, that, by not observing and acting on such indications, and by treating its own notes issued *on securities,* which, like all the note issue, are not legal tender at its own counter, as good cash reserve, the bank trades on too small a margin of actual

cash reserve, and hence is most sensitively affected by the trade in bullion.

7. The first statement issued showed the fact that the Banking Department had transferred to the Issue side £14,351,000 of metal, and had retained, as "*actual*" *cash reserve*, £858,000 against the following immediate, or instant liabilities ; to wit : —

Public deposits	£3,631,000
Other deposits	8,644,000
Uncovered notes	5,825,000
Total	£18,100,000

The bank thus started on the fundamental error of treating its own notes, issued on securities, as good cash reserve, and has so continued to treat them to the present time (which is not sound banking), with less than one-eighteenth of its instant liabilities in *actual* cash. The fault of the law, it will thus be seen, consisted in not requiring all notes issued above the amount of securities, so deposited, to be always kept separate from the others, and all the metal received for them to be held sacred for their redemption to the last pound. As the practice is, the cash is what the managers first lay their hands on to redeem notes, and the securities are left as a *dernier resort*.

8. Before proceeding farther, let us suppose that the law had been so framed as to have required the bank to use the £14,000,000 of securities as trading capital instead of drawing on the stock of metal, — what, in this case, would have been the conduct of the bank? Would it have regarded the £856,000 of coin as adequate cash to hold for immediate calls, and "send round the corner" into Lombard Street, and raise cash on securities, whenever depositors came for cash, beyond the "till money" on hand? It is the "hocus-pocus"

manner of jumbling up in the Act the words "shall be deemed to be issued on *securities, coin,* and *bullion,*" that deceives otherwise good reasoners. The Issue Department of the bank, being wholly separated from the Business Department, is a statutory state-office, acting as *trustee* for the notes issued by it, one portion of which are secured by government stock, and another portion by gold and silver bullion and coin ; and the bank treats *all* the notes exactly as if they were issued wholly on "coin and bullion." It is absurd to suppose that an Act of Parliament can alter a logical fact. I shall presently show that the notes held by the bank are in actual circulation, or the same as if they were held by the public, — that the moment they pass out of the Issue Department they are, in theory and practice, in circulation. But, as the bank itself is liable for them, the *securities* in the Issue Department are the same in effect as if in the Banking Department. They can be used at any time by handing over notes in exchange.

9. The claim that the practice of the bank is the result of the law must be abandoned ; since it leaves it entirely discretionary with the directors to increase or diminish the amount of notes issued on securities, so it does not *exceed* the limitation set by law. There is no compulsion in the matter. Other banks, which keep their trading balances at the Bank of England, being able to use Bank of England notes as legal tender, or cash, are not likely to call for large sums of gold ; and hence the bank might be excused from making it a practice to keep on hand as large an amount of *actual* cash reserve as ordinary bankers. But the root of the evil is unquestionably in the principle of issuing notes *at all on securities*. If it is good trading for a bank to invest all its own capital in long or perpetual securities, it is equally good trading for merchants to do the same thing.

10. In the face of the clear and precise language of the Act, which authorizes the bank to lower and raise the amount of securities in the Issue Department, and, as a matter of course, to make similar changes in the amount of notes issued thereon, the following extract from the treatise of Mr. Thomson Hankey, a former Governor of the bank, reads somewhat strangely : " It must always be borne in mind, that, since the Act of 1844, the directors have had no control over that part of the currency which consists of bank notes ; that is, they have had nothing whatever to do with the *amount* at any time in circulation in the country."

11. This assertion, which lies at the foundation of the error of the bank, is true neither in fact nor in principle. The notes held in the Banking Department are in circulation the moment they leave the Issue Department, just as much as when they pass into the hands of other banks and the people at large, and are only evidences of the bank's indebtedness. They are in no sense cash in the hands of the bank. How, then, can they be so treated ? True it is, by a legal fiction, the bank ceased to be a bank of issue after the passage of the Act of 1844 ; but in fact, and in logical sequence, it is a bank of issue as much as ever, as to the notes issued on securities. The bank is, in fact, liable for all the notes it gives out. The only effect of the Act is to compel the directors, in their capacity as managers of the Issue Department, to hold the " securities, coin, and bullion," on which the law has " deemed " the notes to be issued, as sacred for their redemption. The law cannot change the scientific and actual fact that the bank has all its capital, and the " rest " fund besides, invested in the securities in question.

12. Mr. Leonard Courtney, M.P., author of the excellent article in the " Enyclopædia Britannica," ninth edi-

tion, on Banking, takes the same view in effect on this
subject; namely, that the reserve of notes held in the
Banking Department "are just as much in circulation
as if they were in the pockets and tills of the people."
To have followed this clear and important admission to
its logical result, would have forced Mr. Courtney to the
conclusion I have reached and presented, respecting the
impolicy of the bank treating any notes it may hold *up
to the statutory limitation* the same as actual cash.
Whatever it may occasionally hold, *above that limitation*,
may, in effect, be so treated, because such excess of
notes has gold behind it in the Issue Department.

13. Mr. Courtney, not having a clear perception of the
operation of the Bank Act, but seeing the confusion of
ideas resulting from its interpretation by the managers
and the city, suggests a removal of the note issue to some
other locality as desirable, in order to change the practice
of bankers. He says, "the purely mechanical act of
removing the issue of notes from Threadneedle Street
would make the facts of the situation plain, and would
bring about an alteration of conduct among London
bankers, so that it should conform to the facts thus perceived."

If the present system of issuing notes, and calling them
"Bank of England Notes," and holding the bank legally
liable for them, is to be continued, Mr. Courtney's suggestion seems to me impracticable without a complete
change of the law and practice. But allowing it to be
susceptible of execution, — that is, "the mechanical act
of removing the issue of notes from Threadneedle Street,"
— we will suppose to Whitehall, — the bank itself would
be the first to perceive the error of its present system of
treating the evidences of its own instant or present liabilities as good trading reserve. The bank cannot, on any
principle of legal fiction or commercial casuistry, treat

a security for its own indebtedness as reserve. As to the
securities held by the Issue against the Banking Department, they are, *pro tanto*, a guaranty of the note circulation ; and so many of the notes, in amount, as are issued
on securities, must be held to be only Bank of England
obligations in effect and in principle.

14. As to the claim of Mr. Hankey, "that, since the
Act of 1844, the directors have had no control over that
part of the currency which consists of bank notes," that
is only true as to those issued on metal. The law sets
no limit to the amount of notes issuable on gold and
silver coin and bullion. The issue on gold coin, or for
gold bullion for coinage, is, in fact, the only true and
scientific method of issuing notes ; as I shall fully demonstrate.   I cannot agree with those who point with satisfaction to periods when a large part of the bank's share
of the notes are lying idle, on the ground that the "ratio
between reserve and liabilities" is thus increased ; nor
can I share the alarm which these gentlemen affect to
feel when a sudden demand from abroad, or the country,
for, say, ten of the twenty-five or thirty millions of metal
held in the Issue Department, lowers the ratio of note
reserve to "the danger level," when the managers make
spasmodic efforts "to stop the drain," and bring back the
fugitive metal by raising the rate.   The working of this
plan will be vividly perceptible by going a step farther in
the direction of a coming panic, which has been hastened,
if not originated, by this sudden and sharp rise in the
bank rate above the market rate.   It is then that people
rush in for discounts to meet possible future requirements
for capital, which otherwise might not occur.   Depositors
call for notes and coin to be able to meet apprehended
calls on them.   Thus the reserve melts away "like the
baseless fabric of a dream."   It needs no argument to
prove that this is neither science nor good practical bank-

ing.   The managers and the public have simply mistaken
the cause for the effect.   The conduct of the bank managers has, in fact, been the *cause*, not the *result*, of the
demand for discounts.

15. If the directors, in their capacity of managers of
the Issue Department, were precluded from issuing notes
on the commodity, bullion, and were required to sell
them for coin only, leaving the mint to supply the coin,
as at present, the trade in bullion would be left by the
bank "severely alone," and in the hands of merchants
and brokers.   In this case the ebb and flow into and out
of the bank's cellars would cease to be watched with such
painful interest, in times of industrial excitement, by merchants, and dealers in capital.   The bank itself would
cease to rely on the Issue Department or the Government for aid in the contingency of a drain of a few
millions of metal for export or for the provinces.   The
securities, money and bullion, held by the Issue Department, are a trust-fund for the note-holders ; and when
the bank draws metal only, by presenting its own share
of the notes which it receives because of a paltry loan to
the nation, and which are in no way distinguishable from
the others, it is laying its hands on other folks' goods.
The right thing for it to do would be to draw from its
stock of securities, according to the promissory clause of
the law, and bury its gold in the market, maintaining,
always, an equilibrium between the gold in the issue and
the notes outside of the bank.   In other words, the
bank's share of the notes loaned to it on securities should
not be legal tender at the Issue Department, except in
redemption of securities ; and such notes ought to be
made distinguishable from notes issued on gold.

16. Mr. Hankey has very well described what constitutes a good cash reserve for a banker to hold, and con-
victs the Bank of England of bad banking.   He says, —

"The first clearly admitted duty of every deposit banker is always to retain at his command, *in cash*, a certain amount of his deposits. When this amount has been kept at about one-third of the whole (*liabilities*, he should have added), and the remainder of the deposits invested in what are ordinarily good banking securities, . . . no banker need apprehend difficulty." Again, he says, "The mercantile and banking community must be undeceived in the idea that *promises to pay* at a future date can be converted into immediate payment without a supply of ready money."

17. The point I make against Mr. Hankey and the bank theorists generally, is, that, because the law does not discriminate between notes issued on securities and notes issued on metal, the bank treats the whole issue as if it were made on metal. In this particular the law, as well as the practice of the bank, is at fault. It is my purpose to show conclusively, however, that the bank has it in its power, by diminishing the amount of notes issued on securities, and holding a larger amount of metallic money in its Business Department, to obviate much of the sensitiveness it now perpetually engenders in industrial circles by its efforts to regulate the trade in bullion by raising and lowering the rate. The best thing to be done is to sell all its securities, and bank on cash. That is the only true remedy for the evils in question.

18. To sum up the arguments on which I rest the conclusions I have arrived at respecting the treating of notes founded on securities as good trading reserve, —

1st, The treating all the notes as "issued on securities and gold and silver coin and bullion," as if they were issued *only* on metal, is inadmissible, both as a practical and logical conclusion, and is a fundamental error on the part of the bank.

2d, Notes issued on securities are no better, for a trading reserve, than the securities themselves, which are always lowest in market value when the reserve is most needed, and when their sale in large amounts would greatly lower their market value.

3d, If the plan of investing all the trading capital of a bank in government securities is a safe and good one for it, it is equally safe and good for all business houses, and, as before observed, for all other banks.

4th, This inevitable conclusion involves the absurdity of everybody investing their entire trading capital in such, or equally safe, securities, and conducting their business on borrowed means, as the Bank of England and the national banks of the United States do.

19. Those who accept the dogmas of the Bank of England as infallible, like Mr. Hubbard, who, in a speech in Parliament, said, "the practice of the bank is perfect," and that the evils of the British industrial system "are wholly due to bad trade," will treat these logical conclusions with scorn, simply because they are logical and unanswerable. But there are many excellent and successful business men, who amass a million or more in city trade, who can no more comprehend, either the process or the result of a mathematical demonstration than they can Hebrew or Sanscrit. I am not writing with the slightest hope of making converts of such. I do, however, hope to obtain from some one of this class a reply to one question ; to wit, "What would be the conduct of the bank, in respect to its trading reserve, if the issue of notes were transferred to Whitehall, and the bank's share of notes, issued on securities, were alone delivered to it, and the metal on which the others were issued was held by the Issue Department for redemption only of the notes issued on metal?" I am, of course, presuming that the bank is bound to find the cash for redeeming its quota of notes, just as the United States national banks must do under specie payments. This remark will show the decided superiority of the American over the British system, both of which are fundamentally wrong, and must sooner or later be changed. I furthermore invite all who dissent

from the position taken in this chapter, to read the next two chapters, if not the whole work. They will then be able to compare the present system with one demonstrated to be theoretically perfect.

CHAPTER VIII.

PROFESSOR BONAMY PRICE ON THE BANK CHARTER.

1. PROFESSOR PRICE, in his work on "Currency and Banking" (Henry S. King & Co., London, 1876), it will be seen, by reference to pp. 62 to 68, has fallen into several serious errors, like nearly all writers on the Bank Act, two of which I will notice. At p. 62 he states emphatically, that "In the Issue Department the bank directors have no more authority or right to speak or act than any other person in the kingdom." But I reply, these same directors, or a committee of them, constitute the managers of this same "Issue Department," and by the express terms of the Act, cited at the end of paragraph five of the foregoing chapter, have power "to diminish the amount of such securities" (£15,000,000), "and again to increase the same . . . as they shall see occasion."

2. At p. 67 he has fallen into an equally palpable and *mischievous* error, where he claims that the notes presented to the bank for payment are not the notes issued on securities. Here is what he says : —

"There has never been, since 1844, the slightest tendency of a run upon the bank for the payment of a single one of the fifteen millions of notes." The notes "shall be deemed to be issued on *securities, coin, and bullion ;*" so runs the language of the Act. It therefore follows, in a legal point of view, there is no distinction between notes issued on *securities, coin,* and *bullion*. They are all notes of the Bank of England; and the bank directors, acting as managers of the Issue Department, have perfect and unquestioned power to diminish and increase the amount of notes within the statutory limit of (at present) £15,000,000. Hence, as a logical and incontrovertible economic fact as well as principle, the first notes, in times of panic, or, indeed, on all occasions, presented for payment are notes *founded on securities*. In other words, they are the notes growing out of the business of the bank, not of the Issue Department. Mr. Price seems to have overlooked the fact, stated by Sir John Lubbock in his speech in the House of Commons in 1873, that the Bank of England, *as a bank*, is liable for every note issued from the Issue Office. It is the height of absurdity to claim that the fiction of having a separate issue office has done any of the acts imputed to it ; or that, because this office stores the securities and metal, the Bank of England does not deal or speculate in both securities and metal. If the fluctuations in the gross volume of notes were not within the limits of the amount of notes issued to the bank on securities, the bank would not be so sensitive about the loss of a few millions, or even the whole of the metal occasionally ; and if the directors ever come to understand the true principles of banking, and cease to treat their own share of the notes issued on securities as good reserve, they will at once perceive the gross fundamental error on which they now act. At p. 66 Professor Price correctly says, " The gold stored and kept in the Government Office, the Issue Department, *in no sense belongs to the Bank of England. It is no part of its reserve ;* and it is a great misfortune that the framers of the Act of 1844 should have made the exceedingly unintelligent blunder of mixing up together, in the weekly reports of the bullion at the bank, two absolutely dissimilar and distinct things, — the gold stored away by one office to face the bank-notes, and the gold belonging to the Bank of England as a banker." This is expressed "excellently well."

3. The latter part of the last sentence is what the late Artemus Ward would call "a little mixed." The Act is not responsible for the "mixing up together," but the bank directors, who, like the Professor, treat the notes issued to the bank (the £15,000,000) as issued on gold, and those held in the Issue Department as the veritable notes issued on securities. There should be no dodging or hocus-pocussing in a matter entirely within the limits and scope of scientific demonstration. The facts are: First, the bank has all its share capital and "rest" invested in government securities. Second, it has, at all times, an equal amount (£15,000,000) of notes charged by the Issue Department against it, — the Banking Department, — on account of the securities so held and credited by the said Issue Department. The notes so held by the bank, and used as trading reserve, *must, therefore, "be deemed to be issued on securities alone;"* though the total issues are declared to be on "securities, coin, and bullion." If this is not the clear logical as well as legal construction of the Act, "its framers" certainly *did* commit "the exceedingly unintelligent blunder of mixing up" the entire business. I claim they *did not* do so, but that the bank directors are in error, and do not comprehend the spirit or intent of the Act, or the business of modern banking.

4. But how can Professor Price's declaration, which is logical and true, that "the gold stored and kept in the Government (the) Issue Department in no sense whatever belongs to the Bank of England," be reconciled with his assertion, on the next page of his work (67), that, "there has never been, since 1844, the slightest

tendency of a run upon the bank for a single one of the
£15,000,000 of notes,"— meaning, of course, those
always charged against the bank on account of securities? He might as well have said, "the notes held by
the Bank of England, as a banker, are notes issued on
metal, which the Issue Department holds in trust for the
bank ; and the £15,000,000 of securities, corresponding
in amount with the notes delivered to the bank in addition to those delivered to the bank on coin and bullion,
always remain in the Issue Office, and are there held as
assets when all the metal is gone." The Professor (as
well as the directors of the bank, who are *ex officio*
managers of the Issue Office) *must* accept one horn or
the other of the dilemma. Let them choose which they
like best. If the notes held by "the Bank of England,
as a banker," are notes issued on metal, "stored and
kept in the Government Office," it is a breach of trust,
and a fraud on the public, to treat them as "reserve,"
and demand gold for them. On the other hand, if the
£15,000,000 so held are "to be deemed (as logically
they must be) to be " the notes covered by the securities of which the bank, and not the public, is the owner,
then the Bank of England commits an equal fraud by
drawing metal for them to meet calls on *the bank itself*
for such metal.

5. The present theory and practice of the bank is
only a bungling juggle that ought to deceive nobody. I
repeat, though the entire issue of notes is expressly declared by law to be "deemed to be issued on securities,
coin, and bullion," the bank treats those it holds, and
which it gets by reason of securities deposited, as trading
reserve, as though they were issued on metal alone. So
far as the Issue Department is concerned, this is not
admissible. Much less is it admissible on the part of
the bank, which is bound by law to pay metal for *all* the

notes. It is not permissible in a banker to "blow hot and cold " at the same time.

6. At p. 68 Professor Price declares, that, "in respect of the supposed aims of its promoters, the Bank Act must be pronounced a failure." In this view and in much of what follows I cordially agree, because the facts and the principles are scientifically correct. But I cannot see the enormous advantages, stated on the same page, as resulting from "a saving to the *nation*," as the Professor erroneously calls it, of the paltry sum of £15,000,000, by issuing to the bank that amount, uncovered by metal. I shall show conclusively hereafter (Chap. XXVII.) that gold is the cheapest money, and that paper founded on the same, pound for pound, is the best paper money in the world. I will show that the entire metallic money of the kingdom only costs about one and threepence a head per annum of the whole population, and is as one to fifteen hundred of the annual productions of labor. The saving of £15,000,000, all told, is just ten shillings a head on thirty millions of people ; and the interest at four per cent is £600,000, equal to four and sixpence, — four and six-tenths of a penny per head of the population. The Scotch are said to have made fourpence a head by selling their king. Besides, Great Britain thinks nothing of spending twice £15,000,000 on a negro war in the wilds of Africa.

I wish I could quote all the Professor has said, so well, in favor of small notes issued on gold. But I have tried elsewhere to do justice to this subject in my own way.

7. At p. 74 the Professor suggests an amendment to the Act to remove the Issue Department away from the bank's premises, to Somerset House or Whitehall, and requiring the weekly statement of the issue of notes and quantity of metal to be published separately from that of the bank's affairs. He should have gone farther, and in-

sisted on the notes being made payable by the United Kingdom of Great Britain and Ireland, and to require the bank to buy what notes it requires, for gold coin or bullion, for coinage, pound for pound, as all others in the kingdom now do. In this case the state notes will be good banking reserve, — "as good as gold."

8. I hope that Professor Price, and those who, like him, are willing to tolerate the present British system, with the slight change of removing the issue of the notes to some other locality, will come to agree with me that the *bank note* is at the bottom of all *currency* disturbances. Whether the High Court of Judicature, if the case were brought before it, would decide that the notes to the amount of £15,000,000 used to the bank for its own business purposes, are issued on account of public securities, for which the Issue Department ought not to pay out gold, or whether the bank, like any other holder, could properly demand to be paid in metal, matters not. The issue I make with the system is, that the conduct of the bank, and of all bankers and merchants, so far as such conduct is influenced by the present system, would be very different, if the "surgical operation" I insist on were made. The bank then will recoup its capital now invested in these public securities, and will hold metal in their place for its reserve. A true scientific monetary system will turn over the trade in metal to merchants and bullion dealers, the same as in case of all other commodities, and effect a complete separation of money from finance.

9. I have now only further to ask from the Professor, or some of those who argue as he does, for a reconciliation of the two following passages, one of which has before been quoted, but is again reproduced for comparison. These passages occur in paragraphs 4 and 5, pp. 66 and 67, of his work, "Currency and Banking."

1st, " The gold stored and kept in the Government Office, the Issue Department, *in no sense whatever* belongs to the Bank of England. It is *no part* of the *reserve.*"

2d, " Gold, no doubt, is constantly asked for at the counters of the bank ; but what does the bank do? It sends the notes" (notes, mind, which constitute a part of its trading " reserve ") " over to the State Office, and gets gold for them at once."

If the gold " in *no sense whatever* belongs to the bank," how dare the bank " send the notes over to the State Office and get gold for them?" Why don't some plucky Englishman have the managers of the Issue Department indicted for giving the fellows across the hall gold instead of securities? The case is a serious one. It is hardly better than stealing. It is a penitentiary offence to use trust-funds ; and here it goes on daily, and on a huge scale. " Ignorantia non excusat legem." The directors are warned of their peril.

CHAPTER IX.

THEORY AND PRACTICE OF THE BANK OF ENGLAND FURTHER CONSIDERED.

1. I WISH to remind the reader that I am discussing, analyzing, and applying ascertained principles to the practical business of supplying and regulating the amount of money, metallic and paper, to the demands of industry. The Bank of England, by reason of its great capital, and the prestige which it enjoys and in part derives from the sort of partnership it has with the state, has become the centre of the whole monetary, if not financial, system of the kingdom, and, in a manner, of the world. After

the breaking up of the East India and Hudson Bay companies, and the numerous industrial monopolies fostered for ages by state protection, we have the conspicuous exceptional example of this one great bank, sustained by law, and often by the direct interposition of the Government, carrying out a policy utterly at variance with sound scientific and business principles and with the doctrines of free trade.

2. A careful analysis of the theory and practice of the bank in the conduct of its business will show the truth of these propositions. An extreme sensitiveness, and liability to a panicky condition of trade, has become a chronic disease in the British industrial system; and very clear evidence exists that it has its origin in the practice of the bank, in respect to its efforts to control the trade in bullion and in the note issue. This phenomenon is nearly unknown in France, whose great National Bank, with a much smaller proprietors' stock, holds a vastly larger ratio of actual cash capital to its instant liabilities. This circumstance of itself affords very strong evidence that the policy of continually "acting on the exchanges," in order to control the bullion trade, is as wrong in theory as it is disastrous in practice. The theory itself is so much discussed by business men, and is so well understood from long observation of its working, that the great leading houses, bankers and others, endeavor to predict what the bank will do to-morrow, next day, or in a week, by the export and import of bullion. All are watching with the utmost care the increasing or diminishing tons of ingots held in the vaults of the bank, because these constitute the barometer to the exchanges; and all speculate in their minds on the possibilities and probabilities of the immediate future. I firmly believe, from the actual facts I have mentioned, that the only cure of this diseased state of the monetary and financial system of

the country is a surgical operation which will sever the
present relations of the bank from national financial connection, and the issue of notes on coined money alone,
whether this latter be done by the bank on the bank
premises, or by the State at Whitehall. As I observed in
the last chapter, this will leave the trade in bullion to
those who make a specialty of it; and it will then sink
to the level in importance with the trade in other great
commodities, such as cotton and corn: and people at
large will not grow nervous over it.

3. Let us again examine the facts of the case with a
little more explicitness, without going into historical details, which it is presumed the reader already under-
stands. *The bank has loaned all the proprietors' capital
to the government, amounting to some £11,000,000, for
which the government pays the usual rate of interest,*
and has granted to the bank the right to issue, or, more
correctly speaking, to receive from the Issue Department,
a full equivalent in notes. By lodging an additional
amount of government securities, now making a total of
£15,000,000, it is entitled to receive that amount of
notes; and the portion of this sum not actually passed
beyond the walls of the bank constitute its reserve, except a small amount held in coin, seldom kept up to a
million. This plan of founding a note issue on securities uncovered by gold or silver is at the bottom of the
whole of the evils of the British and American monetary
systems. When there comes a call for bullion for shipment, or coin for the provinces, the portion of these
unemployed notes held as reserve is drawn upon and
presented for payment in gold, and the store of gold
diminishes *pari passu* with the reduction in the volume
of such reserve. With the influx of gold into the vaults
of the bank, the reverse of this happens. The ratio of
reserve to liabilities increases; and a certain, not exactly

defined, ratio between the reserve of notes and the bank's liabilities is considered healthy. When the ratio is lowered suddenly and considerably, people grow alarmed, and become panicky, because it foreshadows a rise in the rate of discount. When it rises above the usual, or, what is considered by the managers, *normal* condition (if any such condition can be considered normal in a machine subject to continual artificial regulation and change), then low rates of interest prevail. There is in such cases a plethora of unemployed capital, which by and by engenders speculative trading and careless and generally bad investments. These are the conditions resulting from the present theory and practice of the bank.

4. By way of illustration, we have only to consider what its policy would be if the bank were compelled by law to act on a different theory in respect to its business. Let us suppose that the Bank Act has been amended so as to embrace a clause like the following, the rest of the Act being made consistent therewith : " The notes issued on public securities shall not be legal tender in payment of public or private debts, and shall be made distinguishable by color and form from those issued in payment of coin ; and the notes issued on government securities shall be held to be notes of the said Governor and Company of the Bank of England ; and those issued in payment of coin shall be held to be notes issued by the State, and shall be made payable by the United Kingdom of Great Britain and Ireland, on demand, in lawful gold or silver coin, according to the requirements of the holder, and shall be legal tender everywhere in said United Kingdom, except by the Issue Department and its agencies."

5. The notes issued by the state, or the bank directors as a board of issue for the state, would then be good

cash reserve for the Bank of England, or any banker or merchant, to hold; but it would, in such case, be equally clear that the bank's notes issued on securities would not, in the bank's own hands, be so considered by Mr. Hankey or any other authority on banking or trade. What the bank would be compelled to do in this situation would be to sell its notes for coin; and if the coin refused to stay, and its notes came back for conversion too quickly, it would have to contract the issue, and sell a portion of the £15,000,000 of public securities to provide adequate reserve. By this method the public would plainly perceive the true position of the paper-money circulation, and the managers themselves would know the exact relations of the two principles involved in the issue, to wit, that of issuing notes on securities and on metal. Such a plan would be equivalent to a mechanical and geographical or local separation of the issue from the business of the bank. The illustration seems to make the question intelligible enough for the most ordinary business man to comprehend.

6. Equally clear would it become, under such an alteration of the law, that the holding of a million of coin, or cash gold and silver, would not be a safe amount for a bank to hold against thirty or forty million pounds of instant or comparatively short liabilities, of which its own notes would form a part, when in the hands of the public. Such "a separation" would be very different from the present statutory separation. The "mechanical separation" of the two departments, suggested by Mr. Leonard Courtney, M.P., in his article in the "Encyclopædia Britannica," with a clause in the Act such as I have quoted, would not be necessary to influence the conduct of other bankers and city men. The Bank of England might still manage the Issue Department without leading to confusion of thought respecting the separa-

tion, and with decided advantage to business interests, as compared with the present plan; though this is not the plan I would suggest.

7. The analysis of the principles involved in the present system of issuing notes and treating them as good banking reserve by the bank, and the illustration I have given of a system that forbids, on business principles, the regarding and treating of such portion of the notes as reserve, seem to me to be demonstrative of the errors that underlie the whole monetary system of the nation. The fundamental error may be traced to the misconception, by the managers, of the power they possess of controlling the volume of notes, and of diminishing and increasing them in amount, within the statutory limit, — at present £15,000,000, — "as occasion may require," or, as I would express it, according to the law of supply and demand, or the requirements of industry. Mr. Hankey truly says that "the more the conduct of the Bank of England is made to assimilate to the conduct of every other well-managed bank in the United Kingdom, the better for the bank, and the better for the public at large."

8. Much has been said about the prudent and safe method by which the Bank of England is governed in the conduct of its business, and the handsome profits which result from such prudence. But these are merits in no way superior to those to which a large number of important joint-stock and private banking concerns, as well as merchants, are equally entitled to lay claim; and in the matter of profit to the proprietors, there are scores of such banks and houses which pay far larger dividends on the capital invested. When it is considered that the Bank pays nothing on the large government balances it holds, averaging over £5,000,000, and the trading balances of joint-stock and numerous mercantile and private

banking houses, while other bankers pay for the depositors' capital they trade on, there is not much for the Bank of England to boast of in the matter of profit to its proprietors.

9. I will now briefly consider the claim set up by Mr. Hankey and the Bank of England managers and *doctrinaires*, that the bank does not aim to "*make* the rate of discount in the loan market," when it raises and lowers its own rate, but only seeks to "keep *in* the market." If this were true, why do the whole of this class of exponents of the policy of the bank continually speak of the necessity or desirability of "acting on the exchanges" by this method? This is, in fact, the avowed purpose of the bank managers in cases where they apprehend a large and long-continued withdrawal of bullion for shipment, when they run the rate up rapidly, one or two per cent at a jump, and get far ahead of the market rate, which follows at a distance. This proceeding is "making the rate," or it is nothing.

10. The matter of fact being disposed of, it is competent for a writer on principles to inquire into the motives, other than those alleged, for the practice, and the effect of the practice on the industries of the people. Some eminent authorities, with much show of justice, allege that the bank finds its advantage in playing with the rate as did the New York "Rings" of speculators just after the great civil war, when, by a powerful combination, they were able to "lock up" so large an amount of capital for a time, as to cause a heavy fall in the price of securities in the market, which the Ring then bought up, and was able to sell at a handsome profit, when they set the "locked-up" capital afloat. It is alleged, and I am assured by high authority, that the bank certainly does take advantage of the fall in public and other securities caused by its own acts, to make heavy pur-

chases. The practice in New York became so conspicuous, that it at length led to the passage of an Act of Congress making such practices misdemeanors, punishable by fine and imprisonment; since which time the practice of " raising the rate " by such means has altogether ceased. But whether such mercenary motives lie at the root of the practice of the Bank of England in thus "acting on the exchanges," on the pretext of preventing the undue outflow of bullion, or not, its injurious effects on industrial pursuits cannot be doubted.

11. The sudden raising and lowering of the rate of discount, or the price paid for capital in the loan market, whether effected by the Bank of England, or by other artificial combinations of capitalists, has the same effect as the rapid fluctuations in an irredeemable paper currency. It strikes directly at the natural regulator of values, supply and demand, and unhinges all business plans. It is the same in its effects on values, as the perpetual " tinkering " with customs and excise duties. Prudent merchants and manufacturers look six to twelve months ahead for their supplies in trade and business. They make bargains for the future; and hence it is of the utmost importance to general trade that there should be no means at the sole disposal of any financial institution, or body of capitalists, capable of causing sudden changes in the price of capital, because the price paid for goods must depend on the rate of interest. Nothing is clearer than this principle, that the price of capital invested in trade and all industrial pursuits, as well as of wages, forms a large proportion of one side of the equation of supply and demand; and hence all artificial disturbances of such *price*, or, let us call it, *market value*, are contrary to public policy, and ought to be counteracted, and not sustained by law.

12. The "acting on the exchanges" by the bank is

the same as if Parliament were to place the power in the
hands of a great corporation, to impose export and import
duties on all the products of industry entering into home
and foreign trade ; and this body, or corporation, for its
own purposes, kept perpetually increasing and diminishing such duties. This will appear perfectly clear if we
consider, that when the bank succeeds, as it often has
done, in raising the market rate of interest in a few days
or weeks, five, six, or more per cent, and then again in
lowering it in a similar way, the merchant must take the
effect into account in making his bargains. The rise so
caused is exactly the same as a tax imposed by the state,
for the time being, on all the trading capital of the country. Such a tax, if made permanent, and not unduly
high, would soon become normal ; and all business would
adjust itself to it, and no great evil would ensue. But
when the bank imposes it, no one can say exactly how
long it will last, or how high or how low it will go. In
this matter the Bank of England has a most decided
advantage over other discount houses and all traders, in
being able to profit by its own secret acts and plans. It
is a large dealer in first-class railway, as well as public,
securities of foreign countries and consuls, all of which
are easily influenced in market value by the practice in
question (note III.).

13. If the bank would avoid these imputations, it
should change its policy of making a flourish of the rate
before the world, and move on quietly with and. in the
market. If its stock of gold is slipping away too fast
for its resources, the true and natural method is to curtail its note issue by diminishing its securities in the
Issue Department, and converting them into gold coin.

14. It is evident from what Mr. Hankey says in his
treatise on Banking, that the bank is losing its hold on
the market. He says, "It has very frequently occurred,

that after a *very long* succession of very *low rates* of
interest, indicated by a great abundance of unemployed
capital, an extent of business has been undertaken, far
beyond what a judicious regard to safety should have
induced : and if, when this state of things is in existence,
any sudden apprehension of an approaching scarcity
should occur, *no rise* in *the rate of discount* will immediately check the demand ; on the contrary, the very
opposite effect may be produced." Mr. Hankey has un-
wittingly laid down the natural law in respect to such
spasmodic and artificial attempts to influence the price
of capital. But he has simply, like the bank managers,
mistaken the cause for the effect.

15. If, in such cases as Mr. Hankey specifies, the
object of raising the rate is to operate *against* the
tendency of the market towards a temporary adverse
condition of the foreign exchanges, and thus to stay the
export of bullion, the effort will be abortive, unless the
bank succeeds in carrying the market rate up with its
own, which it now frequently fails to accomplish, *for the
simple reason that those who find a profit in shipping
bullion always buy it, or raise their capital to buy it, at
the lowest, and not the highest,* or *bank rate,* and because
the market is getting too large to be influenced in this
way.

16. From what has been said, it must be inferred that
the bank, to the extent of its power, perpetually in-
fringes or contravenes the great fundamental principles
of free trade and the free action of the natural laws.
Professor Bonamy Price, in a series of well-written articles published in "The Daily News," in December, 1875,
pointed out the fatuity of the bank policy, in respect to
the playing with the rate, because a few tons, more or
less, of metal had been called for by foreign dealers, and
for use in the Provinces. My own impressions up to that

time had been, that, in this matter, the bank directors were simply acting in ignorance of the principles of monetary and industrial science, and not with the view of profit. I shall devote another chapter to this subject in order to consider the plan suggested by Mr. Ernst Seyd, a German actuary, and statistician of great research and ability, who writes well from those stand-points. It will be seen by those who have examined Mr. Seyd's ingenious and practical method of treating the issue of notes by the bank, that he has reached by actuarial logic the same conclusions, respecting the error of the theory and practice of the bank, that I have done by deduction and inference, or strictly logical methods.

CHAPTER X.

FALLACY OF THE THEORY OF " ACTING ON THE EXCHANGES " BY THE BANK OF ENGLAND. — VIEWS OF MR. ERNST SEYD.

1. Mr. Ernst Seyd, mentioned at the close of the last chapter, who has studied the whole subject of the Bank of England theory and practice from a strictly actuarial stand-point, and has published two works on "The Error of the Bank of England Note Issue," has, since the last two chapters were (May, 1876) mostly written, kindly favored me with his views in writing, and a copy of his printed work last issued. These works embrace a large amount of statistical information, on the entire subject of money circulation in Europe and America, of much interest. He has noticed the circumstance, dwelt on by me in Chap. VII., that the bank has always kept what he calls " the fiduciary issue " of notes predicated on government securities at its " maximum," and

hence has failed to meet the clear intent of the Act of
1844. His reasoning on the failure of the bank to
regulate its note issue, within the statutory limit, by lowering and raising the amount of notes, in order to give
the elasticity necessary to meet the natural laws of industry, or to measure out supply in conformity with demand,
is unanswerable. He has made up numerous theoretical
bank statements showing how, by first diminishing, and
then raising, within the prescribed limits, the amount of
securities held against notes issued to the Banking
Department, and therewith *pari passu*, the volume of
such notes held as reserve would meet the ebb and flow
of supply and demand.

2. This is simply another method of proving that the
bank acts on a fundamental error in treating its notes
issued on securities as banking reserve ; for, if the bank
does not hold a reserve of notes on Mr. Seyd's theory,
it must supply their place by selling the securities and
holding coin as a reserve. The full title of the last
work of Mr. Seyd, now before me, is "Statement of
Accounts showing and illustrating the Error of the
Practice in the Note Issue of the Bank of England."
Not the least important fact, dwelt on by Mr. Seyd with
much emphasis, is, that the bank keeps its surplus funds
invested in long securities. As these funds are borrowed, and constitute instant liabilities, being depositors'
capital, it proves by Mr. Hankey's argument, already
quoted in Chap. VII., that the Bank of England totally
disregards what other bankers consider sound banking.
What Mr. Seyd urges is, that the bank ought to engage
more extensively in discounting short commercial paper,
out of which he claims it would make a large profit for
its stockholders by getting compound interest. He also
points out the risk always attending long investments
made from borrowed capital, which may be called for at

any moment, when such securities may have fallen in market value by reason of crises. The bank statements should be so made up as to show to what extent it is a dealer in debentures and other long securities, in order to enable the public to form a more correct idea of its financial position from week to week, and of its probable course in regard to the rate. The words, " other securities," are by far too indefinite to be of any value for such purpose. There is nothing like short commercial paper based on goods for availability as banking assets. In so far as Mr. Seyd has laid stress on this error of the bank, which is fundamental in banking business, I agree with him.

3. I have already remarked on the fallacious plan of having the entire proprietors' capital locked up in perpetual government securities, and then relying wholly on borrowed capital to trade on. If, in addition to this fundamentally wrong system of banking, a large part of depositors' capital which the bank has borrowed is invested in long securities, liable to wide fluctuations in market value, it is no wonder the intervention of Government is so frequently invoked to save it from making disastrous losses or being compelled to suspend payment. I appeal to the judgment of British statesmen and economists, and to the common sense of the people, whether such a system ought to be tolerated in the present advanced stage of commercial intelligence. If the practice of allowing the Bank of England to suspend in order to save it from making sacrifices to maintain its solvency is a part of the system, it should be made applicable to all other joint-stock banks. " What's sauce for the goose is sauce for the gander."

4. If other large banking concerns would agree to abandon the practice of holding a large proportion of their trading balances or margins on deposit at the bank,

and retain them in their own vaults, it would probably
have a beneficial effect on the loan market in cases of a
panicky feeling threatening a crisis ; and the bank would
then, probably, not have so frequently to pray to Hercules for assistance, and the trade in debentures would
be left to syndicates and debenture companies. It is very
obvious that no part of a banker's trading capital, much
less the capital of depositors, held on call, or at short
notice, can, with propriety, be invested in such long
securities as are liable to extensive fluctuations, or even
consols, which sometimes fall many points in a few days,
as just prior to the Russian war in 1854. As Mr. Hankey has put it, " promises to pay at a future date " cannot
be made to take the place of " a supply of ready money."

5. Should Sir Robert Peel's provision in the law of
1844, for giving to the Bank of England the whole of
the lapsing country bank note circulation, be expedited,
as intimated by the present Chancellor of the Exchequer,
the evils of the bank's fallacious and mischievous policy
will be aggravated to exactly the extent of such increase
in the volume of notes issued on securities. If, instead
of the present " fiduciary issue " of £15,000,000, the
limit be raised to £30,000,000, and the present practice
of keeping the whole in circulation (for I hold with Mr.
Courtney that all " held in reserve in the bank are as
much in circulation as if they were in the tills and pockets
of the people "), it is easy to see how enormously the
already great sensitiveness of the market will be increased.

6. If the bank would change its policy so as to make
it conform to the illustrations of Mr. Seyd, that is, avail-
ing itself of the provision of the law to lower and raise
the amount of notes issued on securities, such a calamitous state of things would be averted, in case the threat
of Sir Stratford Northcote be carried out, to give full

scope to Sir Robert Peel's intentions about the country, Irish, and Scotch banks' circulation. A very little consideration will show the desirability of the suggested alteration in policy. The metallic circulation of the country is a fixed amount, or nearly so, and is wanting in some degree the greater elasticity of a convertible paper money system. The gold coin is not subject in the same degree to the influences of supply and demand, which cause gold bullion, as a commodity, or raw material, to be sent abroad, and hence possesses less elasticity than the commodity which has the whole world for a market. Add to this circumstance the fact that the bank keeps its "fiduciary notes" always at the maximum allowed by law, it will be seen how many elements of a perfect monetary system are deficient.

7. Mr. Seyd inferentially, if not directly, treats the reserve of notes as Mr. Courtney and I do, as, in principle, the same as though they were floating about outside the walls of the bank. The very fact that they are treated by the bank as trading or banking reserve, though erroneously, proves the correctness of this method of regarding such notes. They are held to meet immediate calls for cash, just as those held by other bankers and merchants, and, in the absence of coin, are just as necessary to the Bank of England as to any other bank, so far as the demand for notes is concerned. The bank, however, treats *all* the notes given out by the Issue Department as cash liabilities against that department and not as against itself. In essence and in principle the issue of notes *on securities* is a method whereby a man can own a good investment and possess himself of its value in money, which is an absurdity (postulates 52, 53).

8. One of the best reasoned-out portions of Mr. Seyd's work is where he shows the fallacy of the theory of using the "rate" to act on the exchanges, in order to

influence the trade in bullion, instead of making the note
issue do that work by the means indicated, and allowing
the trade to be governed by supply and demand. He
points out, and illustrates by statements, how the bank first
raises its rate above the market, or natural rate, to attract
a large supply of bullion, and then, when this end is
attained, or the outflow has been arrested, runs the rate
down, often as low as two per cent, in order to drive
it away again, thus causing the utmost inconvenience to
all industries requiring steady rather than high or low
rates of interest. Mr. Seyd's words are, " It is painful,
because it would seem a pity, that, after having made
great efforts to recover bullion and set the issue right, we
should immediately afterwards make efforts to drive it
away again. It is uncertain, because, though we know
that the process adopted must take bullion away, yet we
cannot control or check its effect without occasional jerks
upwards of our rates."

9. While I fully agree with Mr. Seyd, as well as Mr.
Bonamy Price, about the impolicy of acting on the outgo
and inflow of bullion, by playing with the rate like chil-
dren playing at shuttlecock, I propose a more complete
and scientific, as well as practical, remedy. Mr. Seyd's
reforms are limited to the raising and lowering, within the
legal limit, the amount of fiduciary notes ; whilst I insist
on removing the issue wholly from the Bank of England,
and all other banks in the kingdom. But I concede to
Mr. Seyd, as well as to Mr. Price, that they have conclusively demonstrated the fallacy of the theory of " acting on the exchanges," which should be left severely
alone, to be regulated by the only true, equable, and
natural regulator, the demand of the world for all commodities, bullion and money included, on the one hand,
and the market supply of these on the other.

10. After Mr. Seyd's elaborate exposition of the true

intent and meaning of the law, in respect to the power
of the bank to diminish and increase the issue of notes,
Mr. Hankey's assertion, that, "since the passage of the
Act, the bank has had no control over the volume of the
note issue," seems utterly inexplicable. The limits within
which the bank possesses this power absolutely in its
hands, is equal to the whole fiduciary issue of £15,000,-
000, — a pretty wide range in the present scope of industry and general trade. Perhaps, half a century hence,
when the business of the country shall have trebled or
quadrupled, a larger amount to operate on may be
necessary.

11. While conceding so much to Mr. Seyd's exposition
of the fallacy of the traditional policy of the Bank of England, I shall have to take exception, in a future chapter,
to a theory he has attempted to set up for the regulation
of interest. He has published a work on this subject,
entitled "A More Perfect Working System between Bullion and Interest." From a glance over it, I reached the
conclusion that it was simply a new version of the old
Mercantile Theory. Mr. Seyd proposes artificial methods
of regulating the rate of interest, all and sundry of which
are fundamentally wrong; as the natural laws only can
properly regulate the market value of capital and all other
things. The English law of "Let alone," and the American of "Masterly inactivity," express the exact idea of
what is the best method of regulating the rate of interest,
and all kinds of industries.

12. I will only observe, on the subject of this proposal
to establish "a more perfect working system between
bullion and interest," that it is impracticable, and at variance with the true principles of trade and industry, which
thrive best when left to the competition of all the world.
Bullion is simply a commodity, of no more importance in
the industrial system than any other equal in the amount

in which it is dealt in, and exercises no more influence on interest than cotton, in proportion to their respective values. It is simply a question of values, when we come to inquire into the relative influences of commodities. Each one contributes its quota to the great ocean of floating capital, or trading power, which regulates all values, and differentiates the exact proportion contributed by each commodity. In this ocean, gold and silver float on the same level, so to speak, as wheat, corn, and cotton ; and iron, lead, and cotton become as light as feathers or cork. Is it not, therefore, a sheer waste of time to set up pretensions in favor of the "precious metals," which are no more precious, in the vast aggregation of things having market value, than any article for which they are exchanged?

13. I do not wish to raise side issues as to the motives of the managers of the Bank of England in playing with the rate. The alleged reasons for "acting on the exchanges," and influencing the trade in bullion, are sufficient to sustain the basis of reasoning I have adopted in order to demonstrate its fallacy. In a subsequent chapter I shall specially treat of the subject of bullion, and point out very clearly the difference in the uses and principles of bullion and of coined money, — the raw material and the manufactured article.

CHAPTER XI.

MONEY AND BULLION. — WRONG THEORIES RESPECTING THEM.

1. I POINTED out, incidentally, at the conclusion of the last chapter, the circumstance that the precious metals constitute only one of the factors, some more and some less influential, which make up in the commercial world

the great, ever-balancing, but never quite balanced, sheet of human industries. I also pointed out the self-evident fact, that the trading power of these metals differs in no way from that of other commodities, and was simply in the ratio of their gross market values. I now propose to show and prove the scientific and practical difference between money, the manufactured article, and bullion, the raw material.

2. It has been the practice of some of the best writers on economic science, from Adam Smith to the present time, including Mill and McCulloch, and especially of City authorities,[1] *et hoc genus omnia*, to confound money with bullion, or at least not to distinguish between them. Adam Smith says, "Money is a commodity with regard to which every man is a merchant. Nobody buys it, but in order to sell it again ; and, in regard to it, in ordinary cases, there is no last purchaser." Mr. Mill observes, "Money is brought into a country in two ways. It is imported (chiefly in the *form of bullion*) like any other merchandise, as being an advantageous article of commerce. It is also imported in its other character as a *medium of exchange* to pay some debt." ("Elements of Political Economy.") The distinction here made between the two methods of bringing *money* "into a country" is one without a difference ; but my object in citing the passage is to show that he treats bullion and money as one and the same thing. He next says, in express words, "I shall use the term, money, and precious metals, *indiscriminately.*" But, in another sentence, he speaks more accurately, when he says, "in so far as the precious metals are imported in the ordinary way of commerce, their value must depend on the same laws as the value

[1] For the information of American readers, I would explain, that, by "The City" is always meant that part of London in near proximity to the Bank of England, where the chief financial affairs are conducted.

of any other foreign production." The distinction will be apparent, by referring to the causes I have already stated, which give to money other elements of market value, such as being legal tender, and the supply of the *article, money*, as distinguished from the articles, "precious metals." Having approached so near the *rationale* of the matter, it is surprising so good a reasoner should have failed to grasp the entire problem requiring solution.

3. The obvious distinction, both scientific and practical, between the two, consists in the circumstance, that the commodity, bullion, must first undergo the process of coinage, or manufacture, and be made legal tender, before it becomes money. The precious metals, in their two conditions of money and bullion, bear about the same relations to each other as the chrysalis bears to the butterfly. Bullion is the sluggish chrysalis, and money the full-fledged and lively butterfly, swift of motion and lovely to look upon. The comparison may be a little poetical; but, literally speaking, money almost flies, so wonderful are its powers of circulation : while bullion lies hoarded and immobile in the dark vaults of brokers, bankers, and merchants, and is moved only as a commodity.

4. Perhaps, however, the most striking distinction between money and bullion consists in the former being a graduated implement, like a yard-measure, by which we are enabled to measure the values of other things, and mete out, by the scale of denominations, trading power. The stamp of the state guarantees the fineness of the metal, and the divisions and multiples of the unit of value of the various denominations completes the comparison with the yard-measure. All these differing conditions serve to take money out of the *ordinary* category of commodities, to which the precious metals in the form of bullion belong. The pound, the shilling, and the

penny, or the dollar or franc, and the centum, complete the scale of measure of coined money. The reasoner who grasps this distinction will perceive at a glance, that a lump, or nugget, of gold does not act as an implement in the same manner or serve the purpose of a sovereign or a dollar. The nugget itself must be weighed, and its value determined.

5. Under a universal monetary system, such as I have outlined in Chap. XXV., there would be provided a perfect natural regulator of the supply of money; and each nation would coin only so much as was required, and the aggregate supply of coin would distribute itself throughout the world. In other words, no more bullion would be offered for sale at the respective mints, than would afford a profit by being turned into money, and the latter would seldom be meted.

6. I have made this critical distinction, and elaborated it, in order to strike down the erroneous practice of writers of money articles, as well as economists and public men, of confounding the principles and uses of money with those of bullion. There is, in fact, just as wide a difference in principle between the two, as between money and corn, or cotton; and they cannot, without great and utter confusion of ideas, be treated, as Mr. Mill treats them, "indiscriminately" or as synonymous. A bale of cotton is just as much money as a nugget of gold of equal value; and the corn market may just as appropriately, in principle, be called the "money market" as the bullion market may be so called. There will be no possibility of establishing just and true scientific principles in monetary science till these distinctions are recognized. It is simply the same thing as confounding money with capital, which I have already spoken of in my remarks on capital.

7. The habit of confounding money, the measure of

values, with bullion, the raw material, or the sluggish chrysalis with the gorgeous and nimble butterfly, must be got rid of entirely.[1]

8. Mr. Mill has fallen into another most palpable error requiring notice. It occurs in his thesis on the effect of supply and demand on market values. He says, "the supply of money is all the money in circulation at the time, and the demand for money consists of all the goods offered for sale." Again he postulates this fundamental error in these words: "as the whole of the goods in the market compose the demand for money, so the whole of the money constitutes the demand for goods. The money and the goods are seeking each other for the purpose of being exchanged. They are reciprocally supply and demand on each other." If Mr. Mill had substituted TRADING POWER for MONEY, he would pretty exactly have expressed a great fundamental truth, the point of which becomes very clear when we have reached the knowledge that the goods themselves, by means of their representatives, bills, etc., furnish by far the greatest proportion of the capital, or trading power, they are "seeking." The absolute truth is, *the goods in the market are, by means of trading power*, "seeking each other for the purpose of being exchanged." *As for money, it only measures and determines the ratio of value at which the goods shall be circulated in this great ocean of trading power, which constitutes the true circulating medium, and is composed of their own aggregation of values with some addition from accumulations of capital* (postulates 35, 36).

9. Money, in fact, no longer constitutes any considerable element, or factor, in the trading power which distributes goods from the producers to consumers, and

[1] The comparison adopted in the text is all the more appropriate, from the circumstance that the chrysalis of the butterfly is sometimes called "aurelia" from *aurum*, gold.

must itself be treated simply as "trading power." The *true view* to take, is to regard the question as one of *distribution* rather than of *exchange*. It is a pity to see so excellent a general reasoner as Mr. Mill falling into so many fundamental errors. It is so notorious a fact, that bargains are effected between producers of and dealers in goods, and payments are so generally made without the use or thought of money, except to estimate the prices and amounts, that one hardly has patience to refute or eliminate the blunders and bad logic from what is good and true. But it is absolutely needful to dwell on such errors, and to reproduce and repeat, in every logical form, such arguments as I am now using, in order to prepare the ground for the seeds of truth, and for reasoning out sound logical conclusions.

10. The great fundamental truth to be ever kept in mind is, that goods themselves furnish the chief part of their own circulating medium, or, to use the more common though less correct expression, " circulate themselves " by means of their own inhering market value transferred to bills and other commercial instruments, which are turned into trading power by bankers. I strongly urge on future writers on economic science, the desirability of ceasing to speak of the " exchange of goods," as mystifying what is really a very clear subject. Goods, as a practical fact, are not exchanged at all in the industrial world. They are, on the other hand, as an equally practical fact, sold and *distributed;* and the distribution is not at all effected by money, except by means of its trading power : and bullion ranks along with other commodities in the ratio of its market value. It will, therefore, be seen how small a part the precious metals play in the great sum of values acted upon in the various markets by production and consumption, supply and demand. The whole question resolves itself, as business is

now conducted, into this one practical fact, — "Goods are perpetually seeking exchange for trading power, and trading power is perpetually seeking exchange for goods ; and money and bullion are simple factors in trading power." In this view of the actual fact, it would be as well to drop the use of the term " medium of exchange " *in toto*, as well as that of the term " exchange " itself, as applied to trade in goods.

11. Modern banking supplies the methods by which trading power, as I have postulated, explained, and illustrated it, performs its appointed duty of aiding in producing and distributing goods. The instruments invented by bankers and merchants are taken by each trader, or customer, to his banker, and are deposited, or discounted ; and the proceeds, after deduction of interest, are placed to his credit as a deposit. Bankers' ledgers fitly represent supply and demand, production and consumption. One side of the account represents credit, and the other debt, in each customers' account ; and here it is where banking, as now practised, aided by clearing-houses, plays its marvellous *rôle* in effecting settlements and balancing accounts in each community, as well as the world over. Mr. McCulloch well describes the results which are thus brought about by these methods. He says, "among countries and cities having considerable intercourse together, the debts mutually due by each other are found, in ordinary cases, to be nearly equal." So much for the numerous theories and speculations about domestic and foreign trade, and respecting bullion, being a specially desirable object to attract to a country, and for "settling balances of trade."

12. The position occupied by bullion, in respect to foreign trade, in comparison with other commodities, may be formulated thus : "So far from bullion being the best or most desirable article to be used in settling bal-

ances of foreign trade, it is never so used as long as any
other articles yield a paying profit on shipment." In
other words, the profit on bullion is always so small, as
not to be a safe or available investment for export, and
hence is never used for such purposes so long as any
thing else can be sent that will leave a certain margin
of profit. To illustrate : American merchants never send
their bullion or coin abroad to settle foreign indebtedness, or to enable them to buy foreign goods, if cotton,
corn, tobacco, or any other product affords a profit ; nor
do British merchants ever ship bullion to America, if they
can realize even a very small profit on their own goods.
These self-evident propositions push the bullion theory
of settling balances to the *argumentum ad absurdum.*
The use of bullion for such purposes is sometimes necessary, just as it is for a ship-master to carry sand for bal-
last when he cannot find paying cargo.

13. When gold and silver bullion are imported into a
country which produces these articles, it is a certain
indication of poor or non-paying trade ; and general
business depression will, as a rule, be found to prevail
in the industries of such a country on all such occasions.
Capital invested in bullion or money yields no profit,
and hence every good business man will avoid them ;
or, if he has accepted payment of debts or goods in
these non-paying articles, he will seek to get rid of them
the first moment he can find any thing that promises to
yield a profit. It is a principle of trade to make a
double profit, if possible, — a profit on what is exported
and on what is imported, or on buying and selling. But,
when the merchant is obliged to bring home bullion, he
very generally gets only one profit ; and his bullion
diminishes that profit, and must be parted with in exchange for something else before it can be made useful
in trade.

14. In the United States, the leaders of public opinion connected with the press generally view with great satisfaction the flow of bullion, or the return of American gold coin, homewards. It is then claimed to be a sign of the approach of better times; whereas it is only the result of a state of foreign trade that yields no profit, and of unemployed labor and capital, idle mills, and "hard times." It is held to be evidence that "the exchanges are in favor" of the bullion-*importing* country, and of "a favorable balance of trade." The only occasions, in a bullion-*producing* country, under which the importation of the precious metals might be regarded favorably, are, where these metals are attracted, by a demand for metallic currency, to fill the vacated channel of circulation caused by an over-issue of paper undergoing contraction. I have shown that the true and natural method of effecting an equilibrium of value between the metallic and the paper money in such cases, especially in a bullion-producing country, where over-issues have not been excessive, is to await the growth of industry, which acts as a contraction, that will arrest the export of the home product of the metals.

I shall hereafter devote some space to the fundamental errors very generally prevailing respecting the so-called "balances of trade" between commercial countries, and the mercantile theory, which still prevails as an apparently ineradicable idea in the minds of a large class in America and in some parts of Europe.

CHAPTER XII.

POPULAR ERRORS RESPECTING THE BALANCE OF TRADE. — THE NEW MERCANTILE THEORY.

1. I HAVE already alluded to the fallacy of excepting the trade in bullion from the category of commodities to which the principles of free trade have been applied by British legislation; and pointed out that the Bank of England *doctrinaires*, and the city school of economists, have revived, in a new form, identical in principle, however, the exploded "mercantile theory." This theory, as all know, who possess any knowledge of modern political economy, teaches that the precious metals constitute a more desirable and substantial description of wealth than other products of industry, for which those who happen to own them are always desirous to exchange such metals, in the ratio of market values. From this mere assumption they proceed to argue, that the foreign trade of a country should be so regulated by legislation, or the power of the Bank of England, as to attract or retain in it a large supply of these exceptionally desirable metals. As I have remarked, these modern doctrines are identical, in principle, with those so ably overthrown, more than a century ago, by Dr. Adam Smith. It cannot be denied that the plan of "acting on the exchanges," by the bank, is the same, when any effect is produced, as that formerly resorted to by the more direct agency of laws imposing protective duties and taxes on the export of the precious metals.

2. The most feasible explanation that can be offered for such an anomaly, in a country that has unreservedly accepted the doctrines of free trade in their largest and most comprehensive application to all industries, is the

extreme conservatism of those traditional managers of
great city houses and the great national bank. Hence
this branch of political science (which tolerates such an
anomaly as the Bank of England, and its erroneous policy
of seeking perpetually to influence the trade in bullion)
has not kept pace with demonstrated and accepted principles. Any attempt to reform the British monetary system, of which the Bank of England is the centre, and
chief ruling power, meets with the strenuous opposition
of the elders, who constitute the managers of the loan
and money markets. A proposal to demonetize the Bank
of England note, or abolish it, is regarded by many old
gentlemen as little short high treason. It took a third
of a century of the most earnest discussion and agitation
to accomplish the abolition of the Corn Laws, and obtain
an acknowledgment of the doctrines of free trade. The
possibility that the principles involved in this great victory, achieved by logical reasoning over powerful interests and traditional prejudices, might be overridden and
trampled on with impunity by a great financial corporation, nearly allied with the state, by raising and lowering the rate of interest, probably did not occur to the
great apostles of free trade. The Bank Act was passed
in 1844, by the efforts of the statesman who became the
leader in the free-trade agitation, which ended in the
repeal of the Corn Laws, and the general emancipation
of trade, in 1846. It, however, required the experience
of thirty years' working of the Bank Act, under the interpretation (which I have shown to be erroneous) given
to it by the managers, and the teachings of three or four
financial crises, to show with tolerable exactitude the fundamental errors of the theory and practice of that powerful institution. It is also not to be doubted that British
statesmen of the present day have not examined this subject with sufficient care to comprehend the true situation
of the case.

3. The evils of the monetary system, upheld by the Bank of England and Lombard Street writers, have been ably pointed out by Professor Bonamy Price, whose keen dissecting logic and power of analysis have done much to shake confidence in the infallibility of the bank's practice of playing with the rate to influence the trade in the precious metals. As yet, however, the policy remains unchanged ; and the bank managers declare in the most emphatic manner that their system and policy is " perfect," and the evils imputed to it are the result of unsound or " bad trade " (*vide* the speeches and writings of Mr. Hubbard, M.P., and bank director). While the greater part of the practical business men of the kingdom shut their eyes, and refuse to look into a system at which they grumble on occasions of crises, it is not surprising that so much apathy prevails, and that nothing is being done to reform the abuse of a power that only the state through an independent department can satisfactorily exercise.

4. The theory of the bank is, that, when the balance of trade is against the country unduly, there is a tendency to export gold to settle such balances, and the best method to avert this imagined evil is to make trading capital dear. The doctrines of free trade rest on the broad basis that the domestic and foreign exchanges should be left severely alone, to be regulated by the only true and natural power, supply and demand. Now, let us examine and analyze the principles of both domestic and foreign trade, and see how far any artificial interferences are justified. Those principles are generally stated in postulates 40–44, which I will extend and divide as follows, for illustration : —

First, There can be no selling without buying, which the word " trade " implies.

Second, The domestic trade of a country is a trade

carried on amongst the individuals and firms of a country.

Third, Foreign trade is a trade carried on between the individuals and firms of one country and those of other countries.

Fourth, All trade, *in a free market*, tends continually to balance itself, or to equilibrium ; and the so-called "balance of trade" *between nations* is merely a matter of account between trading-houses, which always balances itself with the same accuracy as the two sides of a banker's or merchant's ledger.

To these I here add two other propositions which follow as logical corollaries to the foregoing : —

Fifth, All facilities afforded by law and by bankers and clearing-houses to the free action of the natural laws of industry are fundamentally right.

Sixth, All restrictions imposed by the state, or by corporations or combinations of capitalists, on the free action of the natural laws of industry, are evils, and are contrary to public policy, and fundamentally wrong.

5. The mind that dwells on these simple formulated truths will be unable to resist the conviction that free trade lies at the bottom of all solid and enduring prosperity. These postulates clearly express the fundamental idea, that there is no distinction, in principle, between domestic and foreign trade, and that both kinds continually tend to equilibrium.

6. Although I hope I have overthrown the theory practised by the bank of operating, as it were, against the action of the natural laws of trade, in respect to the export of bullion to settle foreign balances, it may be as well to remind readers of the extraordinary delusion that prevailed in the city and especially in the bank parlors during the long suspension of the bank from 1797 to 1821, that "the bank note was not at a discount.

but gold was at a premium," or had actually risen in the
market by comparison with other articles.   They who
held to this doctrine asserted that the large export of
gold to subsidize foreign armies had caused an actual rise
in the price of the metal, and that the inconvertible bank
note was the true pound sterling.   Though Mr. Horner,
author of the famous Bullion Report, and Sir Robert
Peel, then a young man, pointed out the absurdity of this
theory, the city bankers and merchants obstinately refused to accept their proofs.   The idea that inconvertible
bank notes could correctly represent "the pound sterling" is such a palpable absurdity that even no intelligent
business man of the present day can be found who asserts
the dogma.   Let no man now accept the equally unsupported dogmas of the bank respecting the soundness
of its theory and practice in the management of the
note issue, and its attempts to dominate the loan market.
I say this to such as are prone to accept dogmatic
teaching rather than logically reasoned-out conclusions.
Whilst the traditional fallacy of the plan of seeking to
rule the foreign exchanges, and turn the balance of trade
by means of the bank rate, inheres with great pertinacity
to the city, no one is found willing to insist on the delusion that gold had actually risen in market value, instead
of paper having fallen.

7. The doctrine that the foreign trade of a country, in
order to be profitable, must show an excess of exports
over imports, is one of the most palpable absurdities, and
is the foundation of the old mercantile theory of seeking
by all means possible to attract to a country the largest
possible supply of the precious metals to store away in
the cellars of bankers and traders.   Adam Smith has so
fully considered this question that it is hardly needful to
say much about it.   When the exports of a country are
found very generally to exceed the imports, it is simply

evidence that the exporting country, or the one whose
balance of trade is regarded as very favorable, is indebted to the one having the supposed adverse balance
against it; and the surplus value of goods exported over
goods imported represents the sum applied each year to
the payment of interest and principal.   The class of
economists, especially in the United States, who rejoice
over what they suppose to be large additions to the national wealth, seeing that the foreign trade of Great Britain
shows a very large and increasing balance against her,
prophesy the approaching downfall of the nation.   When
the returns show an average yearly, apparent, balance
against the country of over a £100,000,000, they see in
the circumstance an early condition of national bankruptcy.   The very contrary is the case.   This excess of
imports over exports proves two facts; first, that she is
receiving foreign commodities, including bullion, in payment of interest on loans which her subjects have made
to foreign governments, corporations, and individuals;
and second, that her trade is profitable, and she is real-
izing the profits on her exports which, with the interest
payments, make up the balance-sheet between her subjects
and the citizens of other countries.   The theory that the
citizens of one country lose what those of another make,
as a profit, is monstrous nonsense.   If such were the
case, the same thing would happen in the trade at home
between individuals and firms; and one half the community would be growing rich, while the other half would
be growing poor, which is absurd.

8. If people would get in the habit of simply regarding foreign trade as a trade between individuals, the same
as the home trade, they will get rid of these delusions
about the supposed advantages of having a balance of
trade in favor of one country over another, or against the
rest of the world.   Every sound trader sees to it that he

does not get in debt more than he can pay, and no government or legislative intervention is needed to or can
help individual action.   In fact, all such interference is a
direct evil in its results, as already pointed out.

9. Another equally absurd delusion prevails respecting
" debtor and creditor nations."   Mr. Seyd, who I have
before quoted, in the consideration of the errors of the
theory and practice of the Bank of England, has imbibed
this delusion.   It makes no difference in principle or in
effect whether loans are contracted at home or abroad.
The only things to be considered are the price paid for
such loans, and whether the proceeds have been judiciously expended in productive undertakings.   The absolutely correct theory of trade is, to buy your goods and
borrow your capital in the cheapest market, and sell them
and expend your loans in the dearest market.   That is
just what goes on at home.   No man borrows capital of
his next-door neighbor at ten per cent, if, by going to
the next town, he can get it for five.   Exactly the same
rule prevails in respect to the merchant, and it is the
foundation of all wisely conducted trade.   The protectionist insists on compelling people to buy their goods of
particular classes at home, because he fancies there is
some advantage in having them made there ; though they
cost double the price at which they can be purchased
abroad.

10. If this delusive, and, to some, fascinating, doctrine were really the true principle of trade, it would
follow that each State of the American Union, and each
county and town in Great Britain, should be " protected "
against all the rest of the world.   The people in each
municipal administration should demand the exclusion
from their markets of all goods, and the results of all
labor, capital, and machinery, not produced or expended
within its corporate limits.   Finally, to reduce the matter

to the *argumentum ad absurdum*, every man ought to be compelled by law to make for himself every thing his necessities and luxuries may require him to buy of others, under ordinary conditions of society. He will then have no balance of trade to make him unhappy, as to the means of settlement.

11. The fact that bullion is no better to settle balances of trade than cotton, cheese, or beef, if so good, will appear self-evident when we have come to perceive the fact, that bullion affords the least profit to the dealer, of any product of industry; nor does the miner who produces the article, as a rule, make any higher wages, and very often much lower, than the man that runs an engine to coin it into money. The monster of all delusions is " protection to domestic industry."

12. As a great practical illustration of the folly of treating bullion as an exceptionally available article for settling foreign balances of trade, I refer to the case of France, which paid to Germany £200,000,000 in three years, as a war indemnity, against which she had received no valuable consideration, unless a good beating may be so considered. This huge and unprecedented amount of *capital* was transferred from the " debtor country to the creditor country," without the use of more than ten per cent in gold. The question how the other nine-tenths was paid has been a puzzle to many persons, ignorant of what are called the principles of " international trade." But no one can doubt that the balance, in this case, against France, was actually paid and receipted for. When we analyze the process it will appear very simple. The first instalment was actually, in part, paid in gold supplied by those who took the loans, needful to provide the means of payment. The void in the specie circulation was filled by an increased issue of Bank of France

notes, which, being for the time made inconvertible, were held at par by the demand for actual money, — the notes being also legal tender. All the rest of this unprecedented payment was made through bankers, and the balances were effected by the clearing-houses of Great Britain and the Continental centres of finance ; *and the proceeds were supplied by the credit of France, which anticipated the earnings of* French industry, which it will take many years of toil on the part of the people of France to make good. But Germany did not need or require *gold* in payment of this "balance," though so stipulated in the bond. She took things that were more advantageous, on which there was a better profit than on bullion. Her traders and manufacturers — the latter needing numerous "raw materials" to keep their factories going — took in payment what was better to them than gold ; and *they* paid the German Government the capital in question. The Government didn't want gold, they simply wanted and took "trading power," which they used for such purposes as they intended the loan to effect. It is needless to follow out all the details, to show what became of the indemnity. It is sufficient to know it was not paid in this " exceptionally desirable and coveted commodity," bullion, or in money either. Nor is it needful to point out how all the commercial nations of the world, having trade with France, aided in the great operation.

13. The only true method of arriving at a clear perception of what is called "international trade," is to regard the whole world as being made up of an aggregation of individual traders; and foreign, as well as domestic trade, as being carried on between these, as stated in the postulates of this chapter. The principles discussed in this chapter are of the highest importance

to those who would master the monetary question, and should be gotten "by heart" by all students of the science.[1]

CHAPTER XIII.

MONEY, CURRENCY, LOANS, AND CHECKS. — TRUE AND FALSE PRINCIPLES.

1. ONE of the leading objects of this work is to endeavor to eliminate fundamental errors and currently accepted fallacies from what seem to be well reasoned-out and established principles, which are steadily gaining ground in economic science, so far as they seem to affect that branch known as "Monetary Science." If all who travel over the same ground would act on the same plan, we might hope, by and by, to have a residuum of solid truth, and a system that can be appealed to as confidently as geometry. Like the husbandman who seeks to grow good grain, we must first weed the field of all noxious weeds. Adam Smith, who did so much towards erecting the principles and practice of industry into a science, was compelled to devote a large space to the overthrow of almost universally prevailing errors then dogmatically insisted on, and entering largely into the groundwork of commercial legislation. Many of these principles, overthrown by him by unanswerable arguments, still survive in some form in all countries. But even he fell into many errors, which nearly all the best writers on economic science have failed to detect, and which are thus perpetuated from generation to generation. Let it not, then, be considered that I am devoting undue space

---

[1] *Vide* an excellent letter published by Mr. Charles H. Marshall, an intelligent New York merchant, in "The New York Herald" of Jan. 23, 1878, on the subject of "The Balance of Trade," — note No. IV.

or giving too much importance to this matter of exposing erroneous principles and practices. When all such errors shall be eliminated from the theory and practice of industry, the science of political economy will be reduced to a few simple postulates such as those I have set out with.

2. I have laid much stress on the bad logic and general confusion of thought engendered in the minds of intelligent business men, and even statesmen and professional economists, like Ricardo, McCulloch, and Mill, by not distinguishing the marked difference between money and trading power, or floating capital, and the two elements of which the latter is composed; to wit, the evidences of goods in transit from producers to consumers, and capital accumulated from past industries. Mr. Mill has remarked, on the subjects I am now entering upon, as follows : "The two topics, Currency and Loans, though themselves distinct, are so blended in the phenomena of what is called the money market, that it is impossible to understand the one without the other; and in many minds the two subjects are mixed up in the most inextricable confusion." How admirably this description applies to the whole host of " Money Article " writers in Lombard and Wall Streets ! But is it surprising when we find the late Mr. Bageat, a banker, and the highest Lombard-street authority, accused, by a learned Oxford professor of political economy, of using the term *money* in six distinct senses, and never deigning to point out the perfectly clear and logical distinction between money and capital? This confounding of currency, which embraces money, with loans, or, more properly speaking, what is loaned, which is Trading Power, leads the public, when there is a pressure, or any sudden increased demand for capital, to call out lustily for more bank notes, when trading power is what is wanted.

3. The confusion of thought, referred to by Mr. Mill as being engendered in some minds on the subject of currency and loans, would immediately disappear, like the morning mist before the rising sun, by the inculcation of the perfectly plain method of differentiating all the principles and elements involved in the various processes of utilizing trading power. Money, for instance, differentiates the ratios of all values, or, more correctly speaking, the ratios of the market values of all commodities, lands, labor, etc., in comparison with each other. Money also has the principle, peculiar to itself, of differentiating the value of the material of which it is fabricated, in comparison with other things having market value. That there is any mysterious or other relation between " currency and loans " is a fundamental error, and no amount of reasoning can make out such relationship. When currency forms a part, which it sometimes does, in a very limited degree, of the ocean of trading power dealt in, in the loan market, *it is not in its character as currency at all, but (to the extent of its market value) as trading power.* It certainly requires no great effort of ratiocination to reach this most important starting-point.

4. Adam Smith had a clearer perception than most authoritative writers of the true distinction between currency and loans; but neither he nor Mr. Mill saw distinctly and vividly that currency, which means simply metallic and paper money, holds no other relation to loans than that of so much trading power or capital. Money (I always mean by this word metallic, unless otherwise stated), in its measuring capacity of pounds, shillings, pence, or dollars and cents, performs the same service, in measuring out capital in the loan market, as the quintal or hundred weight does in the grain market. I have repeated this proposition in order to apply it more fully to points I aim to establish.

5. Dr. Smith, speaking of capital, which he calls stock, says, "The quantity of stock, therefore, or, as it is commonly expressed, money, which can be lent at interest in any country, is not regulated by the value of the money, whether paper or coin, which serves as the instrument of the different loans made in that country, but by the value of that part of the annual produce, which, as soon as it comes, either from the ground, or the hands of the productive laborers, is destined, not only for replacing a capital, as the owner does not care to be at the trouble of employing himself." Dr. Smith evidently meant the accumulated profit arising from the various industries of such country, which, as stated in postulate 36, forms a part of the floating capital, or trading power, from which loans are drawn; but he has nowhere shown that he had grasped the fact that goods themselves supply by far the greater part of that reservoir of capital (not money) out of which the commercial world at large draws supplies to keep all those productive industries in constant motion, or to carry on reproduction in perpetual succession.

6. There is something indefinite in the term "market." We speak of the "loan market" as if it were some particular place, where all who have capital in any form to lend, and all who want to borrow, meet together, and make their bargains. But in effect the same end is achieved by a very different process. The loan market is, in fact, composed of the aggregation of all that portion of the people who have any thing they desire to lend, which very generally is held by bankers on deposit, and those who have bills given them for goods sold. The latter class are, through the aid of the banker, in a sense borrowers of their own capital; since they furnish the very trading power they are enabled to borrow, through the magic intervention of the check.

When the borrowed capital is drawn for use, the check passes it over to pay a debt or complete a purchase. When the bill falls due, which the bank has transmuted into purchasing power, the maker pays it by check. So every thing is carried on in perpetual succession by check, and seldom is any money drawn. These checks are daily balanced against each other at the various central clearing-houses, which I shall by and by more particularly describe. This, then, is the loan market, or " trading-power market."

7. The money market is quite a different affair. It is everywhere where money is bought and sold, where money is actually paid over the counter for goods, and goods are paid for money. Adam Smith very well expresses it when he says, " Money is a commodity, with regard to which every man is a merchant." It is, in fact, in the small dealings by retail, and in the payment of wages, and largely for farm produce, and fares on steamers, railways, etc., where actual *cash* is paid, that the money market becomes conspicuous. It is in these dealings that the demand for money arises ; and the supply will always be properly meted out under the system I have proposed, especially if that system should be extended, by treaty arrangements, so as to embrace all the great industrial nations of Europe and America.

8. One of the most deceptive and alluring errors of amateur economists of the " practical school," and extensively prevailing among the rank and file of politicians, is the doctrine that Government is bound to supply a certain amount of metallic and paper currency *per capita*, or to average it at so much a head for every man, woman, and child in a country. This is statistical lore brought into the regions of scientific principles. The question of population has no special relation to the volume of currency needed to conduct the industries of a people, other

than so far as it can be made to indicate the number and
amount of transactions requiring the use of money. No
doubt a larger supply of actual money is needed to
conduct rural than town industries, in relation both to
population and transactions. This arises from the fact
that farmers and country people do not, as a rule, keep
bank deposit accounts; and the money thus circulates
more sluggishly than in towns and cities. But the *per
capita* plan of regulating the supply of money is not much
better than to form the estimate on the number of codfish
taken out of the sea, which probably does not vary much,
one year taken with another. The true scientific and
practical regulator is the law of supply and demand; leaving the coinage as nearly free as possible, and placing the
issue of paper money in a State Department, such as I
shall more particularly describe in a later chapter, and to
which I have already frequently alluded.

9. It will pretty clearly appear to those who have
followed my course of reasoning thus far, that there is
no more relationship between currency and loans than
there is between sugar and cheese. They are, as Mr.
Mill says, "quite distinct things." This being settled,
the theory that banks of issue are necessary to regulate
the supply of paper money, so as to equally meet demand, becomes a meaningless assertion. This is a very
favorite argument with a large class, especially in America, a class whose interests lie in supporting the National
Banking System, so far as the issue of paper money is
concerned. These philosophers hold exclusive control
of a large number of influential journals in the United
States, and urge their opinions with great pertinacity.
The truth is self-evident, that banks of issue are the very
worst parties to be intrusted with the duty of regulating
the laws of nature; for that is the absurd proposition involved. Their interests disqualify them for the duty, and

hence the issue of paper money by banks should be
abolished. This proposition, however, will require more
extended examination in a future chapter on banks of
issue.

10. The theory that there is a natural rate of interest,
about which the market rate revolves, or oscillates, is
another fallacy. Both Adam Smith and Ricardo have
fancied the existence of such a rate ; and Mill, remarking
on their theories, says, "the natural rate is some rate
about which the market rate oscillates, and to which it
always tends to return." There is certainly no *such*
natural rate, which would, if it existed, be a permanent
fixed rate. A single moment's reflection will convince
any logical mind that the *market rate* is the only *natural
rate* of interest, because it is the market that is acted on
by the natural law of supply and demand. I have stated
this proposition in postulate 38. It is self-evident that
the market rate of interest is regulated by the supply of
capital *to*, and the demand *for*, capital in the loan market ; and hence the natural rate is the market rate. I am
afraid I am upsetting a great many long-cherished fundamental errors, which will have to be eliminated out
of the received theories of industrial science ; and possibly many more must follow.

11. I shall maintain, as a correct principle, that all
bankers and traders who require currency should buy it
at the market price, and for the full expressed value.
The plan of lending to banks a government guaranteed
paper circulation on national securities, as in the United
States, and to the extent provided by the Bank Act of
1844 to the Bank of England, is a violation of sound
principles of public policy. It is the worst kind of class
legislation, and has no justification in principle ; while it
is palpably evident that it is a false system of paper
money, which should be based only on metal.

12. There is no distinction to be drawn between metallic and paper money, in respect to the parts they respectively perform in the general operations of industry, other than that the former regulates the supply of the latter, so as to exactly meet the demand for it. In practice, a sovereign or a half-eagle serves no better purpose in making a purchase or extinguishing a debt than a pound or a five-dollar note. *It is simply a matter of convenience, and hence the public will generally prefer the note to the coin.* Such notes are easier and more safely carried, and, when the security is ample, will, as a rule, be preferred to the metal. Mr. Scott Russell, the eminent shipbuilder, mentioned to me as a fact, that, in Scotland, he found great difficulty in getting the country people to take sovereigns in payment of travelling expenses. He said more than once his host or hostess pushed the gold coin back to him in disgust, saying, " I nae want that thing.   Gie me a poond note."

13. One of the chief obstacles to the progress of scientific principles is interposed by what are termed " vested interests."   Every step towards reform in monetary science, or in giving effect to its teachings, is certain to meet with strenuous opposition from those who have real or fancied individual or class interests likely to be effected by the change. There are some, however, whose education in old dogmas and teachings lead them to resist from what the Rocky Mountain men call " pure cussedness," which may be translated to mean pure obstinacy and preconceived opinions. In the matter of issuing paper money, a certain class seeks to make a profit by issuing such money. In the case of a note issue founded on and guaranteed by public securities, which makes bankers reckless in regard to keeping on hand an adequate reserve or trading balance in cash, the temptation to embark in banking as a mere speculation is very

great. The securities draw interest, and the notes are
used to make another and larger profit by lending or
discounting commercial paper. It is a nice method of
"being able to eat your pudding and have it too." Possibly a time may come when such a system will not be
so advantageous, or sufficiently popular to maintain its
existence.

CHAPTER XIV.

MONEY, CURRENCY, AND BANKING, AND THE ECONOMY OF PAPER MONEY CONSIDERED.

1. I PROPOSE to devote this chapter to the subject of
money and currency in connection with banking, and the
extravagance in metallic money; and the first thing to
which I shall turn my attention is the fallacy that prevails
among a large class of economists and practical business
men, both in America and England, respecting the policy
of delegating the prerogative of the state to joint-stock
companies and private parties to issue paper money.
Professor Bonamy Price seems to be a representative man
on the side of those who favor this policy. He says in
his "Treatise on Banking and Currency," published in
1875, "There is a very solid and serious distinction between a private issuer of notes and a government. The
property given to a solvent banker for his notes *is not
lost to the nation.*" (I italicize the passages that seem
to me to be palpable errors of fact, as well as of principle.) "The banker lends, if he is a good banker, to
persons who do not waste or destroy. The public pays
exactly the same for the tool of exchange, whether it
procures it from the miner or from the bank. *But when
the wealth is given to the miner he consumes it.* The
nation retains, no doubt, an equal value of gold; *but it is*

lost as capital beyond the work of exchanging, in buying
and selling.   Its services as a tool are all that the nation
gets from it.   The same services are procured from the
bank note, only it costs but sixpence to the *banker and
the nation*.   Compared with a £5 note, wealth to the
extent of £4 19*s*. 6*d*., *which must have been sent away
to a foreign miner, now remains in England.   But government issues are directly connected with consumption.
The Government spends and consumes what it procures
with its notes.*

2. The reasoning in the above paragraph is so palpably
fallacious that it is difficult to credit it to the same acute
mind that has so ably in the same work analyzed and
reasoned out the business operations of a banker, and let
in such a flood of light on a subject just beginning to be
clearly understood in all its multifarious operations and
influences on the industries of the world.   There is, no
doubt, "a very solid and serious distinction between a
private issuer of notes" and a state issuer; but the
reasoning of Professor Price is a simple, plain, *non
sequitur*.   Nothing is more self-evident than the fact that
if the Government, as the agent of the state, can purchase the articles it consumes in the maintenance of the
army, the navy, and all departments, and can pay for the
services of its hundreds of thousands of employees, with
the notes of the state, it saves the nation just so much.
The note is no more a tool of exchange than an equal
amount of any other trading power; and, in the light of
trading power, or capital, it is not of the slightest importance whether it be issued by the state or by a private
issuer, save only the considerations, which are the safest
issuers? which supplies the best and most trustworthy
tool?   These considerations being conceded to be equal,
it only becomes a question whether the state, or, say, the
whole people, shall have the profits of the issue, or one

favored corporation, or two thousand, as in the United States. "Government issues" are no more "directly connected with consumption" than "private issues."

3. It resolves itself, then, into the simple question as to who shall have the profit; that is, so far as any principle is concerned in respect to the work which "the tool of exchange" performs. This is as true as any proposition in geometry, and Professor Price's conclusions fall to the ground. The £5 note, if issued by the state, will cost no more to the state than to a bank; and the £4. 19s. 6d., which the Professor assumes to be the profit of the note, will belong to the state, if the state acts as the issuer, instead of giving it away to the bank. Mr. Price's argument as to the comparative advantage of utilizing the issue of notes as substitutes for gold can only be allowed as an incident connected with paper money. The main object of such money being to secure to the public a more convenient tool than gold coin, the matter of profit must be kept strictly in subordination to that object. It is only when a larger accumulation of metal takes place than is needed to secure the convertibility of the issue of paper money, that a portion of the gold can be parted with and sold to the public or to foreign states and traders. Again, I desire to impress on Professor Price's mind that neither kind of money is one whit better than an equal amount of any other kind of trading power needed in the industrial pursuits of the people, and the latter is really the element in which the banker "lives and moves and has his being." The supply of trading power is the specialty of the banker, as the supply of money, metallic and paper, should be of the state. I hope the Professor will set himself right on this question, and, when he issues a new edition of his valuable "Treatise on Banking and Currency," will make a note of the error he has so palpably fallen into in his reasoning on this subject.

4. In respect to Mr. Price's comparison of notes with gold, he has also fallen into an error. The market value of gold is regulated exactly the same as that of any other commodity. But I have shown, that, when converted into money, the law of supply and demand acts on it in *its character as money;* which, if there were limitations set on the supply, would raise its market value above that of gold bullion. On the other hand, if more is coined than is needed, the surplus coin will presently find its way into the melting-pot. The goods sent to the "foreign miner" to pay him for his labor are no more lost by his "consumptive" habits than goods exchanged for any other valuable product, at home or abroad. So long as people and nations want gold, and are willing to pay for it, the foreign miner is as good a consumer as any other worker. Who can deny this fact?

5. Then, as to the substitution of paper money, as far as is practicable, if that principle is admissible at all, the advantage will still be in favor of the nation's retaining the issue in its own hands. But why has my much esteemed and distinguished friend mixed up the two questions, — that of the *best issuer* of paper money with that of *the economy* of the two tools, paper and metallic money? They are quite separate and distinct; "there is a very solid and serious distinction between" the two things. If the tool bank notes and the tool state notes are equal in efficiency, and the state is equal in solvency to a bank, we have only to balance the profits and advantages of *paper money* against those of *metallic money*, so far at least as the former can be safely used as a substitute for the latter.

6. The point which Professor Price has attempted to make in favor of delegating the prerogative of the state to private issuers of paper money, — in which I have shown he has failed, — is diametrically opposed to the plan of

separating the Issue from the Banking Department of
the Bank of England. This separation, he claims, — and
I admit the claim to be good, — makes the Issue Department just what the Professor calls it, "a state issue
department conducted by the Bank of England directors
on the premises of the bank." I quote from memory,
but the quotation is right in substance. The Professor is
therefore inconsistent with himself.

7. I take exception also to his argument against en-
couraging the importation of gold, as being contrary
to the principles of free trade. I have already refuted
the theory that the *consumption* by the foreign miner of
the wealth given in exchange for his product is a loss
to the nation. "The wealth given in exchange" for any
foreign product, whether of utility or of luxury, is also
consumed. But what has the matter of consumption to
do in either case ; that is, in respect of gold or of any
other article of trade? The only question for the merchant and economist to consider is, whether the trade is
profitable. *It is simply an exchange of equivalents in market value, — nothing more, nothing less.* It is a very common delusion, even among practised economic writers,
that it is advantageous to a country to produce precious
metals rather than other valuable commodities, or than
to buy them abroad with other products. Now, there is
only one case where the home product of these metals
is more advantageous than importation from abroad ;
namely, where they can be produced cheaper at home.
If the labor and capital employed in their production
at home afford a better profit than when employed in
producing other things, which can be exchanged for the
needed supply of the metals abroad, then home mining
is advantageous. It is simply a question of profit and
loss to those engaged in the business, or how labor and
capital can best be invested.

8. It will be seen hereafter, in Chap. XXVII., paragraph 7, that the claim set up by Adam Smith and most economists to the present day, that the substitution of bank notes for coin is a great advantage to a country on the score of economy, is a complete, though an almost unchallenged, delusion.   I shall show that the best currency for a country is one composed of metallic coins and paper, issued pound for pound, dollar for dollar, on such metal, the two being interconvertible at the pleasure of the holder, and claim that to the public such currency is the *least expensive*.

9. There is no certain, or even near approximate, method of ascertaining the amount of *circulation* in a country where it is made up of mixed metallic and paper money; though the *issues* of the latter may be estimated.   Good authorities assume the circulation in the United States (May, 1879) to be, paper, $650,000,000; gold, $250,000,000; silver, $50,000,000; subsidiary coin, $50,000,000; total, $1,000,000,000.   The coin, on this estimate, is $350,000,000 against $650,000,000 of paper, — not very far from two dollars of paper to one of metal; and if we discard the $50,000,000 of subsidiary coin, which is so much overvalued, and class it with paper, we shall have $300,000,000 of metal against $700,000,000 of paper and other token money.

10. According to Mr. Ernst Seyd, an able German actuary and statistician in London, the circulation of Great Britain stood in 1876 : —

In sovereigns and half-sovereigns . .	£105,000,000
Silver and copper coins	16,000,000
"Provincial," Scotch, and Irish notes .	15,000,000
Bank of England notes	37,000,000
	£173,000,000

Mr. Seyd adds, "Of this, the metallic currency may be taken as all *in circulation;* but of the country bank notes there may be but £12,000,000; of the Bank of England, but £27,000,000."

Mr. Seyd probably means *active* circulation; for, in his work on the "Error of the Note Issue of the Bank of England," he treats the notes held by the Bank as "reserve," as being in circulation. This is the correct method of regarding all notes or metal held as reserve by bankers and merchants. But, in comparing the amount of paper and metal in order to see how much is saved by paper, we must take account of the metal held in reserve to meet conversions of notes. This will make the matter stand thus : Bank of England notes uncovered by metal, $15,000,000; country notes, less one-third held for reserve, $10,000,000. We thus find the excess of notes above the bullion and coin held for conversions is just £25,000,000, against £121,000,000 of metal. But inasmuch as the metal held in the Issue Department of the bank is nearly all in the form of bullion not counted by Mr. Seyd, and which would be promptly coined to fill the vaccuum that would ensue if the £27,-000,000 of notes issued on metal were withdrawn, we must add that amount to the coin circulation, less, say, £3,000,000 in coin, held by the issue. We shall now find the metal to stand as £145,000,000 against £25,-000,000 of paper, or nearly six times as much. Great Britain thus saves the sum of £25,000,000 by the use of paper, or as a financial gain, the interest on which, at three per cent, is £750,000; and this does not go to the whole people, but to a select few bank-stock holders.

11. I am now speaking only of the use of paper money as a *financial expedient,* which I insist is a *secondary,* and in no case properly a *primary,* consideration. Its primary object is to supply a better tool of industry that is more convenient and readily available than metal. I discard *in toto* the theory that paper

money should be used to create new capital, or as an auxiliary to financial operations, and shall hereafter demonstrate that money and finance ought to be wholly separated, in thought and in practice, from each other (Chaps. XXIV.–XXVI.). The banks of Amsterdam, Venice, Hamburg, and Sweden were pure and simple banks of issue, and did not at first lend the metal received in payment of notes; and it was only when they did so that they involved themselves and the public in disaster.

12. The comparison between the two systems, that of Great Britain and America, shows this result, that the metallic circulation of the former is as about six to one of paper; and in America the metal is about as one to two of paper. This will be further considered hereafter (Chap. XXVI.), where the highly inflated condition of the currency and business in the United States will be pointed out. My object is to show, that, so far as financial gain is concerned, by the issue of paper money, it bears no comparison to the benefits arising from a sound monetary system. I think, however, that, by means of a state issue department, automatic in its action, experience may show that a portion of the gold received in exchange for notes may be used to reduce the public debt say a third or a half; but such use will tend to inflate the currency, and must be so gauged as to spread the sales over a long period, or be confined to the annual *increase* of the demand for *currency*, created by the annual *increase* in the industries of the world. I will, in treating more specifically of the organization of such a department, point out how the uses of metal may be minimized in Great Britain by the issue of one-pound notes, which, as I before observed, must be left to experience and the demands of industry for notes to determine.

CHAPTER XV.

BANKS OF ISSUE, DEPOSIT, AND DISCOUNT. — THEIR ORIGIN. — THE ISSUE OF PAPER MONEY NOT LEGITIMATE BANKING. — CANNOT PROPERLY BE DELEGATED TO BANKS.

1. THE subjects to be considered in this chapter are of extreme interest in monetary science. They bear down strongly on what are termed vested rights, legal and equitable, and traditional prejudices. Such considerations always crop out, and oppose themselves to every social and industrial reform. They are creatures that die hard, and live down, very often, several generations of men. In order to show, demonstrably, that the issue of paper money is not legitimately the prerogative of bankers, I propose to point out the distinctive features of the three kinds of banks mentioned at the head of this chapter, and ascertain what connection banking, as now conducted, has with metallic and paper money. I shall show that all sound and good banking is confined to receiving and holding on deposit " other folks' " capital, and discounting commercial paper, or bills given in payment of goods in course of production and distribution, as pointed out in postulates 35, 36.

2. I can add nothing to the clear analysis made by Professor Price of the business of a banker; but he has overlooked the manifest distinction existing in theory and practice between the issuing of notes to take the place of money, and that of dealing in trading power, a small part of which only is made up of money. He has, however, in a few words stated the exact and legitimate business of a modern banker. He says " The bank and its great instruments, the check and the bill of exchange, transfer the ownership of wealth from one man to another.

But banking *is not currency*, and hopeless confusion
must result if it is regarded *as currency*. Indeed, the
referring to currency as the cause of many of the most
important events in banking is, to this hour, the fatal
cause of the unintelligibleness of that really simple
matter, currency. The practice of banking leads to a
vast diminution in the use of currency in the quantity
of coin and bank notes employed; but they are essentially distinct instruments, precisely as a plough drawn by
horses is a different tool from a spade worked by a man,
though they both perform the same service of digging up
the ground."

3. The legitimate offices of a banker, then, are to facilitate the " transfer of wealth," or, more correctly speaking,
trading power, or capital, which he has found out how to
do, by utilizing the value of goods in course of production
and distribution. The circumstance, that by far the larger
proportion of this business is conducted by non-issuing
banks, and is effected with the use of only one-thirtieth
part of paper money, is demonstrative that banking has
no practical or theoretical relation to the issuing of
notes. Furthermore, it is a question hardly to be disputed, that these non-issuing bankers find their profit in
not issuing notes. They earn, and, as a rule, return, a
better profit on the capital invested, than such as distract
their attention, and occupy their time on a business of
a totally different character, and which probably, on the
whole, has caused more loss to the public, the stockholders, and individuals connected with the issuing of paper
money, than all the profits that have ever arisen therefrom. It is one of those illusory methods of seeking to
make wealth, like the prospecting for gold and diamonds,
that numbers its victims by the thousand, while those who
have been successful count by hundreds or tens. Any
one who will take the trouble to investigate this subject,

going back a hundred years, will be amazed at the enormous sacrifices of capital that banks of issue and wrongly
managed government issues have inflicted on the world.
Still, the delusion clings to business men and economists
that banks of issue are the right things, and that they,
and they only, know how to mete out currency in conformity with supply and demand.   But a careful analysis
of the business, and the objects actually attained by and
through the instrumentality of banking, as conducted at
this time, disclose two important facts : *First*, that nearly
all the advantages, and they are enormous, which have
inured to society from banking, have proceeded from
banks of deposits and discount irrespective of notes ; and
second, that nearly all the evils inflicted on mankind by
bankers are directly traceable to banks of issue, and the
issuing of notes.   These are solid reasons for putting an
end to the issuing paper currency by banks, and remitting
the prerogative back to the state.

4. But I must now proceed to point out the distinction
between banks of deposit and discount, and such as issue
circulating, or currency notes.   "The hopeless confusion
of ideas " respecting the issue and use of paper currency,
or money, in connection with banking, is, no doubt, due
to the circumstance, that until lately in the United Kingdom, and still very generally in America, banks of deposit
and discount have also been and are banks of issue.
Whenever the state assumes and exercises the prerogative
of issuing paper, as it always has exercised it in respect
to metallic money, and the name of *bank note* is abolished, then " the source of unintelligibleness " will disappear.   So long, however, as there are banks of issue and
bank notes, the public will continue "to connect currency
with banking."   To logical reasoners and economists, as
a rule, the distinction between the printing and issuing
of notes which the banker engages to pay in money, on

demand, and the *using* of such notes, which represent
the banker's credit only, and not goods, appears perfectly
clear.

5. The comparison of the plough and the spade well
defines the distinction in question.   The banker in his
proper sphere is at the same time a borrower and a
lender.   In a sense he lends a man his own capital, when
he discounts his bill founded on a sale of goods.   But he
also borrows his depositors' capital, and lends it to traders
along with the proceeds of their own bills, which, by the
magic power of the check, he is able to do.   When the
banker lends his own notes, he simply trades on his own,
and not other folks', credit.   This is a manifest and fundamental distinction between banks of deposit and discount
and banks of issue.   The cases of the Bank of England
where the Government, in effect, lends the bank the
credit of the state, on public securities, to the extent of
£15,000,000 in the form of notes to trade on, and of the
United States where the Government lends to all national
banks, without limit, ninety per cent of paper money fully
guaranteed, which is the same thing as lending the public
credit, on all Government securities lodged with the
Treasurer of the United States, are anomalies in banking
and currency.   Yet neither the Bank of England nor the
national banks of the United States are any more successful, or possess greater ability to promote industrial
pursuits, or to earn profits for their shareholders, than
non-issuing banks and bankers.   The question of the
Government, as the agent of the state, lending notes to
banks to trade on, excluding all other classes, will occupy
more attention hereafter.

6. That there is a marked distinction between a banker's trading on his own and on that of his customers'
credit, and on the security of goods, must, I think, be
admitted.   The one case is trading on credit *pure* and

simple; the other is trading on actual capital. Though a man's credit may and does serve the purposes of capital, it is unlike actual capital existing in the accumulated savings of industry, and actual goods represented by bills. It is this difference that marks the boundaries between banks of issue and of non-issue. The issuing banker trades on his own credit to the extent to which he can circulate his notes; the non-issuing banker has solid capital to trade on. If this were not true of the issuing banker, he would have no motive of profit in circulating his own notes, instead of notes of the state. It is true, when the notes are paid out, they are used, by the public at large, *as money* and trading power in by far the greater number of transactions where they are used. It is only *as money* that such notes can be kept in circulation. If they reach the hands of a trader, he puts them back into his bank; and they presently return to the issuer. Traders, in their regular course of business, seldom draw notes or coin. They use checks in perpetual succession, as I have somewhere else shown. Genuine banking is, in fact, as Professor Price has shown, simply acting as a broker between producers of goods and consumers, between buyers and sellers.

7. I have, I trust, sufficiently demonstrated, that the issuing of paper money is, in reality, what Professor Price says of it, not banking at all, though he insists that banks ought to issue it; and that a banker can trade as well on notes issued by a state, like the greenbacks of the United States, or notes of the Bank of England or France. Let us briefly notice the origin of banks, as we now know them. There were bankers and "money changers" in ancient times, but they were very different affairs from the banks of modern times. The first examples of what may be called issuing banks, were those of Amsterdam, Sweden, Hamburg, and Venice. These banks were started in the

fifteenth and sixteenth centuries, and originated in consequence of the great abuses that had crept into the monetary systems of most parts of Europe. The practice of clipping, filing, and *overvaluing* metallic coins, by professional rogues and fraudulent kings and legislatures, had become intolerable. These banks were established to remedy those abuses, and were pure and simple banks of issue. What they did was to receive metal by weight, at its market value, deducting the cost of coinage and management. For all such deposits they issued their notes, or, in some cases, receipts, to be held while the metal was being recoined. McLeod says, " none of these banks did any business on their own account by way of discounting bills or making loans. Thus we see the peculiar function of all these banks, which were pure banks of deposit, was to issue promissory notes, payable to bearer on demand, which, however, did not exceed the quantity of the bullion they were substituted for." The notes were mere vouchers for the deposits of metal.

8. The Bank of England, established in 1694, was the first bank of deposit and issue in England. But it was also a bank of discount. Mr. McLeod says the names, " bank and banker, were utterly unknown in England in the time of Charles the First." Those who dealt in money and loans were then, respectively, known as or called " money changers " and " money scriveners." The original capital of the Bank of England was £1,200,-000, all of which was lent to the Government for the privilege of issuing a like amount of notes, uncovered by specie, and having also granted to it the right to receive deposits and lend capital and money on commercial paper and other securities. This was the origin of the bad system of founding an issue of paper currency on public securities, and treating notes as good cash reserve, which still clings to both the British and American na-

tions with desperate tenacity. It was a plan which enabled the supposed lucky lenders of capital to get the current rate of interest on it, and have it, too, to trade on in the form of notes or paper money.

9. The prestige which the first British bank acquired, by its sort of partnership with the State, made the bank a great success, and has been the parent of all the manias that have so often and so violently raged in Great Britain, until the year 1844, for the establishment of banks of issue, deposit, and discount, combined. In the American Colonies, now the United States, the practice in question received its highest and culminating abuse, where the issue of paper money became a burlesque on monetary and financial concerns. During the latter part of the last and beginning of the present century, up to 1844, the multiplication of such "money-making" banks, by bad and reckless competition, and the over-supply of paper money, leading to inflation and overtrading, brought stupendous ruin on large bodies of stockholders and the general public.

10. In Great Britain there were three epochs, during the period last mentioned, when these manias for issuing paper money prevailed; namely, from 1810 to 1819, from 1823 to 1825, and from 1835 to 1838, each ending in hundreds, if not thousands, of failures, and the loss to shareholders and the public of sums of startling magnitude, and the destruction of business houses and industrial interests beyond estimate. These disasters led to the passage of the Bank Act of 1844, prohibiting the issue of paper money by any new companies or firms, and totally abolishing banks of issue (except the Bank of England) within fifty miles of London.

11. The banks of Amsterdam, Sweden, Venice, and Hamburg, being restrained from issuing any more notes than the value of the gold on which they were issued, and

not being allowed to trade, were pure and simple banks
of issue, *in effect,* being compelled to hold all the gold
received for the redemption of their notes.   Thus no possible harm could arise from the issue of notes fully covered
by metal; and their greater convenience, as a tool of industry, than metal, soon made their notes very popular.
There were also many circumstances which conspired to
render the Bank of England both popular and successful
from the start.   These circumstances led to its receiving
a large line of deposits, which amply supplied it with metal
and trading capital, for which it paid no interest.   There
were some other advantages which it enjoyed.   1st, It
was under the management of wealthy and experienced
men, who could influence business.   2d, It had no competition, except from private houses.   3d, It held the
government balances, and had the prestige of being considered a national bank, and managed to a large extent
the government finances, and negotiated government
loans.   It has ever since enjoyed these and other great
privileges; but competition has long since set a limit on
its profits, which are far below those of the Bank of France,
— the only bank of issue in that country, — and numerous
joint-stock banks.

12.   Having conceded so much to the success, character, and standing of the Bank of England, I am led, from
all that I can gather respecting the embarrassments so
often brought on it by its *note issue,* at present of
£15,000,000, on securities, to the irresistible conclusion,
that, on the whole, such issue has been an injury to the
concern.   I think a clever actuary and accountant, like
Mr. Seyd, who had the time and patience to go into a
close analytical investigation of its affairs from the beginning, could demonstrate that the Bank of England
has been a large loser by its issue of notes instead of confining itself wholly to trading on its own and other folks'

capital, including £5,000,000 of free government deposits. Furthermore, from a pretty careful study of the history of British banking and currency, I am led to think that economists, from Adam Smith to Ricardo, McCulloch, Mill, and Price, have exaggerated the value, to the banking classes at least, of paper money, for the reasons I have assigned; that is, the enormous periodic losses, and the restraints that the issue of notes impose on legitimate banking. What advantages might have arisen from or may hereafter arise out of a well and ably conducted state issue department is quite another matter.

13. I lay it down as a self-evident and fundamental principle, that paper money, being simply a more convenient tool than metallic, ought never to be issued for the direct object of profit, or for the creation of private or national resources. When the main object of issuing currency notes is gain, as it always has been, till the Bank Act of 1844 set a limit to the issue on securities, the tendency is to over-issue, or keep out more notes than can be made safely to circulate. In order effectually to guard against the possibilities of over-trading in paper money, the principle I have laid down is, that the first object to be aimed at, is to secure an adequate, and only an adequate, quantity of more convenient tools than sovereigns or other gold coins. The profit must only be regarded as of secondary importance, and incidental. That is, if it shall be found that the note issue of a state money department shall bring about such an economization of metal as I have pointed out in a former chapter, then the state may avail itself, in a limited degree, of such profit, and use it as resources. It cannot be doubted that a well-conducted state department, in such countries as Great Britain and the United States, would not only supply the best industrial tool, in the form of paper

money, but would incidentally yield a larger profit than
any bank, or number of banks, all of which would purchase their supplies of paper money from the state
department. Notes issued by the state, and held within
the strict limits of supply and demand, would require very
little gold, comparatively, to maintain their market value
and hold them at par with gold : besides, their convertibility would be guaranteed by the whole resources of the
nation ; whilst those of banks, unless aided by Government, command only a very limited amount of backing.

14. The question soon coming up for consideration
by British statesmen is, whether the present Bank of
England Act, on renewal, shall be so amended as to
transfer more promptly than is now taking place the entire country, Scotch, and Irish circulations, to the Bank
of England, to be made available by lodging in the Issue
Department an equal amount of dead securities ; or
whether a state issue department, pure and simple, shall
be created, and established at Whitehall. The great success of the India State Issue of notes, under very serious
difficulties, should encourage a hope that the latter course
may be adopted.

15. If the Government of the day, taking a narrow
and mistaken view of the important principles and still
more important public interests involved, determine to
enlarge the present plan of issuing notes on securities,
the limit of such fiduciary issue will be raised to £30,-
800,000. To this extent, then, would the evils I have so
fully pointed out in the chapters on the Bank of England
theory and practice be increased. The policy of Lord
Beaconsfield's government, so far as it has been developed, seems to favor the carrying out fully Sir Robert
Peel's intention of gradually transferring the entire note
issue of the kingdom to the Bank of England. That
such a result would lead to an increased sensitiveness in

financial affairs, and, by the increased power conferred
on the bank, to still more dictatorial interference by it
with the loan market and the trade in bullion, I think
cannot be doubted.

CHAPTER XVI.

BANKS OF DEPOSIT AND DISCOUNT, OR LEGITIMATE BANK-
ING VERSUS BANKS OF ISSUE AND CLEARING-HOUSES.

1. At the risk of being charged with prolixity, I feel
compelled to draw occasionally from the fountain of
truth deductions already made and applied, in establishing other fundamental and collateral branches of the
subject, or used to overthrow errors. Professor Price
has so fully examined and pointed out the operations of
legitimate banking that I am spared much labor, and
what I shall say in this chapter presupposes a well
grounded knowledge of the subject so ably treated by
him. That legitimate banking, in the present age, has
nothing in common with the *issue* of notes or paper
money, I accept as a demonstrated truth. The bank,
whether it be a single individual, a firm, or a joint-stock
company, must possess an adequate amount of cash
capital, — that is, actual money, and accumulated capital,
which can instantly be turned into money, to serve as a
margin of security to customers. Mr. Hankey, who is
excellent authority on that matter, thinks one-third of all
deposits should be held in this form, as cash reserve. The
next step is to accept the deposits of all and sundry customers who may have accumulated capital or desire loans
or discounts on the security of goods. It need scarcely
be added that the selection of customers, by a bank,
other than those who simply desire to leave in a banker's

hands surplus balances of capital, is a matter of prime importance. As a rule, with but few exceptions, a bank should never lend capital, its own or its customers', on what is known as "accommodation paper." Commercial paper should always represent commodities in course of production, or in transit from producers to consumers.

2. In the accounts established between banks of deposit and discount and their customers, the banker debits himself with his own and his customers' capital, whether the latter consists of accumulated or earned capital, or of the "proceeds" of bills discounted. When money is deposited, it simply counts as so much trading power in the general mass of that article. It is, however, an asset, of which we have seen a prudent banker will take care to have an adequate supply at command, in his own vaults, or at easy call. This "cash," together with the discounted securities, makes up the other or credit side of the ledger.

3. By this brief statement of the organization of a bank of deposit and discount, it will be seen that the funds on which he trades consist: *First*, of his own capital (money being treated merely as capital). *Second*, of the balances of other people's capital, left with him for safe keeping, on which he may pay interest, a little below the market rate at which he lends it, or not, according to the exigencies of customers. Most sound and well-managed banks have a pretty large "line" of customers who do not care to tie up their balances for specific periods, in order to get interest thereon ; and on such the banker makes a clear net profit, without any cost to himself, by lending to good customers. *Third*, the largest and most important part of the banker's trading fund consists of the proceeds of bills representing goods, which have been discounted ; that is, the interest has

been deducted or subtracted from the face of the bills, and the balance has been debited to the banker, or credited to the customer as a deposit of capital. The "discounted" interest forms also a part of the trading fund, being the banker's profit; and the method of getting paid in advance is equivalent to getting compound interest.

4. That "mighty instrument" the check, as Professor Price expressively calls it, is the talisman by which the common pool of trading power, described, is made available. Though the check purports to be payable in cash, and can at any moment be convertible into cash, it is only so done in the ratio of three per cent on the gross amount of trading power handled; and of this, only about the half of one per cent is handled in coin. In referring again to this fact, it must not be supposed that I undervalue the offices of either metallic or paper money as tools of industry. This half of one per cent of trading power, handled by bankers, in the shape of money, or coin, is indispensable to a sound monetary system. It is the "governor" of the industrial engine, and as a measure of value can no more be dispensed with than the yardstick, and measures of length generally, as well as of weight and capacity. But, in conceding these most important functions to money, let us not undervalue trading power wielded by bankers through the bill of exchange and the check, in manner already fully set forth. If money corresponds with the governor of the steam-engine, trading power represents the boilers and the rest of the engine in the mighty machinery of human industry; and the clearing-house serves, like the safety valve, to indicate the amount and pressure of steam, or the force applied. It may here be noted, that, when the banker pays the check, he credits himself and debits the drawing customer.

5. To make the subject still more vividly clear, I must state what constitutes purely and simply a bank of DE-POSIT. This will separate the operations of modern banks, so as to show more precisely the dividing-lines between the several kinds. I have sufficiently explained (Chap. XV. par. 7) what a bank of deposit and issue, pure and simple, is, and will let Mr. J. B. McCulloch state what a simple bank of deposit effects. He says, " When a public deposit bank is established, those who make use of its services deposit with its officers the money " (Mr. McCulloch means capital including money) " they must otherwise have kept at home, in order to meet their current demands upon them ; and when the individual who has obtained a bank credit has a payment to make to another person dealing with the bank, — and the principal traders in most towns in which a public bank of deposit is established belong to it, — it is made by a transfer of so much credit, or *bank money*" (trading power), "from one account to the other ; and it is only in the event of a person having to pay *money* to a stranger, that he has any motive to withdraw his deposit from the bank. In this way the circulation of money is rendered all but superfluous for all but the smallest payments."

6. It will be seen what an immense utilizer of *money* a purely deposit bank, by the use of the check, can be made ; but it will also be seen that its dealings are confined to the one description of capital resulting from the profits of industry defined in postulate 36, and to actual money in a very limited degree. The discount of bills is the greatest utilizer of money, as by far the largest part of floating capital is derived therefrom. Add to this the potency of the check, which, though used to aid the operations of banks of deposit, pure and simple, only finds its highest efficiency in transferring and measuring out trading power in banks of discount.

7. Though the business thus described constitutes by far the greater part of the general business of banks of deposit and discount, there are other and kindred operations to which they devote themselves profitably. Most of such banks, through agents and correspondents, make remittances for their customers by letters of credit, certificates of deposit, certified checks, and bills of exchange to all parts of the country, and receive similar remittances, pay drafts, etc. In most large cities, and more especially in London, and many cities in America, this kind of business is extended to foreign countries, and is engaged in by all other kinds of banks.

8. Still further to facilitate the operations of bankers and the settling of commercial accounts and balances, both domestic and foreign, the next, latest, and perhaps most marvellous invention is the CLEARING-HOUSE — Balancing-House would give to ordinary minds a more exact idea of the nature and offices of these institutions. All business men, however, know what the clearing-house is ; but it is only in London where this method of balancing accounts receives its highest development. When a clearing-house has been established in a town, a clerk from each bank belonging to it meets similar clerks from all the other "clearing-house banks," and a general exchange of checks is effected in a few minutes ; and in London the balances are settled without the transfer of a pound of money, by each one having balances to pay drawing a check on the Bank of England, where all keep a portion of their trading power, or reserve. This plan of checking on the Bank of England went into operation in 1856, and now (1876) the annual clearings reach the enormous sum of *sixty-six thousand millions of pounds ;* or, put it in dollars, *three hundred and twenty-five thousand million of dollars,* — a sum too large for the mind to grasp.

9. From what I have shown, it has been seen that the business of a bank of deposit and discount consists in receiving the surplus and temporarily unused balances of accumulated and other floating capital awaiting more permanent investments, — whether it consists of money, checks, bills, or credits on other banks or commercial houses of standing, — and out of the common fund of trading power thus collected, to lend to all customers, having good security to offer, such as bills founded on goods being preferred. The "unused balances" referred to, which nearly all large customers who borrow generally hold at their bankers, it will be seen, form a considerable part of a banker's reserve and discount fund, and become an important element in his profit.

10. In London, excepting the Bank of England, this kind of business is regarded as almost the only legitimate as it is nearly the universal system of banking. So perfect is the system, that, but for the strenuous efforts of the Bank of England to dominate the loan market and counteract the operation of the natural rate of interest, there could hardly be any thing to desire. As a bank of discount, the Bank of England stands, I believe, about fourth rate ; and it is entirely within the power of the other joint-stock and private banking firms to put a complete and final end to the power of that institution by the establishment of a bank of deposit, pure and simple, wherein to keep their trading balances, and on which they shall all draw to settle clearing-house accounts. This bank might be called "The Clearing-House Bank ; " and a certain amount of the deposits might be invested in public securities, which would yield an income, and pay the expenses of management. It might also perform the offices contemplated by the " Check Bank," which would have been a success had it been started on the plan suggested. The idea is well worth the consideration

of London bankers, if it has not already seriously engaged their attention.

11. It will also have been seen that the issue of notes is in no way necessary to the success of banks of deposit and discount; and it is certain none of the successful ones in the kingdom would engage in the practice, now that the fallacy as to the profitable nature of the business has been demonstrated by abundant experience. But, as I have before remarked, the delusion still prevails, mostly in America, that banks of issue sustained by government securities are advantageous, and necessary to the industrial interests; and I regret to find such good financiers as Mr. Spaulding, the father of the Greenback, or National Currency Law, and David A. Wells, the able advocate of free trade, and Edward Atkinson of Boston, all sound on the question of trade, with the one exception of paper money, advocating the manifestly unsound practice of the nation connecting itself with and aiding private parties to circulate government guaranteed notes for profit to themselves. If these gentlemen were not national-bank presidents, or otherwise connected with the interests of those national pets, directly or indirectly, and, I may add, were younger men, I might hope for their conversion to true demonstrated principles. But the public mind of America is gradually becoming aware that bankers ought not to be the only class favored with the plan of drawing interest on a good investment, and having ninety per cent of its value in "ready money." The great danger now is, that the so-called Greenback party may push the money question to the *argumentum ad absurdum* by carrying out the "interconvertible" plan, and running into wild extremes of inflation.

12. As an exception to the rule, in the United States, I wish to mention the name of the late John E. Williams, for many years a large shareholder and president of the

Metropolitan National Bank, the largest in New York, whose personal acquaintance I had the pleasure to have. Mr. Williams was a warm advocate for the abolition of the national-bank circulation and confining it to greenbacks, or national legal-tender notes. His writings on the subject were able ; and he pointed out clearly the desirability, and the advantage it would be to the national banks, to give up their circulation voluntarily, and sell their securities, on which they can realize a handsome profit, and use only legal-tender notes. When the silver mania runs its course, possibly these numerous pet banks may see in Mr. Williams's self-abnegation and patriotic course, and in his powerful arguments, that a true, sound, and permanent monetary system is better than one that excites public hostility, and is founded on a total misconception of monetary principles, and of the uses and offices of paper money.

13. I ought also to mention Gen. F. A. Spinner, late United States Treasurer, whose name has been appended to so many hundred millions of the legal-tender notes, great and small, from the inception of their issue, till he was forced out of office, near the end of President Grant's administration, by the national-bank influences in Congress. He was always opposed to the principle of lending the public credit to bankers to trade on, however good security they were able to give in the shape of national bonds.

14. Hon. Mr. E. G. Spaulding, before referred to, president of a national bank at Buffalo, on the contrary favors this plan. This gentleman has, however, contributed a valuable work on the "Financial History of the War," which explains the origin of the legal-tender, or greenback, money, and the reasons for establishing the national-bank system, which is a decided improvement on the old State banks. This, and Mr. Spaulding's

"Centennial Address to the Bankers' Association," are excellent works of reference on the subjects of banking history and statistics in America; and they embody the opinions of many of America's leading statesmen on the questions of issuing paper money, and general banking. Mr. Spaulding's address states the number of national banks in existence in the United States then (beginning of 1876), at 2,118, having a paid-up capital of $505,485,965. There were also 907 chartered State banks with a paid-up capital of $164,366,669. These, and 2,375 private bankers, were *non*-issuing banks, showing a large development of legitimate banking.[1]

CHAPTER XVII.

"THE PRIMARY OBJECT OF PAPER MONEY IS TO SUPPLY A BETTER TOOL OF INDUSTRY THAN METALLIC MONEY. — INCIDENTALLY ONLY CAN IT BE PROPERLY TREATED AS TRADING POWER, OR RESOURCES" (*postulate* 49).

1. I HAVE, in the last chapter but one, laid down the broad, well-defined distinction between issuing paper money simply to create trading power, or national resources, and of using it as a more convenient and efficient tool of industry. The subject relating to the "taking up of loans" from the public, by the issue and circulation of paper money, seems of importance to those who seek, by scientific methods of reasoning, to reach sound fundamental principles. If the position I have laid down in postulate 49, placed at the head of this chapter, is well taken, its acceptation by economists and legislators will lead to very important results. If the proposition is fundamental and true, it overthrows all

[1] The three last paragraphs were written in 1878.

the past theories of economists and statesmen respecting the primary end gained by the use of paper money. It has hitherto been and is still the universal theory that the primary object of such money is to create trading power, or national resources. Banks of issue think of nothing but the profit to be derived from putting notes in circulation ; and states have generally used such money as resources to prosecute wars. It has always been considered as a legitimate method of making two pounds out of one, or, as I have expressed it elsewhere in homely language, as a plan by which a man "may eat his cake and have it too."

2. This was not originally the purpose of the inventors of bank notes, as I have shown by the practice of the first banks of issue before cited. It was reserved to British ingenuity to enlarge the uses of bank notes by granting the right to issue them, to be used as money, to the Bank of England, as a consideration for a loan made to the state. It was due, however, to the fertile mind of the eminent Scotch financier, John Law, in the next generation to enlarge this fascinating method of creating wealth ; and "Lawism" still clings to the public mind with as much tenacity as that other delusion, the "mercantile theory." If a bank could lend its entire capital to the nation, and receive the current rate of interest for it, and be able to recoup itself by taking up loans from the public on a security susceptible of performing the office of money, it is not surprising that ingenious minds should presently seek to improve on it by issuing notes without having either gold or securities behind them. They argued that the tool paper money was so much more convenient than the tool metallic money, beside being so much cheaper, that the public would not stop to inquire particularly into the nice distinctions of monetary science. Law was not so wild in

his theories as others, who improved on them. It was argued, that, if government securities formed a good basis for issuing paper money, lands and goods might serve an equally good purpose. Thus the question of providing a better tool of industry was treated as of secondary importance, or altogether lost sight of. The Bank of England still acts on this false theory, otherwise it would sell the government securities (£15,000,000) in which it has its capital and "rest" invested, and would let the *note issue* rest on metal, as it did in the cases of the banks of Venice, Sweden, Amsterdam, and Hamburg. The national banks of the United States were founded on the same erroneous principles, otherwise they would sell their public securities, and trade on greenbacks and their own capital, instead of on notes founded on securities.

3. One of the inconsistencies of this theory, that the proper office of paper money is to economize metal, or make the issue of notes merely a matter of profit to the issuer, is, that banks alone should have this advantage. Indeed, Professor Price has attempted to show that only "private issuers" *can* make *a profit* in this way ; that when the state takes up loans by issuing notes, the proceeds of such loans "are lost to the nation" (see Chap. XIV.). I have already shown that this is an unsupported inference. On it, however, is founded the claim that *a bank* may properly take up loans from the public on the security of its notes, but a *government* may not, for the reason, that, when a government does so, the loans are *consumed*, and there is no residuum of profit left to the nation. Now, I am showing that profit is only a secondary consideration, — a thing to be made subordinate to the higher and much more important office of supplying a better tool than metallic money. But the plan of issuing paper money on government securities

is, in effect, to allow the bank to raise government loans
on its own notes, and lend the proceeds to the Government at the market rate of interest.   In other words,
the bank has borrowed its whole capital stock from the
public.   It is a plan of organizing and starting a bank
without any capital of its own.   Hence, like a large proportion of the American national banks, the very notes
authorized to be issued on securities are used to pay for
those securities.   The plan is a total reversal of the postulate I am enforcing.   It makes profit the primary object
of issuing notes, while the main office of notes is wholly
ignored.

4. The idea of substituting a certain quantity of paper
money for metallic money, which may thus be sent abroad
and sold to foreign countries for other and more profitable articles of value, seems to have taken a deep hold
on the minds of even great reasoners like Adam Smith,
Mill, and others.   This method of "making haste to
grow rich" seems so fascinating that it is almost a pity
to attack it; but it certainly belongs to the same category in economic science as the "mercantile theory,"
overthrown by Adam Smith himself.   True science cannot be limited to national boundaries; and we cannot
permit other countries, scientifically speaking, to take our
old tin kettles and pans because we have found out how
to do without them.   This would be a fraud on the whole
outside race of barbarians.   If we have found out a substitute for money, we are bound by honorable principles
to publish the recipe to all the world.   If we can make
one pound or one dollar do the work of two, and can
extend the process to millions on millions, all nations
should have the right to the secret.   But this theory is
something like that of the Hindoo idea, that the world
must have something to rest on; and so the big turtle
was invented.   If we palm off our useless metal on other

nations, on what are they to rest *their* foundations of
wealth, and what becomes of the universal money we
have heard so much of ?

5. It is safe to say that this alluring theory of making
profit, or *creating value*, by issuing paper money has led
the commercial world into all those dire disasters of which
I have already spoken in treating of banks of issue.   It is
a theory that lies at the bottom of the fallacy that money
can be created out of nothing, — that the Bank of England and the national banks of the United States can turn
their investments in government securities into money,
in order to draw the interest on such investments and
trade on the value thereof at the same time.   It is, in
fact, Lawism in all its worst features ; though the idea
was invented before Law's time.   It is, *par excellence*, the
root of all the evils that have grown out of the uses and
abuses of the delegated prerogative of states to private
individuals and corporations to manufacture and emit
paper money.

6. It is hardly going too far to claim that a large
proportion of all the issuing banks established in Great
Britain and Ireland up to 1844, and in the United States
and the British Colonies up to the present time, have
had their origin in the fallacious and tempting idea that
a man may, by a single stroke of the pen, double or very
largely increase his wealth by becoming a stockholder in
a bank of issue.   In Great Britain a limitation has been
set on such issues, which has resulted in a vast expansion of the true system of non-issuing banks, which have
demonstrated by their success and efficiency that the
issue of notes is not necessary or a legitimate office of a
banker.   But in the United States a law has been passed
setting no limit on the issue of bank notes except that
set by the entire national debt ; and this Act is entitled,
" An Act to provide for the Resumption of Specie Pay-

ments, and for a System of Free Banking." As banking
was free before, it is a manifest misnomer. It should
have been called, "An Act for the Free Issue of Paper
Money *to all Bondholders of the United States.*"

7. While the English and American systems remain
what they are, the really important question to consider,
by professional economists and statesmen, is, whether
private issuers can be trusted, in any case, with "lump-
ing" sums of notes, even when guaranteed by the state.
Mr. J. B. McCulloch says, "The widest experience proves
that *no man, or set of men,* ever had the power to make
unrestricted issues of paper without abusing it, — that
is, without issuing it in inordinate quantities. . . . The
re-enactment of the restriction on cash payments at the
Bank of England, and the rendering it perpetual, would
have no perceptible effect on the value of bank notes,
provided their quantity were not at the same time increased. But *there cannot be a doubt, that, under such
circumstances, it would be increased*" (also Daniel Webster's speeches quoted in the Appendix).

8. The arguments adduced seem to me to give the
coup de grace to the claims set up by a large class of
economists, and a still larger class of interested *practical*
men, in favor of the plan of issuing notes on government
securities, which I have shown is a plan of having your
capital and the value of it in money at the same time.
But the same temptation, to use the emission of notes
by the state, to create public or national resources, has
often led to the most serious disasters, even worse than
in cases of private issues. The old "Continental money"
of the United States, and the issues in France a few
years later (during the fever of the great Revolution) of
assignats and commandats, are examples of this extreme
fatuity of rulers on the subject of issuing paper money
to create resources. Until the principles I am contend-

ing for are recognized by statesmen and legislators, and
are made the base-work of laws prepared to carry them
into effect, there never can be a sound monetary system
in any country. If neither private nor public issuers
have been able to put proper restrictions on the issue of
paper money, it is because no properly constructed issue
department has ever been devised. The issue of the
Bank of France, during late years, and of the State Issue
Department of India, have come the nearest to well-
regulated monetary management of any on record, unless
it be those of the first four banks of issue, already several
times quoted, as they were first organized. The cure of
the evil, if ever it be cured, must be by the removal of
the issue from all temptation, on the part of managers,
whether public or private, of using paper money chiefly
as a method of creating either public or private wealth,
otherwise than for supplying a more effective and convenient tool than metallic money, into which it must
always be made convertible on demand, to steady its
market value, and regulate supply exactly to suit demand.

9. To effect this end, — to afford adequate guaranties
against the abuse of flooding the market at one time,
and denuding it at another time, of this valuable improvement on metal, for circulation, — and to insure convertibility at all times, the issuing board must be wholly
removed, alike from the influences of bankers and merchants, and from the control of the finance minister,
who is too often tempted to tamper with the paper currency, to meet emergencies in national affairs, *and must
sell notes for metal only.*

10. The fundamental principle being thus established,
the question arises as to how an issue department should
be constituted to meet the necessities of the case. This
will be made the subject of another chapter. Without
anticipating what I have to say on that subject, I may

here remark, that paper money issued by such a department will cost traders and all classes just as much as
metallic money, which is the correct thing. Bullion
dealers, bankers, merchants, and miners, the owners of
the precious metals, will take them to the money department, as they now take them to the Bank of England, the mint, or to brokers, and will sell them for
notes or for coin, as they may need, each party — the
state and the owner of metal — trading on market values
the articles they have to exchange. Thus there will be
a perfectly self-regulating or automatic machinery established. There will be no more metal coined than is
needed by the public, no more notes issued than will
stay in circulation, no more metal taken to the money
department than will afford a profit, however small.
The equation of supply and demand will find its nicest
equipoise. The equilibrium will be as perfect as the face
of the ocean. The waves and ripples will always tend
towards an exact level. If a profit occurs to the department from the issue of paper, it will belong to the nation,
and not to individuals. The profit, it will be seen, under
such a department, will simply be an *incidental* circumstance, and not a *primary* object. The profit can only
arise from a sale of a part of the metal on which I have
doubts.

11. I have now, I hope, demonstrated by logical reasoning the distinction between issuing and using paper
money, for the purpose of affording a more convenient
and effective tool of industry, and for creating trading
or national resources. *When the necessities of the state
or of individuals drive them, or either of them, into the
market for loans to meet emergencies, the proper thing to
do is to borrow on the best security available, and at the
lowest rate of interest practicable.* But science and
experience most amply prove that the issue of paper

money, as a means of raising loans, is wrong. Practice has always demonstrated the falsity of the theory; and it is time the statesmen of England and America should master and settle this question, demonstratively and finally. The solution of the problems of monetary science, now so extensively agitating the industrial world, must be sought in a plan that will give absolute freedom to the laws of trade, which I have shown are the laws of nature, as active and well defined as the law of gravitation.

12. A class of interested economists, especially in the United States, for want of a better argument against the issue of notes by a national department, have descended to the small trickery of politicians in raising "a cry" against the practice. They cry out on all occasions, "The Government must not be allowed to trade, or to follow the business of banking." But I have shown that the issuing of paper money is not trading or banking; and, by limiting its issue to the offices of an industrial tool, I have knocked this senseless cry to the ground. The Government no more trades by issuing paper than by coining metallic money. This is undeniable, and I challenge its refutation.

13. M. Michel Chevalier, the eminent French economist, has done good service in the cause of sound monetary and industrial science, by advocating the right of the state to issue and possess the profit, whatever it may be, of paper money. Two letters which I had the honor to receive from him some years ago on this subject will be found in the Appendix, and I have great satisfaction in directing attention to them. I also invite attention to letters I had the honor to receive from Lord George Hamilton, Under Secretary of State for India, written at the request of the Marquis of Salisbury, then Chief Secretary of State for India, showing the satisfactory working of the

India State Issue Department. The successful experiment suggests that the issue of small notes, as low as one or two rupees, would immensely increase the success and the usefulness of paper money in India. It is due to the one and two dollar greenback notes, issued in the United States, that these treasury notes have become so popular, that the people will not readily consent to their retirement, and the substitution of silver, or of bank notes issued on securities.

14. The great evils of a silver standard of value have of late led British statesmen to seek a remedy in the demonetization of that metal in India, except for a limited amount of subsidiary coins. If the note issue could be enlarged by introducing small notes, which are particularly adapted to the small, frugal dealings of the laboring and middle classes of India, the profit incidentally resulting from such issue would probably make up for the depreciation in the market value of silver, and the disastrous effects of having a metallic circulation that fluctuates as violently as ever the Bank of England note did during the long suspension of that institution.

CHAPTER XVIII.

SUGGESTIONS FOR STATE ISSUE DEPARTMENTS IN GREAT BRITAIN AND THE UNITED STATES, AND CONSIDERATIONS CONNECTED THEREWITH.

1. AFTER the very clear exposition of principles as well as the functions that would devolve upon an independent, or perhaps, more correctly speaking, scientific, money department, set forth in the preceding chapters, it may seem almost a work of supererogation to indicate a method for organization. Besides, the details

seem to lie on the very surface. Already they exist in most countries which issue coined and paper money. All that is required is, to bring the scattered elements together, and construct a homogeneous edifice. The Issue Department of the Bank of England, and of the Treasury at Washington, will furnish able and experienced men for the management of the note issue; and the respective mints can supply the clerical and mechanical forces for the production of coin. All that is therefore required is, to bring the whole — the mints and the issue of notes — into one building, and place them under the direction of a single board. The laws needed in each country to bring about this object would prescribe the number of managers, and their duties, which would be automatic.

2. The department may be called the "Money" or "Currency Department," the latter being, strictly speaking, the more comprehensive and expressive term, from a scientific stand-point; but either is good, and "Money" is a more popular term. The business that would devolve on such a department would be very large, and would require commodious and separate buildings. The working of the proposed automatic system will be found more definitely referred to in subsequent chapters, explaining and defining the principles and the objects that will be attained (Chaps. XXIV., XXV., and XXVI. in particular).

3. It will now be seen how little there will really have to be done to organize a scientific issue in the two most powerful industrial nations, — those whose foreign, if not domestic, commerce is the greatest. In France the change would be no greater; and, as far as the result would affect the people, they would not have a prejudice to be moved by the change. The same coins and nearly the same style of notes would be supplied. The bank

notes alone would disappear; and in their place, in Great
Britain, the new note would run something like this:
"'The United Kingdom of Great Britain and Ireland
promises to pay the bearer ———— pounds in coin on
demand, at the issue office of the State Money Department, or any of its branches or agencies." In the
United States, there will need to be no change from the
"greenback." The same plates may be used as at
present.

4. The business of the department may be briefly
summarized: —

First, To provide and pay coin for all the gold bullion
offered, seeing that such coin is of the specified fineness.

Second, To provide and pay notes, of the denominations specified by law, for gold and silver to all who bring
such metal, coined or uncoined, to the issue office, or its
branches or agencies.

Third, To provide silver, and subsidiary coins of all
kinds, and sell the same to all comers for gold or silver
coin, or silver bullion, at its market value, or paper money,
at the option of the parties applying.

Fourth, To redeem all notes and silver and other subsidiary coins in gold coin, on presentation at the several
places specified for that purpose.

Fifth, To establish agencies at such important centres
of business as experience shall indicate.

Sixth, To take charge of all cash held by the Bank
of England, or the Treasury Department of the United
States, held for the redemption of paper money, and
redeem all such paper money on presentation.

Seventh, To receive, hold, and pay out, on check, all
sums of money, — metallic and paper, of a specified
amount, of private individuals and joint-stock associations, — but paying no interest therefor.

5. The question as to the policy of using any part of

the large amount of coin that would accumulate in time in these departments, for the retirement of so much of the public debt, is one involving very nice considerations, as well as the retirement of the present bank issues. In the case of the bank of England, the Government would have to pay the bank the £11,200,000 of old debt, and the bank would take up and cancel its notes ; or this may be done by the new Issue Department taking all the coin and bullion in the Issue Department, and retiring with new state notes the entire issue of bank notes, leaving the bank in possession of the securities on which the £15,000,000 of notes are issued, and striking and settling the balance. It is only a simple matter of account, requiring time and skill to accomplish, so as not to change the volume of the currency or disturb values. The bank will have no demand for compensation. The present arrangement was not intended to be permanent. It was made when the Government wanted means, and it has always had a right to pay off the debt at its pleasure. These securities are now (May, 1879) worth nearly their face in gold.

6. Whether the country banks in Great Britain are entitled to damages for being compelled to withdraw their circulation is also questionable. They are in the same position of those in America, which issued notes before they entered the national banking system, to some extent at least ; though the former were not obliged to furnish any securities, which the American banks in most states were, — such securities being then state obligations. Such securities being good, the banks putting them up would get back their capital invested in them, to trade on. They would then do business on sound principles. But the settlement of these matters, probably, will not form any part of the difficulty in the way of a change for the better. The real question that underlies the whole

money problem is, how to overcome the blind prejudices of a class of great influence in the community, who do not wish to have the present order of things disturbed. To counteract this, is really what has to be done ; and this can only be done effectually by non-issuing banks, and the community at large.   In the United States public opinion, at this time, is nearly equally divided on the question of substituting " greenbacks " for bank notes.

7. In Great Britain the currency is only swelled above one of pure metal, about £25,000,000.   In carrying out the new plan, if none of the metal coming into the Issue Department were to be disposed of, a contraction of that amount of the currency would ensue ; and to that extent, at least, it might be desirable to part with the gold held for notes, *pari passu*, with the retirement of bank notes now issued on securities.   In America the measure would have to be consummated more slowly, to avert currency disturbances.   The present system might have to be got rid of, by substitution in full, or nearly so, of the national, or greenback, circulation for bank notes.   It will be shown hereafter (Chap. XXIV.), that the currency is still in a highly inflated condition.   How to get an adequate supply of metal behind the note issue, and hold the whole present volume of $650,000,000 in circulation, is a problem requiring time, skill, and determination to accomplish. Perhaps another great and overwhelming commercial crisis may be needed to sicken the people of a system that always breaks down when stability is most needed.

8. With regard to introducing a scientific (which is the true) system of issuing and regulating the supply of metallic, paper, and subsidiary currency, according to supply and demand, into the United States, the large amount of bank notes issued on public securities, and the small amount of gold held by the Government to sustain their convertibility into gold, interpose serious but not

insuperable difficulties to it. In the present anomalous
relationship between the Government and the national
banks, the whole burden must necessarily fall on the
former to maintain specie payments in a crisis. It is a
system in which the Government has all the responsibility
and risk, and the banks the lion's share of the profits of
the issue. Only a portion of the American people perceive the error of this plan of supplying paper money.
They do not take heed of, if they perceive, the fact, that
the public at large pay full gold price for these bank notes,
which cost the banks only one per cent " tax on circulation," and a mere nominal price for fabrication. When
this fact, and a better knowledge of the advantages of a
circulation founded wholly, or for the greater part, on
metal, shall prevail, there will be no serious obstruction
in the way of gradually bringing about a change that will
be permanent, because it will be scientific.

9. I have pointed out the danger there would be in
selling any considerable amount of the accumulations of
gold in the Issue Department, in retirement of the public
debt, in consequence of the inflating effect such sales
would have on the volume of the currency. To the
extent, however, that the new system would operate contraction, I have suggested, as to Great Britain, such sales
might be expedient. In the United States, I cannot
help regarding the volume of paper currency, which now
(May, 1879) constitutes a very large proportion of the
actual circulation outside of the banks and the treasury,
too large, — in fact dangerously large, because of the
vast amounts of deposits, or capital held on deposit,
which in crises will be the first demand for metal. The
note-holders, feeling that they have the government guaranty, will, for a time at least, remain passive and indifferent. These pertinent considerations should all have due
weight on the part of currency agitators. What I would

strongly urge in regard to the United States, is, that a gradual contraction of paper money should take place, so as to *bring back gold to the channels of circulation without forcing the Government to buy it by increasing the interest-paying debt, as Secretary Sherman, acting on the authorization of a law prepared by himself and passed by Congress under his dictation, has done.* I propose that the laws of industry shall provide the means, and then the burden will fall equally on the whole country (see postulate 61).

10. There is another circumstance incident to the adoption of a single national issue department which may justify the use of a portion of the great metal fund for retiring portions of the national debt. There is a regular annual increase of business transactions in each of the two countries under present consideration, demanding an increase in the currency. We have no right to suppose there will be a stop to this increase. On the contrary, the steady development of industrial pursuits, caused by improved methods of production and transport, and the growth of wealth, lead to the almost certain fact that this demand will increase in a considerable ratio. Now, the demand for more currency may be turned to account by the sale of a portion of the accumulating gold, equal to one-half, or even to the whole, *increased* demand for currency for a few years. There will then be no *unnatural inflation*. It will be a substitution of so many notes for so much gold, without disturbing the working of the automaton.

11. In the chapters treating of a universal monetary system, I have advocated the issue of notes as low as the lowest gold coin. This I hold to be very desirable for convenience, and in a scientifically organized issue department, worked automatically, I think the public demand should be complied with. If the people don't

want small notes, they will not buy them, but take metallic money. Such a department as I have outlined will
completely set aside the objection to small notes, because every note issued must be paid for by metal at its
full face value. Small notes are almost infinitely prefer-
able to silver dollars, the weight of which is very objec-
tionable. But give the public the choice. If they prefer
silver dollars, let them have them. There is nothing so
democratic as money. There is no commodity that demands the application of free trade so strongly as money,
and no system can approximate perfection that does not
yield to the idiosyncrasies, so to speak, of those who use
this indispensable tool. "Money," says Adam Smith,
"is a commodity of which every man is his own merchant." Then give to each money-merchant the commodity in such denominations and form — metal or
paper — as he requires, or fancies most.

CHAPTER XIX.

SIR ROBERT PEEL'S POSITION ON THE NOTE ISSUE. — MR.
GLADSTONE CLAIMS THAT IT BELONGS TO THE STATE
WHEREIN THE ACT OF 1844 HAS FAILED.

1. I DO not attach much importance to the mere unsupported *opinions* of even the highest authorities in
economic science, or the greatest statesmen. It is only
when such opinions are backed up by close logical reasoning that they can be accepted as good conclusions.
Of how much value are the acts of Sir Robert Peel, we
may decide when we compare his theory with his practice, which I shall presently do. This, however, we may
concede to him, that the Bank Act of 1844, putting an
end to the unlimited issue of bank notes, and providing

for the ultimate absorption of all the country and Scotch
and Irish bank paper circulation, by the Bank of England, and separating the Issue from the Banking Department of that institution, effected an immense improvement on the old system. An equally important, and,
considering the circumstances, still greater, revolution in
currency was effected in the United States by the Act
of Congress authorizing the issue of the national legal-
tender notes called "greenbacks." Had the national
banking system not been tacked on to the currency, and
the issue of legal tenders been kept within the limits set
by specie value, the United States would to-day have
an approximately scientific and perfect system of paper
money.

2. The object of the issue, in the United States, was
to create national resources : and hence the finance minister, Mr. Chase (Secretary of the Treasury), failed to
grasp the fundamental principle, that nothing is gained
by the nation or the people by inflating a legal-tender
paper circulation ; and the plan he adopted, of afterwards
dividing the issue with banks, was a blunder as serious
as that committed by Sir Robert Peel, in continuing
the privilege to the Bank of England to issue notes on
government securities, which Mr. Chase copied, and applied to the national banking system. Nothing is more
true than the fact, that neither statesmen nor nations,
as a rule, can readily free themselves from the traditional errors of past generations ; and even good thinkers
and reasoners are prone to accept the opinions, principles, and 'practices of business men without sufficient
distrust of their soundness.

3. That Sir Robert Peel had a very clear perception
of correct theoretical monetary principles, is shown by
his speeches, and the latitude he provided in the Act
of 1844, to enable the managers of the bank to exercise

a discretion as to the amount of the notes they might call for and use on account of securities. The following extract from one of his speeches, to which my attention has been drawn by the eminent French economist, M. Michel Chevalier, is proof of this fact.

"Some have contended, and I am not one to deny the position, that if we had a new state of society to deal with, the wisest plan would be, to claim for the state the exclusive issue of promissory notes as we have claimed for it the exclusive privilege of coinage. They consider that the state is entitled to the whole profits to be derived from that which is the representative of coin ; and that, if the state had the exclusive power of issuing paper, there would be established a controlling power which would insure, as far as possible, an equilibrium in the currency."

It is quite evident that Sir Robert had a deep conviction of the true principles of monetary science. He had examined the subject very carefully while a member of the Bullion Committee in 1810, as a young and rising statesman, and under the able tuition of Mr. Horner, who prepared the report of that committee, which embodied sound principles, and which the majority of the House of Commons were incapable of understanding.

4. Before citing his motives and reasons for continuing the issue of notes by the Bank of England, notwithstanding his very evident conviction that it was not the right, or theoretically the best plan, I wish again to point out to the reader the absurdity of the system. When Sir Robert introduced the Bank Act of 1844 to Parliament, we find the Government owing the Bank £14,000,000, including the original loan of £11,200,000, for which it paid the current rate of interest. This covered the whole capital of the bank, and its "Rest" in addition, leaving the bank without any cash capital to use as trading reserve, or for a margin. Of course this had been going on from the inception of the bank in 1694. But

the proprietors were applying for an extension of their
charter, and all the country, with a few exceptions, had
become inimical to the unrestricted issue of bank notes;
and Sir Robert was in sympathy with the people, and hit
on or accepted the plan of limiting the issue to what it
then was, and, accordingly, prepared his bill so as to
stop all issues immediately of all banks, except the Bank
of England, within fifty miles of London, and authorized the merging of all lapsed circulation in the country,
and in Scotland and Ireland, into that bank, expecting
that arrangements would be made by mutual consent to
absorb the whole gradually, and perhaps speedily. Since
then, however, barely a million pounds of such circulation has fallen in, making, as elsewhere stated, at the
present time, but £15,000,000 as belonging to the bank,
out of a total of £30,800,000 notes issued in the kingdom.

5. Sir Robert Peel, therefore, contemplated a time
when the bank would become the owner of £30,800,000
of the public debt; and the Act provides that the bank
might then increase its issue on notes to that extent.
This would exceed the present paid-up capital by £19,-
600,000. I wish now to point out the exact effect of
increasing the note issue to that amount, — £30,800,000.
It would be simply to compel the bank to use, according to its present policy, the sum of £15,800,000 of additional notes, issued on the additional securities required
to be lodged in the Issue Department in payment for the
same. This is what has been done, to an immense extent, in the United States; that is, the national banks
have used the notes to pay for bonds. But let any man
of ordinary reasoning powers examine this proposition,
which the Bank Act, as it now stands on the statute-book,
involves, and he will be forced to the conclusion, that
either this will be the result of giving effect to the inten-

tions of the framer of the law, or else it will compel the
bank proprietors to raise the sum in question by the issue
of new shares, or to change its policy, and diminish its
issue in manner pointed out in Chap. VIII. The present fiduciary issue of £15,000,000, resting on public
securities, already exceeds the entire bank's paid-up capital and rest-fund together by about a million pounds ;
and, leaving out the " Rest," it will make the whole excess
up to nearly £20,000,000. If this is sound banking, then
it is a method whereby banking capital can be created
ad libitum. This, then, is the proposition which the
present Chancellor of the Exchequer has intimated to
be the intention of the present administration to give
" more immediate effect to."

6. The following apology was offered by Sir Robert
Peel for not acting on his convictions as to the true principles of the note issue, stated in the extract from one
of his speeches already quoted. " The true policy in
this country is to work as far as possible with the instruments you have ready at hand ; to avail yourselves of
the advantages which they possess, from having been in
use — from being familiar — from constituting a part of
the habits and usages of society. They will probably
work *more smoothly than perfectly novel instruments, of
greater theoretical perfection.* If we disturb that which
is established, let us have some good practical reason for
the change."

7. It was lucky that Sir Robert Peel found two years
later, in the urgency of Messrs. Cobden and Bright and
their following, " a good practical reason " for overthrow-
ing " old established usages of society," when he changed
front, and helped to pass the Act repealing the " Corn
Laws," which broke down the traditional theories of protection. But I have shown that " instruments of greater
theoretical perfection " may be created without " disturb-

ing that which is established," in my proposal in last chapter to transfer the entire clerical machinery of the note issue, and the management of the mint and the national debt, from their present offices, where they would be no longer of use, to the new state department. It is only right to say, that the real lion in the path is the Bank of England. Such a suggestion strikes at the consideration and importance of the bank managers. To take away the name of "Bank of England note," and substitute therefor the title of "The United Kingdom," and to remove the public deposits, and the management of the public debt, these gentlemen would consider as worse than highway robbery. That is where the shoe pinches, and Sir Robert didn't care to tread on other people's corns at a time when his fame and power were at the highest.

8. I have already noticed the views of M. Chevalier on the subject of the right of the state to issue the entire paper money needed by the people, and to receive the profits. His letters stating those views will be found in the Appendix. Mr. Gladstone expressed himself very decidedly on the question under consideration, in 1866, when he introduced a bill into the House of Commons to indemnify the bank against the over-issue of notes during the crisis of that year. He declared emphatically, as he has always done when acting on well-grounded convictions, "The whole business of issue is in the state; and, what is more important, the responsibility also belongs to the state." It was not an occasion when he could give effect to his words, or express more explicitly what he would do if the opportunity should be presented to him for carrying out his convictions.

9. This being a work on principles, I have not felt it necessary to quote *mere opinions* unless the reasons have been advanced by their authors for expressing them. I

regard monetary science as too far advanced to rest on mere empirical *dicta,* or the unsupported dogmas of any man.   Hence I have not felt called on to quote the *opinions* of numerous and often voluminous writers on the Bank Act.

10. I have conceded to Sir Robert Peel the credit of having, by the Bank Act of 1844, given to the country a greatly improved monetary system, in comparison with those which had existed from time immemorial.   His failure, looking from the stand-point taken by him, was clearly due to leaving it in the discretion of the directors to issue, and hold in the Banking Department, the whole of the so-called fiduciary notes, — those issued on securities, from which practice they have never once deviated to the present time, — always treating such notes as cash in the banking business.   I pointed out, in the chapters on the Bank of England, that the law left it optional with the directors to "diminish and increase" such securities, and, *pari passu* therewith, the cash in the Business Department.   The real evils, therefore, of the system, as carried out, are due either to the greed, or the ignorance and misconception of true principles, on the part of the directors.   I have shown what the effect will be if Lord Beaconsfield's government should carry out the intimation of the Chancellor of the Exchequer, to give immediate effect to the provisions of the law for merging the whole note issue of the kingdom into the Bank of England.   Unless the bank changes its policy, it will promptly issue the whole £30,800,000 of notes on securities, *purchased with the notes themselves ;* for it cannot be supposed that the proprietors will assess themselves about 160 per cent on their present shares, or by the issue of an adequate amount of new shares, to furnish capital wherewith to purchase the additional securities.

11. I have alluded to this point again, because I have nowhere seen it raised, nor have I anywhere seen its probable, I may say certain, effect on the policy of the bank in such a contingency as is alluded to, stated. The additional notes, issued on securities, or a portion of them, would no doubt go into the channels from which the country notes were taken. Now, a large proportion of these country and Scotch notes are for one pound ; and the bank only issues as low as five pounds. This would call for an enlarged supply of sovereigns ; and there would, hence, be severe periodic drains on the bank for metal : and the effect on the rate would be frightful. We should have a change every few days, to stop the demand for metal in the provinces ; and the whole trading community would be kept in a worse state of uncertainty, about the price of capital, than they have been for the last thirty years. "Go," said the Swedish chancellor to his son, "and see with how little wisdom the world is governed."

CHAPTER XX.

BANKING AND CURRENCY IN THE UNITED STATES. — EVILS OF A SYSTEM OF UNLIMITED ISSUE OF NOTES. — CENTENNIAL ADDRESS. — ONE HUNDRED YEARS OF BANKING IN THE UNITED STATES.

1. FREE trade in respect to the issue of paper money, and protection to domestic industry, — the one as fundamentally wrong as the other, — have very generally been characteristic of American legislation ; and the two evils still rival each other in the number and influence of their adherents. In these two important national considerations the United States stands to-day about where Great

Britain stood half a century or more ago. I am not writing history, however; and those who desire information on this assertion must look for it in the records of British and American commercial legislation. As the title of this work implies, its object is to state and elucidate principles, and apply them to existing institutions and practices, in respect to monetary science. I shall therefore proceed to describe in general terms the sort of monetary system that prevailed in the United States for over half a century prior to the outbreak of the great civil war in 1861.

2. Concurrently with the disasters inflicted on the British public, referred to in former chapters, by the unlimited issue of paper money and over-trading in the banking business, and prior to the Bank Act of 1844, almost exactly similar events were happening in the United States, in perhaps a more aggravated form, and with more calamitous effects on industry. These were brought about by the operation of similar causes, and were stimulated by the same class of motives, — the desire to make two or three dollars out of one. Every State in the Union had its own system of banking laws; and these enabled a small coterie of persons, very generally seeking to create salaried positions for themselves, to organize banks of issue, discount, and deposit. To start a bank, we will say with a capital of $50,000, which was a very usual amount outside of large cities, and in many cases only $25,000, very little actual cash capital was required beyond what was necessary to fit up an office and pay for engraving notes of the most improved and fancy styles of art. The subscribed capital was paid, in part or wholly, by the partners giving their notes, payable to and indorsed by each other, at the brand-new bank; and these were afterwards paid by the notes of the bank when they were got ready, or were renewed until the big

profits realized finally retired them. The organization of
a bank on this plan was often only the work of a few
days, which were necessary to send some hundreds or
thousands of miles to get the notes engraved and printed,
and to file the articles of association at the State capital.[1]

3. Up to the outbreak of the civil war, the right to
charter banks was universally claimed to be, as it still is
by a large class, a "State's right." Prior to this event,
the Constitution of the United States was held not to
confer the authorization on Congress to grant such charters, the Bank of the United States being the single
exception to the rule. The elasticity of this instrument
had never been tested, until then, by so strong a moral
force as the necessities of a great war, involving the existence of the nation. The sword had to settle the question ; and it did it effectually, as to how far State's rights
overlapped the boundaries of national powers and interests. The Gordian knot having been cut by the sword
of necessity, the present national bank system sprung
into existence, like Minerva from the head of Jupiter,
"full armed" and irresistible. But I am getting ahead
of my subject.

4. The new bank having been opened, and the talis-
manic word of "Bank" written in large letters over the
door, and a few hundred dollars in gold and silver being
secured, and not unfrequently exhibited in the window,
to add at least the appearance of solidity to the "institution," the public were invited to open deposit accounts,
and accept, and use as money, the new and crisp notes,
in exchange for labor and goods ; and, for want of any
thing better, the public very generally did accept them,
without questioning the ability of the bank to pay them.

---

[1] These facts are based on a statement made to the writer by the late United
States Senator, Hon. J. M. Howard of Michigan, and had reference to all the
Western States.

It was a common practice in various parts of the country for these mushroom banks at a distance from each
other to exchange notes, to prevent their being returned
too rapidly for payment; such reciprocating banks thus
giving each other moral standing. The facilities for
rapid travelling did not so generally prevail at the time
of which I am speaking as at present; and these banks
possessed wonderful facilities for getting large amounts
of their notes in circulation, and were not particularly
nice about having much specie on hand to meet them,
if some unforeseen event brought them home faster than
was agreeable. On the fundamental principle laid down
by Mr. J. B. McCulloch, that "the people must have a
circulating medium," or some kind of money, to transact
their business, and as the nation had made no adequate
provision for supplying such money, either metallic or
paper, they accepted the only tool that came to hand
that would serve the purpose of money.

5. That such a system should have prevailed for so
long a period, and over nearly all the inland States, may
seem to have been a reflection on the intelligence or
business capacity of the American people. But such a
charge would come with a bad grace from·Englishmen,
whose longer experience has failed, even yet, to master
the problem of issuing and properly regulating the supply
of paper money so as accurately to meet the demands
of industry. Another excuse may also be made for the
United States, in the matter of its paper-money system :
the Union, in many things relating to domestic administration, was scarcely better than "a rope of sand," until
the great civil war broke down some of the absurd theories about "State rights" which grew out of the right of
States to own and deal in human beings.

6. In 1842, when Charles Dickens was on his American travels, the currency troubles, which had culminated

in 1837 in the breaking of hundreds of these paper-money
factories, had left the Western and most of the Southern
States without even such indifferent tools of industry;
and no better substitutes had been provided by these
sticklers for State rights.   He observes in a letter to one
of his friends, that he had to carry about with him "an
uncomfortable," and certainly an inconvenient, amount
of gold, say £250, or $1,250.   But his real difficulty
consisted in the total absence of small change; there
being nothing of the kind in many localities, — especially
in Ohio, — but "shinplaster" notes, as they were called,
issued by local traders, as low in denominations as ten
cents.   He says, "Apropos to this golden store, consider
at your leisure the strange state of things in this country"
(he was then in Ohio).   "It has no money, really *no
money*.   The bank paper won't pass, the newspapers are
full of advertisements from tradesmen who sell by barter,
and American gold is not to be had or purchased."   He
says he bought sovereigns at first, but· subsequently was
unable to get these, and was compelled to buy French
gold and silver coin.   The least odious terms used to
characterize the paper circulation were "Shinplaster,"
"Wildcat," "Wolverine," and "Red-dog money."

7. Passing over the period of colonial existence, and
the issue of "Continental money," which is full of interest to the student of monetary science, and pregnant with
unheeded admonitions, we find that the issue of bank
notes in the United States, which stood in 1830 at $66,-
628,898, was increased by the year 1837 to $149,185,890,
or about 125 per cent in seven years.   Then came the
great commercial and financial crash, which led to the
stoppage of nearly every bank in the Union, 180 of
which became total wrecks, including the Bank of the
United States, which had advanced large sums, exceeding its paid-up capital, on State securities, a large pro-

portion of which were afterwards repudiated. The country was only just beginning to recover from these great
calamities, brought on by the excessive issues of bank-
paper currency, at the time Dickens was writing his
"American Notes." The losses from circulation alone,
during the five years from 1837 to 1842, were estimated
by statisticians at $100,000,000; and they fell most
heavily on the portions of the country and the people
least able to bear them. The losses to general industry
must have been three times the above sum, arising from
deposits, and the ruin brought on all traders by a complete suspension of business. Crops lay unmoved in the
granaries of the farmers, and consumers had to pay exorbi-
tant prices for the necessaries of life. President Jackson,
an obstinate, self-willed political partisan, with a large
following in Congress, had succeeded, during his eight
years' administration, in preventing the adoption of any
measure by the General Government to supply the people with an adequate metallic or paper circulation to
meet the demand for paper currency; and the whole
question was left in the hands of ignorant State politicians, and for a new crop of bank speculators to settle as
best they might. In New York, Massachusetts, and many
other States, banking laws were passed to authorize the
issue of notes on state and other securities, deposited in
the hands of an officer, known as State Comptroller, who
acted as trustee for such banks as might fail, and to
whom reports were required to be made. This plan
was a decided improvement on the systems that preceded it, especially in such States as had not repudiated
their obligations. It was copied from the practice of the
Bank of England, from its inception in 1694, and afterwards was transferred by Mr. Lincoln's government in
1864 to the national banks, substituting national for
State securities. Banks, however, organized on the State

plan, were required to redeem their notes in specie, and afforded, perhaps, more security to note-holders than the States could give.

8. There was this difference between the State-security banks and the national banks created by Mr. Lincoln's administration. The States did not guarantee the full face of the notes, as is the practice of the National Government in respect to the national bank notes. If a bank failed, the comptroller sold the securities; and, if they realized enough to pay all notes in full and expenses, they were fully paid: if there was a deficiency, then there was a *pro rata* dividend; and the notes were valued in the market accordingly. As I shall devote one or two chapters to considering the national banking system, I will only here remark on one peculiarity, which seems to have been devoid of any special object or good purpose. It is that which requires the one kind of national currency issued to banks to be convertible into the other kind made legal tender, and issued directly to the people. Both kinds rest on the same basis of security.

9. Mr. E. G. Spaulding, in an address delivered before the United States Bankers' Association at Philadelphia in 1876, remarks on this kind of redemption as follows: —

"There has been recently established a Bureau in the Treasury Department at Washington, for the purpose of assorting and enforcing redemption of national bank currency. This operation furnishes clean notes for those that are worn and defaced, but it is in no sense an efficient redemption." In another paragraph of the same address, he says, "This is practically no redemption at all. It is merely swapping one kind of paper currency for another of about the same value."

10. The only difference between the two kinds of notes consists in the requirement that the bank notes must be redeemed on demand in the national or greenback

notes. But *cui bono?* The national bank notes are practically made "legal tender for all taxes, and other debts to the Government, except principal and interest on the funded debt; the law also makes them receivable by each national bank for all ordinary debts due them " (see same address, p. 61).

11. Mr. Spaulding's Centennial Address gives a brief summary of the progress of banking in the United States for the first century of the country's history, and supplies a large amount of valuable information of interest, especially to those who do not care to wade through the numerous works containing more specific details. It would be quite impossible to enter into such historical considerations in a work devoted mainly to the elucidation of principles, and their explanation and application to monetary systems as they exist.

12. The claim put forward by Mr. Spaulding in this address, and in his valuable " Financial History of the War," that the national legal-tender notes ought to be redeemed, or bought back by the Government and cancelled, because he, in introducing the legal-tender bill into Congress, and others in advocating its passage, had declared it was to be only a temporary "war measure," is not good logic. No doubt Mr. Spaulding did not desire a national system of paper money to become permanent, as it was seen by him, as a shrewd banker, believing in banks of issue, and by the whole class of bankers, that it would diminish *pro rata* the bank circulation. None of these gentlemen then anticipated, what has since happened, that the people would give a preference to this new method of providing an indispensable tool, and that they might think that what was good in time of war might be good in times of peace.

13. Mr. Spaulding, in speaking of the greenback currency, at p. 57 of his address, remarks, "this currency

did not *grow out of industry and production*, and was not therefore a legitimate commercial currency." Now, I have laid down in the postulates (54 and 55) the self-evident propositions, that " paper money only represents and takes the place of metallic money," and that " both metallic and paper money represent value, and not goods, labor, or other things for which they exchange." It is simply absurd to claim that " money grows out of industry and production." It was invented to measure, and " handle " (so to speak) as a tool, labor, goods, lands, and other things, but more especially, perhaps, trading power. Mr. Spaulding has evidently fallen into the common error of confounding money with capital, or trading power, a preponderating part of which *does* " grow out of industry and production " (postulate 35). If this should meet his eye, I hope he will frankly agree with Professor Price in what he says in respect to this postulate. While bills of exchange, bills of lading, warehousemen's receipts, and other devices of bankers for the transference of debts and credits, do most clearly "grow out of industry and production," money as certainly does not. It simply represents value, and, by its scale of denominations, measures the value of other things. It is a common measure of values, as the yardstick is of lengths ; and these securities given for goods, by being expressed in such denominations, are turned into trading power by bankers. Bankers must learn to make these distinctions before they can write clearly and intelligibly on the principles of money.

14. It is this confounding of currency with banking that lies at the bottom of half the popular errors on the money question. Fortunately the public have come to the plain, practical, common-sense view of the purposes served by the greenback currency ; and they are not likely to give up this valuable creation of Mr. Spaulding and his politi-

cal co-laborers who invented it. But few people, outside the national banking influences, believe that a national bank note "grows out of industry and production" any more than a greenback; and, though both are guaranteed by the nation, the mass of people have a preference for the latter.

15. Again, the national bank note, as it now stands secured under the law, "grows out of" a long interest-bearing security on which it rests, instead of on metal, and is only "bogus" money after all.

16. I grant that the greenback has been badly used by its inventors, who now seek to cry it down as the "rag-baby." But the ill-usage has come from their hands. Its good qualities have been overslaughed by the inflation caused by an excessive issue of national bank currency. But for the over-issues of the latter, for which the National Government bid an enormous premium in the shape of national securities, which enables a corporation of bankers to own a fine investment, and to possess themselves of its value, very nearly, in money, the "rag-baby" would have been a full-grown giant long ago, and at par with gold. See next chapter about the origin of this *sobriquet* for the legal-tender notes. Mr. Spaulding puts *all* the blame on the over-issue of these favorite notes of the people, with how much justice or consistency will appear, when we take note of the fact, that the greenback currency antedates the bank currency by two years. This sort of disingenuousness may do for politicians, but it is inadmissible in economic science. *As a simple, undeniable matter of fact, the inflation of the paper money of the United States was chiefly due to the enlargement of the bank circulation from $150,000,000 in the loyal States, at the beginning of the war, to $300,000,000 under the national banking law* (in 1864), *which Mr. Spaulding so much extols.* The moment Mr. Spaulding and all good

reasoners come to perceive that banking has no connection whatever with the issue of paper money, the scales will fall from their eyes, and they will no longer "see men as trees walking." The Government gained nothing by compelling the banks to buy public securities, which it could not have gained better, and by an immense saving of interest-bearing debt, by issuing greenbacks instead of notes to loan to the banks at one per cent taxation. Had the national bank Act limited the issue of national currency to banks to $150,000,000, the amount of State banks' circulation at the time the Act was passed, the inflation and depreciation of notes would never have become so great an evil.

17. I am now, before parting with Mr. Spaulding's theories about money, compelled to take close and serious issue with his assertion that the true plan to have been pursued at the close of the war would have been to fund the whole $400,000,000 of greenbacks, and of course the fifty millions fractional currency, into a six-per-cent bond. He says, "If the right to fund the greenbacks into six-per-cent gold bonds had not been abrogated, no financier or practical business man, *whose opinion is worth quoting*, can doubt that we would have gone to specie payments within two or three years after the close of the war." His expressed reason for this opinion is, that the individual "indebtedness in the country was but small." Now, with all due respect to the excellence of Mr. Spaulding's historical writings, I have to say to him, and those who think as he does, that the possibility or impossibility of returning the currency to a specie basis, in one, two, or three years after the war, does not rest on *any man's opinion*. The first thing to be ascertained is, to what extent the inflated currency had inflated the value of labor, commodities, and real estate. Real estate was the last to feel the full force

of the stimulus (as it has been the last to feel the effect
of contraction), and probably did not reach its culminating point of value, as measured by legal-tender notes,
till 1867, when goods and labor had already begun slowly
to recede under the upward turn in the value of the
paper (then perceptible), partly from actual contraction
by Mr. Secretary McCulloch, and partly by the contraction of increased demand. But as good judges as
Mr. Spaulding have shown from actual statistics that all
values except real estate had doubled at the close of the
war. Take labor as the best gauge of value, and we find
it had risen from one dollar to two dollars per day on
the public works and railways. I am adding to this
chapter in April, 1878, when labor all over the country
has sunk back, under the slow contraction in the value
of the currency, to one dollar, and paper money to par
of gold. It is not a matter of *opinion* at all, but of
demonstrated fact, that, had this contraction taken place
in one, two, or three years after the war, it would have
broken every bank and trader in the United States, ending most likely in a great social revolution. This will
appear most self-evident when it is considered that all
traders, including banks, trade on margins of capital vary-
ing from the stock speculator's five or ten per cent to the
banker's twenty-five, thirty, or fifty per cent. Let Mr.
Spaulding take the deposits of his own bank, and ascertain whether he does not regard what Mr. Hankey sets
down as safe — say about one-third its liabilities — as a
good average margin to hold. He will therefore see, that
by reducing the value of all goods, and consequently of
all bills given for goods, from one hundred to fifty cents
in the dollar, in so short a period, would produce universal bankruptcy. The truth is, the entire trading community in America, with a very few exceptions, trade on
five, six, and up to ten per cent *only*, of actual cash or

immediately available capital. A man with $10,000 seeks to turn over $100,000 every year.

18. Inflation is like intoxication. Everybody fancies they are growing rich under its delusive and flattering inspiration. On the other hand, contraction acts like the effects of drink passing off, and delirium tremens setting in. "No man, whose opinion is worth having," can doubt the absolute truth of the facts I have stated. The country is just now finding its way out of the interminable vortex into which the mistaken policy of those who are responsible for inflation led it, during and just at the close of the war of the great Rebellion. The monster of mistakes rests on their shoulders, and not on those who opposed rapid and ruinous contraction. It is clear, that, had Mr. Spaulding's theory been carried out, it would have caused all but universal bankruptcy.

CHAPTER XXI.

THE NATIONAL BANKING SYSTEM OF THE UNITED STATES. — ITS ORIGIN. — GOOD AND BAD FEATURES, AND POSITION IN AMERICAN POLITICS.

1. THE monetary and financial systems of the United States occupy so large a space in the industries of the world that they require special notice in this work. I write this chapter on the eve of a great and exciting presidential election, in which the currency question forms a conspicuous element. On one side stand the combined forces of over two thousand national banks, which are nearly a unit in favor of absorbing the entire legal-tender note circulation; and on the other, a vast conglomeration of interests and theorists, from Governor Tilden, the Democratic nominee, who rides two hobbies

at the same time, — the national bank and greenbacks, —
and Governor Hendricks, the proposed Vice-President
on the same ticket, whose faith is in "Greenbacks made
equal to and convertible into gold," to the class who
propose to cut loose altogether from metal, and use
stamped pieces of paper for money, to be made convertible into other stamped pieces of the same material,
purporting to bear interest, and these again to be re-
convertible into the former kind, with interest added, —
the interconvertible system, in fact. But, in justice to
both parties, I ought to say, they are both more or less
tainted with these wild theories ; though both have a large
number of sound thinkers and solid business men, who
agree with Governor Hendricks, that a state issue of
notes, convertible into gold, is the safest, and, theoretically and practically, the best, paper currency for the
country. I ought to mention that a third candidate is
in the field, — the venerable Peter Cooper, who, like a
second Nestor, is wrestling for the greenback and interconvertible prize at the age of eighty-six. The result of
this memorable contest will be known before these pages
are sent to the press ; but the settlement of the money
question in the United States, as in Europe, will be deferred for many a presidential election yet to come.

2. I have pointed out, in former chapters, that the
legal-tender notes of the Government were, like the Revolutionary, or "Continental money," issued to supply resources to carry on the war. The law authorizing the
issue was passed by the largely preponderating Republican
party, under a pledge of the Government that the notes
would be retired and cancelled when peace was restored ;
but the Democrats in Congress to a man opposed its passage, on the alleged ground of unconstitutionality. I will
just observe, *en passant*, that the parties in question, as
parties, have changed positions on this question. At

least four-fifths of the Republican members in the present
Congress are crying down their own child, under the
sobriquet of "the rag-baby;" while about the same proportion of the Democratic members, now in the ascendency in one branch of the national Legislature, — the
House of Representatives, — as lustily cry out in favor of
the *infant.* So much for political party principle and
consistency in the United States; and so much for the
opinions and knowledge of monetary principles among
American statesmen.

3. But, to come to the question under consideration,
Mr. Lincoln's government needed means to raise, feed,
clothe, and put in the field half a million of men; and
Mr. E. G. Spaulding, aided by the Secretary of the Treasury, Mr. Chase, who was "cudgelling his brains" for ways
and means, secured the passage of the legal-tender Act,
referred to at the close of the last chapter, and subsequently, in 1863, the national-bank Act. The several
legal-tender Acts, passed in 1862, authorized the issue, in
all, of $400,000,000 of notes of one dollar and upwards,
and $50,000,000 of "fractional currency" below one dol-
lar; and the national-bank Act, which went into operation
in 1864, added $300,000,000 more notes, to be secured
to the Government by government bonds lodged in the
United States Treasury. When the legal-tender notes
began to be paid out in rapid issues, the banks were, as
might have been expected, compelled to suspend specie
payments. The bank circulation of the loyal States, at
the time of the passage of the legal-tender Act, was estimated by Mr. Chase to be about $150,000,000; and
these continued to circulate, under suspension, till the
beginning of 1864, when the larger part of the old banks
organized under the national law, in order to avail themselves of the opportunity of getting ninety per cent of their
investments in public securities in national currency money.

As the sole object of issuing the legal-tender or greenback notes was to create resources, in violation of the sound principle I have before laid down, that the first object should be to provide, under proper limitations, a more perfect and convenient tool of industry, that end would have been better reached by compounding with the banks for their circulation, and to have issued only greenbacks instead of " national currency " to banks.

4. Prior to this period, the experiences of the people, especially in most of the Southern and nearly all the Western States, had been, as I have shown in the last chapter, most unfortunate in respect to bank paper money; and when the greenbacks were found to answer all the purposes of money, and circulated everywhere in the country at a uniform price, they became exceedingly popular. Those issued to the banks, though legal tender for every thing except certain dues payable to Government, and being also convertible into legal tenders, or greenbacks, circulated on the same level of value. The only distinction in principle between the two kinds of paper money was, that the one was legal tender in payment of *all* debts and taxes, except customs dues, made payable in coin (which exception lowered their market value) ; and the other kind, the notes loaned to the banks, was legal tender only for certain things, including all other Government dues : and the Government itself acted as trustee for banks that failed. The effect of this was, that, after the whole $300,000,000 had been issued to the banks, the notes of failed banks were eagerly sought after, and were sold to new banks at a premium, at one time as high as ten per cent. There was also the distinction, that the "legal tenders " were issued directly to the public in payment of supplies, material of war, salaries, and the wages of all employees of the State ; while the bank notes were at first issued in the course of general business.

After they were in circulation, however, both kinds were paid out and received indiscriminately by the Government, the banks, and by the public, except in the one case of customs dues.

5. The great question before the American people now is, Shall the greenbacks be retired by the increase of the interest-bearing debt of some $350,000,000; or shall the national banks be compelled to surrender their circulation, which was raised a few years ago to $354,000,000, on the absurd pretext of "equalizing the currency"? as if a currency that circulates at the same level of value everywhere in the Union needed "equalizing." Those troubled with nice scruples about the fundamental law, argue that the measure authorizing the issue by the Government of legal-tender notes was only justified by the exigencies of the war. "It was a war measure;" and the very Secretary of the Treasury, Mr. Chase, who secured its passage, had decided, when made Chief Justice, against the majority of the court, that that which was barely legal in time of war was shockingly illegal in time of peace. But the greenbacks are still too popular to be thus annihilated in this way, or by act of Congress; and the prospects now are, that the contest will end in the separation of the greenback-men from both the old organizations, and that a new party will result: or that the Democrats will capture Republican greenbackers, and the Republicans will make reprisals on their opponents by capturing the Democratic bank-men; and thus the issue will be taken by the present organized parties.

6. It is a singular thing that no one has yet raised in the courts the constitutionality of the issue of notes to the national banks. The national organic law authorizes Congress "to coin money and regulate the value thereof," but is silent about the issue of paper money, further than to secure loans. No one, I believe, claims

that notes issued in payment of debts owed by the nation are illegal, provided they are not made "legal tender." But there is "a very solid distinction" between the issuing of notes (which serve the purposes of money) in payment of Government expenses, and lending such notes to the national banks to trade on for gain. If the Constitution does not expressly forbid this sort of dealing between the Government and the banks, the principle is certainly fundamentally wrong. It is so manifestly wrong for the Government to lend its notes to one class of traders, and refuse them to all other classes on equal security, that a high national court would be justified in declaring such relations to be void on grounds of public policy, irrespective of the silence of the organic law on the subject (*vide* extracts from speeches of Webster, Calhoun, *et al.*, in Appendix).

7. Leaving the legal question where it is, I will briefly point out wherein Mr. Lincoln's administration failed to meet the requirements of a very nearly perfect system of currency. When it was found that the state banks' circulation stood in the way of the legal-tenders, the right plan was to compound for it, and, if more paper money was really needed, to have filled the channels occupied by the old bank notes with additional greenbacks, as before stated. As a financial expedient, this plan, it is not to be doubted, would have saved to the nation about the entire $300,000,000 loaned to the banks on its own interest-bearing securities. To put the matter in plain English, Mr. Chase made the banks a present of $300,000,000, subject to an annual tax of one per cent, and raised the amount by the sale to the banks of $330,000,000 of six-per-cent bonds. But the most serious blunder committed by Congress was the authorizing the issue of so large an amount of irredeemable paper, which shortly reduced its market value at one time to forty-five per cent of the

face of the notes. Better far to have raised the ways and means by paying a higher rate of interest and to have held the value of the notes at par of gold by limitation of volume. The effect of the over-issue was presently felt, by a sudden rise, to double their former prices of all supplies for the army and navy and the wages of all the employees of the nation. The huge loans were thus squandered, and the permanent debt nearly doubled. The theory acted on was, that, in order to raise loans at all, it was necessary to diminish the trading power of the currency, which never ought to have been regarded in the light of ways and means, except incidentally, in supplying it for convenience of use and to meet an increase in demand. The absurd theory was acted on, that the rate of interest must not be made higher than six per cent, and that the loans must be sold at par ; and, in order to sell them at par, the market value of paper money had to be reduced to fifty cents on the dollar. All this has had the effect of building up the national banking system, and making it master of the Government and the country, instead of subservient to the nation. It is no wonder that the party, at one time all-powerful, which carried out such a policy, should now be tottering to its fall.

8. Here was the great opportunity, such as Sir Robert Peel regretted he did not possess, — "a new state of society," in which "a more perfect theoretical system of currency" might have been established ; and the Government then had a plenary power to execute its purposes. But one of the great obstacles to American Parliamentary Government is the want of leadership. It is a government of *juntas* or committees, without the necessary cohesion of leading and commanding statesmen holding seats in the Houses. Hence the possibilities of wise legislation seem to diminish in the inverse

ratio of the increase in wealth and population. Washington is a good field for the investigation of future chancellors' sons seeking to "see with how little wisdom the world is governed."

9. Having made these critical observations on the American system of paper money and banks, it is proper to point out some of their good points. If Mr. Chase's currency measures fell short of perfection, they were certainly a great improvement on those they superseded. They were born of necessity, "the mother of inventions;" and though the legal-tender notes were intended simply as a war expedient, to create resources, they served the purpose of enabling the Government to send nearly all the gold in the country, together with the current product of that metal, to foreign countries to purchase war-supplies. So good a purpose did the greenback currency serve, both by enabling the Government to use the gold it had driven out of circulation, for foreign purchases, made through traders, and in supplying the people with a better tool of industry than any they had ever had, the originators of it may be forgiven for its over-issue, which discredited it at home and abroad. Its popularity has not abated one iota in more than a dozen years, and its opponents are chiefly those interested in the national banks. The so-called "Act to provide for the Resumption of Specie Payments, and for a System of Free Banking," was passed with the view of doing for the national banks what Sir Robert Peel intended his Bank Act to do for the Bank of England; namely, to give to these banks the whole paper circulation of the country, on Government securities. The circumstance that the plan is predicated on the perpetuity of the public debt is an argument against its correctness. The temper of the American people, at least, is not in favor of a perpetual national debt; and

hence a banking system founded on such a debt rests on no durable basis. This national antipathy to a permanent public debt arises from the instinctive distaste for an aristocracy of wealth, or of any other kind, which they have come to connect with the public debts of Great Britain and European countries generally. I again also direct attention to the provision in this "free banking law" which permits the formation of national banks with no other limit than the whole national debt; and it is as certain as the earth revolves round its axis, that this practically unlimited issue of national banking currency will lead to new inflations whenever manias for bank speculations arise. The Act is a thorough stultification of its authors, and is most absurd in principle, and must prove most mischievous in practice. The Act itself can only be regarded, by those who carefully examine its principles, as a bonus offered by the Government of the United States to speculators in paper money founded on public securities, and a premium on inflation.

10. This latter view of the effect of the national banking system has not before been noticed by writers on the subject, and I invite special attention to it. It is a powerful incentive to capitalists owning United States bonds, or having uninvested capital, to organize banks of issue. Thus a tendency is engendered to divert capital from other industrial enterprises, and to maintain an unhealthy supply for banking purposes. Only men ignorant of economic science will claim that there cannot be too much loanable capital. What is so much clamored for, namely, "cheap capital," is very generally a great evil, and is indicative of bad times, cheap labor, and low profits. The one condition is the result of the other. Men who cannot see the force of this reasoning are incapable of comprehending the subject, and their clamor is utterly unworthy of attention. The plan of governments

paying bonuses to any branch of industry has the effect
of denuding other branches of a portion of the capital
that naturally belongs to them.   If it does not, why is
the bonus offered?   Now, the result of all such induce-
ments to invest in particular branches not only counteracts the natural distribution of capital and labor, but
in the long run injures the laborer.   Adam Smith has
pointed out the damaging effects on industry of government bonuses and monopolies with great force.

11. There is another striking feature in the national
banking system that has not been so conspicuously urged
by others as its character deserves.   It is what I have
several times referred to as the result of the Act for
the resumption of specie payments ; to wit, the provision
which does away with the limitation on the issue of
paper money.   Since 1844 there has been a complete
limitation set on the issue of paper money in Great
Britain uncovered by gold or silver.   There is not a
pound more than when the Act of that year was passed,
except what is so covered.

It may be questioned whether there exists any branch
of industry, or any pursuit, where the bounty principle is
so obnoxious as in the case of banks of issue.   It has
always happened, when panics have broken out, that the
causes are directly traceable to the overtrading in bank
capital.   These cyclones have ever been preceded by
low rates of interest and overtrading in discounts, and
are as invariably followed by severe contraction and high
rates for loans.   The last paragraph I have added, in
May, 1879 : and I may observe, that, though specie payments have been reached, the rate for loans in New York
ranges from two and a half to four per cent ; and the
prospect of a definite settlement of the currency question
in the United States is as much muddled and apparently
more uncertain as to the future, than ever.

CHAPTER XXII.

CURRENCY AND BANKING IN THE UNITED STATES MADE SUBSERVIENT TO PARTY ENDS AND INTERESTS.

1. NOTHING is more discouraging to those who seek to establish true scientific principles as the basis of currency, than the efforts of partisan politicians to make political capital out of that which should, above all other things, be made to yield to sound methods. I propose to point out in this chapter, written in the latter part of the summer of 1876, pending the canvass of the presidential election, how the currency question has been seized on by both parties to forward their purposes. I am compelled to point out how the President of the United States abandoned the principles he had for many years earnestly advocated, because he saw, or thought he saw, it would promote the success of his party. Being a soldier, he might have been excused for not knowing much about a question involving numerous difficult and complicated principles. But he had evidently studied it; and what he did, he did from purely partisan subserviency.

2. President Grant had lost no opportunity, from the time of his first message to Congress in 1869, till the spring of 1874, to magnify the excellence of the greenback currency. In each recurring message he made special allusion to it, telling Congress it was "the best currency the world has ever seen" (his own words), and urging the adoption of measures to raise its value to the standard of gold, and to provide for its convertibility on demand. Suddenly, however, during the latter year, he obtained new light, imparted to him, it was said in the newspapers, by Senator Jones from the great silver State

of Nevada, which resulted in his handing the senator
for publication a memorandum on the currency question,
in which he proposed to abolish the entire greenback
circulation, and fill the channels then occupied by it with
national bank notes and gold. His method of accomplishing that great feat was, to purchase $400,000,000
of gold in Europe by the sale of government securities.
The idea of waiting a few years for its production from
the mines of California and other gold-producing States,
was too slow for the President's impetuosity to get rid
of "the best currency" in the world. He never stopped
to consider what an Herculean task it would be to sell
so many bonds for nothing but gold, or what effect its
withdrawal in a short period of time from the European
bullion markets might have. But a part of the plan was
to pass laws that would "turn the balance of trade" more
strongly in favor of the United States. If these remarks
should ever meet the President's eye, I invite him to
read the chapters on bullion and the balance of trade
(Chaps. XI., XII.).

3. Nor did President Grant allude to the large addition that would be made by his proposal to the public-
interest debt, increasing the annual taxation say, of $15,-
000,000 a year. But such conversions are not unusual
among American statesmen, — especially on the currency
question. The future historian will perhaps find ample
causes for the readiness with which the President and
most of his party changed ground with their opponents
on the matter of retaining or abolishing the greenbacks.
As in England, "a cry" to go to the country with on
each recurring presidential election is necessary ; and each
party, in convention or through the party papers, gets
up one to order. The Republicans scented victory in
the present bitter contest, in an alliance with the " Money
Powers," — the national banks ; and their " cries " were,

"Hard Money," "Honest Money," and "Rag-Baby," with "Democratic Repudiation" thrown in as a make-weight. On the other hand, a large part of the Democratic party have all along formed a mine of political capital by an alliance with actual repudiators of public, if not private, obligations, — a class pretty numerous in all communities ; and the popularity of the word "Greenback" has come to be the enticing cry of this wing of that once more rising party. With them the term means, unlimited issue of irredeemable paper. Another Democratic "cry" is sympathy with what they call the "debtor classes," who, they allege, have been ground into powder between the upper and the nether millstones of the "moneyed" or "creditor classes." This exposition of the positions occupied by the two great political parties in the United States at this time, September, 1876, on the currency question, will hereafter be read by economists and other investigators with the feeling that inspired the Swedish chancellor, when he sent his son to see for himself "with how little wisdom the world is governed." The reader will probably see the propriety of my introducing this episode in American politics, in that it relates almost exclusively to the money question, and that the final settlement of that question is yet many years, if not generations, off, both in England and America.

4. It has been shown, that in the United States the one party appeals to the power of wealth, the other to that of the laboring millions, for sympathy and support. This is a dangerous issue to be made in such a country as the United States. It discards from consideration great fundamental principles which teach that capital and labor, wisely directed and left free from legislative restraints, will always harmonize and work together like twin sisters. In civilized and industrial communities the one

can no more exist without the other, than animal life can
be sustained without air, food, and water, and, in the
case of the human race, than they can do without clothing, houses, and all the other accompaniments of civilization.

5. Beside a mere record of facts, I have been led to
make these statements, which are historically and literally
true, not because American politicians are worse than the
average public men of England or other countries, who
are not over-scrupulous how they rise to power, but to
show how desirable it is to have the money question
definitively settled, and taken out of the whirlpool of
party politics and all interested business influences. This
most desirable object can only be attained by a general
agreement among the educated and thinking men of all
parties, and combining on a correct theory as to the real
offices of money, metallic and paper, and adopting some
method that shall leave the natural laws to indicate and
accurately serve out an adequate supply of both kinds to
meet the actual demands of industry.

6. In Great Britain the omnipotence of Parliament
alters and changes the unwritten constitution ; and an Act
of Parliament, passed and acquiesced in by the people,
settles such questions as the issue of currency, and almost
every thing else, as far as any human concerns can be
definitely settled. In the United States little if any thing
short of an amendment of the Constitution, which though
a solemn is a tedious proceeding, affords any assurance
that what is done one year will not be undone the next
year. This is a very difficult process with nearly equally
divided parties. Party interests, in the United States, very
generally overtop national interests or considerations of
patriotism. But possibly this currency question may yet
find its solution, and more definite if not permanent settlement, by an amendment of the organic law of the

nation. Congress at this time having one party in the ascendency in one House, and the other party in the other, seems powerless to effect any settlement whatever. Both candidates for the Presidency are, by antecedent associations and utterances, in favor of surrendering at discretion to the national bank influences, and to give the whole paper currency to those banks; but a powerful counteracting influence is at work against this policy in the popular branch. I have before, through influential journals in the United States, suggested to the people the desirability of agitating the question of an amendment to the Constitution, to authorize and make it obligatory on Congress to create by law a National Issue Department, clothed with discretionary power, within prescribed limits, to have charge of the coinage of metallic money and the issue of paper money, in manner suggested in the chapter on a State Issue Department.

7. The plan of lending notes, at one per cent tax on the circulation, is so evidently unconstitutional, and contrary to public policy, that it must sooner or later come to an end by continued agitation of the question among the masses of the people. Moderate men, of all shades of politics, would do well to sustain a plan for a change in the fundamental law of the nation. Questions of this kind become dangerous elements in governments when left alone too long. Just now the entire influential press of New York, of both sides of politics, have closed their columns against those who favor a continuance of a national paper currency, though issued on a gold basis by and for the nation. These journals, one and all, do nothing but cry out, "rag-baby," "rag-baby." In the West, nearly all the press is in favor of the "rag-baby," and opposed to the bank theory of currency; and the question seems to be taking sectional ground. I have already pointed out the dangerous theories that have

taken deep root in the West and South, where I have had many personal opportunities to learn the state of public opinion. The desire to have a new era of inflated values, by an excessive issue of inconvertible paper money, seems to be at the bottom of the agitation in all parts of the South and West that I have lately visited. It is not difficult to foresee, that the bigotry of journalism referred to tends to foment a much-dreaded evil in the American body politic, — another sectional schism.

8. One of the phases of the money question, which has its serious as well as ludicrous sides, is the tendency that its incessant discussion by mere charlatan writers and speakers is the one already alluded to as fostering communism. There are numerous cheap weekly journals, extensively sold and read throughout the whole country, whose sole object is to foment the (so called) conflict between capital and labor. The one idea put forward, is to influence the election of members to the various legislatures and the national Congress favorable to the passage of laws aimed directly at the rights of property. These philosophers, not content to leave the natural laws to regulate the price of labor and commodities, aim at imposing restrictions of all kinds on all industries not in sympathy with the particular class to which they belong. I hope and believe that the body politic in the United States possesses sufficient cohesion, and that there is enough wisdom and moderation left in it, to settle these questions on some satisfactory basis. The costly lessons of one great civil war should be sufficient, at least for a century, to admonish public men of all parties not to press for extreme measures calculated to keep up sectional jealousies and hatreds of any kind.

9. The issue of paper money is still regarded by nearly all public and business men in the United States, as it was in Great Britain till the passage of the Bank Act of

1844, from the one stand-point of creating trading capital.
The idea of producing a better and more convenient tool
of industry than metallic money hardly ever enters into
the discussion of monetary topics. The cry is for " more
money," when there is too much paper money already,
and what is needed in reality is more capital. The circumstance that modern banking has turned into available trading capital goods in course of production and
transit to consumers is overlooked, just as is the great
fundamental truth that only a limited amount of *actual
money* is needed for industrial purposes. As a proof of
this *proposition*, — self-evident to good logicians, — I desire to point out the fact, that, during the universal cry
for " more money" raised by a large class all over the
country in the years 1875 and 1876, there has been a
voluntary surrender, by national banks reducing their
circulation and getting back and selling their securities,
of over forty million dollars ; thus showing conclusively
that there was *too much money*, — more than the people
needed or would buy, and more than was profitable to
the banks of issue. During periods of industrial stagna-
tion, resulting from preceding periods of inflation in
business and over-production, people always complain
of " hard times," of " scarcity of money," and so on.
The Government is very generally then held, somehow
or other, to be responsible for the cause of these great
public evils. I am free to admit that unsound legislation
has much to do with the causes of periodic crises in the
industrial world. Laws that interfere with the free action
of the natural laws no doubt produce spasms in the industries of the people which never would be perceptible
but for these artificial restraints set on industry.

10. It will have been seen, by those who have followed my course of reasoning on this subject, that I
propose to have perfect free trade in money as well as

in all industries, as far as is practicable, with a due regard to the levying of taxes to support the Government
and other local administrations.   In respect to money,
the only tax on it admissible, in a true theory, is the cost
of production and management.   When more metallic
money is needed, it will be indicated by a rise in the
exchange value of money, — that is, the price of metallic
money will rise sufficiently above the market value of
bullion to cause the owners of bullion to take that article
to the mint, or the money department, and sell it for
money.   On the other hand, if the price of money falls
below the market price of bullion, the occurrence will
immediately make itself known by the fall in the exchange value of metallic money.   The latter will soon
begin to be sent abroad, or be put into the melting-pot.

11. I have before stated these phenomena in the phi-
losophy of metallic money more than once, and again
revert to the subject as one that American public men
have not generally considered.   It lies at the very threshold of any sound system, and therefore will bear repetition.   Then, as to paper money, let the state — by
which I mean the nation — supply *all that the people*
(through bankers, brokers, and traders, or otherwise) *require*, and are willing to pay for at the full metallic value,
and no more.   This is free trade in money.

12. I have perhaps already said enough about the incidental use of a part of the metallic money that may be
paid to or be coined by the money office.   Only ample
experience (such as the Bank of France alone, of all the
issue offices of the world) can determine how much of
the accumulation of metallic money may be used and
sold as capital, without disturbing the equilibrium of
values.   This well-managed issuing bank, it is thought
by many, holds quite an unnecessary amount of metal on
hand ; and if it held only coined money, instead of a

large supply of the raw materials, half of the seventy or
eighty millions sterling held by it would serve every purpose of the convertibility of its notes. But, as I have
before said, this may be a violation of natural principles,
which I am always ready to respect.

CHAPTER XXIII.

CURRENCY AND BANKING IN FRANCE. — THE BANK OF FRANCE.

1. In no country, perhaps, in the world have the delusions respecting the availability of paper money for creating wealth taken deeper hold of the public mind than
in France, at various periods and in many forms. The
epochs of these delusions, however, were not so numerous as in Great Britain and the United States ; but they
present the subject in its most serious as well as most
ludicrous aspects. The state of public feeling, and the
madness of all classes, when the eminent Scotch financier, John Law, was at the height of his glory in Paris,
rivalling the king himself in the magnificence of his re-
ceptions, has never been reached in any other country,
or during any other popular mania in France. I assume
that the reader has made himself familiar with that marvellous mania in French society, when the highest members of the most ancient and proud nobility of Europe,
of both sexes, patiently awaited the arrival of the great
man at his grand reception hall, to beg for shares in his
vast paper scheme known in after-times as the "South
Sea Bubble." Mr. Charles Mackay has given quite a
melodramatic turn to Law's remarkable success in stir-
ring up the lowest depths of avaricious greed, and his
account of the matter, in that very readable and instructive work, "Popular Delusions." But when the bubble

burst, and brought ruin on all concerned, " none was found so poor to do him reverence ; " and it required the whole power of the king, who had, as he thought, improved on Law's theories of finance, to protect him from mob violence.

2. Though the ruin in which Law's paper-money scheme involved immense numbers of the wealthy *bourgeois* and of the ancient nobility, left a deep and lasting impression on the public mind, the idea that a man or a nation may possess valuable property, and at the same time utilize its market value by means of paper money representing it, just as the Bank of England and the United States national banks seek to do with respect to government securities, continued to have its zealous believers. Hence, when the French Revolution was in progress in 1792 and 1793, the assignats, which were notes secured on lands and real property confiscated from the nobles and the Church and owned by the State, were proclaimed to be the real solution of the money question of the day. But the history of this paper bubble, and that of the commandâts which followed, and took the place of the assignats, are too well known to need further allusion. They simply proved the fundamental error of investing your capital in things having market value, and possessing yourself of that value in money. These French monetary experiences, however, must have produced a more profound and lasting impression on the minds of French statesmen than on those of most other countries ; for France has not since been a good field for speculations in banks of issue, and has long tolerated only one such, — the Bank of France. Thus she has been exempt during the whole of the present century from those numerous over-issues of paper money which so frequently culminated in national disaster, through unlimited competition among hundreds and thousands of issuers in Great Britain and America during the same period.

3. After the assignats and commandâts, came hard money, supplemented by occasional issues of what may be termed treasury notes for temporary expedients, until the Bank of France came into existence in 1800, under a charter authorizing a capital of 45,000,000 francs, say £1,800,000, which was soon subscribed and fully paid. In 1806 the bank received a new charter, and underwent a more complete organization, and its capital was increased to 90,000,000 francs; but this was subsequently reduced to 67,000,000 by the bank's own act in buying in and cancelling the excess of shares beyond this sum. It stood at this until the year 1857, when the amount of its capital was again raised to the sum of 182,000,000 francs, or say £7,300,000, at which it now stands.

4. Like the Bank of England, the French National Bank has passed through many severe trials, but has very generally been prudently and ably managed, and has yielded much larger profits to its proprietors than the Bank of England. Its success in this respect may, to some extent, be due to its having always possessed a monopoly in the supply of paper money; and its dividends have not unfrequently been at the yearly rate of from 150 to 250 francs on the 1,000 franc share, or from 15 to 25 per cent.

5. I have alluded in a former chapter to the marvellous manner in which the French Government, through the intervention of this powerful and generally well-managed institution, paid off the German indemnity, and showed that very little actual money or bullion was used to pay it. It may here be remarked that about nine-tenths of the 5,000,000,000 francs (£200,000,000) were paid by the transferrence of "purchasing power" raised on the national credit. The Germans, being possessed of this power, could use it to buy gold, or any thing else they

needed; and as gold is only useful for what it will exchange for or buy, but little of the sum total, probably, was ever invested in that commodity. Now, what the Bank of France did to aid in this prodigious financial operation, was to lend the Government out of its own trading resources in 1870, 1,363.000,000 francs, nearly £54,000,000 sterling. To do this, it was authorized to suspend specie payments, though I very much doubt whether it was, in point of fact, necessary; still, as a prudential measure, it was perhaps the best thing to do. It is sufficient to know that the result was, the successful raising, through great loan agencies all over Europe, of the entire loan of £200,000,000, and the repayment, within five years, of the whole sum advanced towards it by the Bank of France.

6. As an aid to these great financial operations, the National Assembly in 1872 passed "a stay law," which enabled acceptors of bills held by the bank to suspend payment for a year; and it has been stated authoritatively, that this measure was most salutary in its effects, and that scarcely any loss was sustained by the bank in consequence. The same thing was done in several of the Southern States at the close of the American war. If the British Government finds it wise, for the sake of securing a "breathing-time" for the Bank of England, to suspend the Bank Act in periods of crises, may it not be wise to extend the suspension to all traders for one or two months, till the fury of the financial cyclone has had time to subside? "What's sauce for the goose is sauce for the gander."

7. I have directed attention to the issue and management by the Bank of France of paper money as being more theoretically and practically perfect than that of the Bank of England, or any other issuer of such money. The obvious reason for this nearer approach towards a perfect system seems to be, that the bank does not issue

notes on public securities, and always keeps on hand an adequate supply of cash money to meet all its obligations. It does not treat its own notes as good reserve, and discounts commercial paper freely; whilst the Bank of England deals much more largely in long securities, liable to material fluctuations in market value in times of great depression or unsound speculation and general inflation of values, and overtrading and "production."

8. But, after all, much of the success of the French Bank is unquestionably due to the circumstance that it has a monopoly of the issue of paper money, and is free from the effects of sharp competition, which exists whenever there are a large number of licensed issuers in a country, whose chief aim is to make a profit out of the business. Hence, for these and other reasons of a prudential nature, the Bank of France affords the best example, on a large scale, of a sound and scientifically conducted system of paper money on record, unless it be that of the State Issue Department for India, which is a pure and simple issuer of convertible paper money.

9. In making these comparisons, I ought not to omit the Treasury Issue Department at Washington. Under the able and honest administration of Gen. F. E. Spinner, a very perfect routine business became early established; and no possible fault can be found with the business machinery for issuing and renewing notes. The fault is in the inception of the plan of issuing demand-notes not redeemable in coin, and in over-supply, in total disregard or ignorance of the fundamental principles of money or currency. No national issue department can be safe in the United States, that does not provide effectually against the temptation of a finance minister to use the issue for *financial* instead of for purely *monetary ends;* and it *must* be kept out of party politics as effectually as the national banks of France and England. In the

United States, the party machinery seems to have become
a part of the State itself. Party organizations are permanent fixtures on the body politic ; and the dominant party
is always unscrupulous as to what it lays its hands on to
maintain itself in power, and is not over nice about the
provisions of the Constitution when a crisis in its affairs
arises. Hence greater safeguards are there needed than
in most other countries.

10. At this time, in France, the only really important
question seems to be, whether the body of shareholders
composing the Bank of France shall have the profits of
the issue, or the nation. If the capital or the circulation
of the bank were taxed in some ratio correspondent with
the profits derived from the note issue, perhaps a change
in favor of the State might not be expedient. The principle of " farming out " the issue of paper money to private
parties is not sound, and, unless very good reasons can be
shown for it, ought not to exist. The most eminent of
French economists, M. M. Chevalier, is a stanch advocate in favor of a State issue, or of selling the notes for
their full market value (*vide* his letter in Appendix).
His views and arguments have been frequently set forth
in the columns of the leading journal of Paris, the " Journal des Débats ; " and he claims, as I do, that the State
can no more properly delegate its prerogative to bodies
of incorporated capitalists to issue paper money, than it
can the right to coin metallic money, or to regulate the
weights and measures of the nation.

11. There is one defect in the currency issue of France,
that I cannot pass by without notice. It is the want of
notes of lower denominations than one hundred francs.
There should be issued all the twenty and forty or fifty
franc notes the public may be willing to buy. It is especially inconvenient, in travelling in France and in other
continental countries, to be compelled to carry sums of

metallic money, and especially silver change.   In a pretty
extended tour I made, some years ago, through France,
Belgium, Germany, Switzerland, and the Austrian Tyrol,
I found the Bank of France note as good as gold, but
often experienced difficulty, especially in "posting," to
get a hundred franc note changed.   If the world comes
to regard paper money in the light of a more convenient tool of industry than metallic money, the prejudice against smaller denominations will yield to practical
utility and the wants of the people, and lead to the issue
of notes to represent the gold coin commonly used in all
countries, and an immense saving of capital now invested
in such coin.

CHAPTER XXIV.

HOW THE VOLUME OF CURRENCY AND OTHER THINGS AFFECT
THE MARKET OR EXCHANGE VALUE OF COMMODITIES. —
PRESENT INFLATED CONDITION OF THE CURRENCY AND
BANK DISCOUNTS IN THE UNITED STATES (MARCH, 1879),
AND WHAT IT PORTENDS. — NICHOLAS BIDDLE ON CUR-
RENCY.

1. THIS subject has been treated generally in Chaps.
IV. and V. ; but, in consequence of the attempt recently
made by some American economists in the "New York
Commercial Bulletin," a journal circulating in mercantile
circles, to controvert the doctrine that the prices of articles are influenced by the volume of currency, I propose
a further examination of the subject.   If the doctrine
attempted to be set up by these writers is correct, then
postulates 3 and 4 are incorrect, and not self-evident
propositions, as I affirm them to be.   No. 3 says, "Money
is a commodity, and has a market value independent of

the material of which it is made ; and, like such material, its market value is governed by its volume, or supply and demand." No. 4 : "The value of money or any other commodity is in the inverse ratio of its volume." These propositions embrace most important fundamental principles, underlying the whole edifice of economic science. Hence I propose to leave no grounds for denying their correctness.

2. In respect to currency, the postulates simply mean, that when currency, usually composed of coin and paper money, is increased in amount, its trading power, or exchange value, is correspondingly diminished in the same manner as that of other commodities ; on the other hand, if the volume be diminished, its trading or exchange value will be increased, *pari passu*, with such diminution or contraction. It is not denied that this law is absolute and fundamental as to other leading commodities, such, for instance, as iron, corn, wheat, cotton, and indeed the whole category. But currency, after all, is the most conspicuous example, because with it we measure and differentiate the value of all other things dealt in, in the markets. But the theorists I am referring to contend that currency is an exception to the rule, and that there is never too much or too little of it. But that assumption is not to the point. The question of " too much or too little " has no bearing on the proposition itself.

3. The theory is simply founded on a misconception of the services rendered by currency, and in opposition to an equally glaring fallacy that the market value of any given commodity is determined without reference to other factors in the great sum of human industries. In treating this question, I am considering currency in the light of coined money, and paper convertible into coin at the option of the holder. Such currency, I have shown, is very often inflated where the limit of the issue

is allowed to run far beyond the amount of metal kept
as reserve for its conversion ; but it is, nevertheless, less
liable to affect other values, as measured by itself, than
inconvertible paper.   In other words, its effects are not
so immediately visible as those of the latter.   Hence
some have concluded, without reasoning, that the volume of metallic and convertible paper together does not
influence values at all.   The question to determine is,
whether the prices of goods have risen, or the price of
currency has fallen, — for it is a question of relative
values, — when the one falls, the other appears to have
risen.

4. The question is complicated by other circumstances
and things.   It would be erroneous to affirm, that, if the
volume of currency were doubled in a short time, the
market value of goods, as measured by it, would in like
manner be doubled, for the simple reason that currency
is but one, and by no means the largest one, in the great
volume of things which act on and affect market values.
In postulates 35 and 36 I very clearly presented the elements which enter into this question in modern industrial communities, and really determine the relations of
value among the whole category of commodities.   In 35
I showed, that, by the agency of banks of discount, the
market value of goods in course of production and distribution was turned into trading power without the aid
of currency, and constituted the larger proportion of the
loans discounted to traders, manufacturers, and speculators.   In postulate 36 I stated what composed the
balance of such loans, including money, or currency.
Now, currency only forms about five per cent of the
gross amount of trading power in a commercial country
like the United States ; and *it is in its capacity or office
of trading power that it plays its part in the general
category of things which stand for capital.*   But, though

metallic money is one of the smallest factors in the sum, it is the most important, because of its greater stability under the operations of supply and demand. Currency may be likened, in this respect, to " a little leaven which leaveneth the whole lump." When its stimulating effect is set in motion by unusual issues of bank or government notes, without regard to the quantity of metallic money behind them, it suddenly causes a rise in the market value of other and grosser things, as the leaven causes the mass of dough to rise.

5. The question as to whether gold has risen or goods have fallen, or *vice versa*, is one of easy solution. If there occurs a period when there is a general rise along the whole line of leading commodities, — such, for instance, as cotton, corn, wheat, iron, etc., — it is evidence that trading power, including currency, is abundant and cheap. When one, or two, or three articles have risen, and the general category of goods remains unchanged, it is a sign that trading power, or capital, maintains its equilibrium, or that supply and demand balance each other, and the change in the exceptional articles will be found to be due to other causes, such as over or short production of the particular ones.

6. When it is seen that metallic money alone is not chargeable with fluctuations in the market value of commodities, but forms only a small part of the things responsible for them, it will also be seen how important it is to hold our currency as close as possible to one of pure metal, using paper as a substitute for it, for convenience. Metallic money never fluctuates violently or suddenly, and, unlike inconvertible paper, and discounts and rediscounts of goods, or goods discounted several times over through resales, does not tend to inflation and overtrading and production. Many good reasoners have indulged and speculated much on the effect on market

values produced by the great discoveries of the precious
metals in the United States and Australia during the last
thirty years, and founded thereon predictions of a large
increase in such values in respect to labor and the entire
category of the products of labor. These predictions
have not come to pass, because, contemporaneously with
the increased production of these metals, a still greater
increase has taken place in the production and consumption of nearly every thing else. This latter result
has been brought about by the important improvements
and facilities in communication, and the distribution of
commodities of the most bulky descriptions, and cheaper
and more improved methods of production and manufacture. Consumption has likewise kept pace with production, in consequence of the general expansion and
distribution of wealth.

7. A due regard to these considerations leads irresistibly to the logical conclusion that the ratio of values
between the precious metals and of the general category
of commodities has been wonderfully maintained. Silver
has fallen most, owing to very large amounts being suddenly precipitated on the markets of the world by the
Germans, who have wisely adopted the sound policy of
not forcing on the people a currency so clumsy, and so
liable to sharp fluctuations. During the thirty years in
question, the product and stock of gold and silver have
been doubled : but the other productions of labor have
been trebled by railway and steamship transit, and improved methods of production and manufacture ; and with
these *the ability to consume has fully kept pace.* Thus
the equation between supply and demand has been, as
already observed, wonderfully maintained.

8. It would appear from these considerations, that, but
for the contemporaneous increase in the production of
gold and silver during the last thirty years, their market

value, or trading power, must have considerably increased. But had their quantity remained stationary, being only five per cent of the capital used in conducting the industries of the world, including the paper money used with the coin, the market value of other things would not have fallen in the same ratio as that in the respective things we are comparing. The perturbations in the market value of labor and commodities, produced by the action of supply and demand, are, therefore, brought to a scientific or logical solution. It is the essence of absurdity to claim that labor, or any article dealt in, in the markets, is exempt from this universal law. Bullion, the raw material, and money, the manufactured article, are alike subject to it; and the plan I have reasoned out, and shall more fully state in the next two or three chapters, of maintaining a close approximate value between bullion and coin, is the only true, scientific, and practical method in existence, or which can be devised for the supply of currency. I make this broad claim, because science is inexorable in its requirements. It has not two ways for reaching the same result. All deviations from its teachings are violations of natural laws, and all legislation to override its precepts is erroneous and mischievous.

9. I have, in many places, endeavored to disabuse the minds of thinking men of the habit of treating money and capital as synonymous. I wish now to inculcate the equally important truth, that fully three-fourths of the capital used in conducting the industries of the chief commercial and manufacturing countries consist of the market value of goods in course of production and distribution. This capital is made available by banks of discount and deposit, by means of bills representing goods, and checks used for transferrence. This easy process of turning goods, before they are ready for market or have reached consumers, into capital, tends mightily to stimu-

late production, and, to the same extent, to increase the general volume of trading power ; and, unless consumption keeps pace with production, the increased quantity of goods tends directly to diminish market values, including that of labor. If it is the general volume of capital, acting on labor and goods, that influences their market values, it follows, as a logical sequence, that any extraordinary addition (by production) in one or two articles, — such, for instance, as gold and silver, — only tends to increase that volume in the same ratio that these articles bear to the whole. The same rule applies to other productions, such as cotton, corn, wheat, or iron. In this respect the most perishable articles having market value add just as much to trading power as the " everlasting metals " of M. Cemuschi. These principles will serve to illustrate the perpetual changes that are taking place in the market values of commodities.

10. I will now further consider the part played by paper money not fully covered by coin. It has already been demonstrably shown, that mere convertibility of paper for " occasional calls " in " flush times " is no guaranty against over-issues of such money by banks and governments. The security given by banks against loss by the abuse of the privilege does not prevent the recurrence of periodical break-downs, and long derangements to the industries. At this time (March, 1879) gold and silver coin in the United States are at par with each other, and with paper money. The coin amounts to about $350,000,000, in the hands of the Government, the banks, and the people. Some estimate the total higher, but I prefer to take the lowest figures set. The entire paper is in excess of $660,000,000 ; and all must be treated as in actual circulation for financial purposes. To reach a clear estimate of the forces that act on the industries of the country, we must get at and add to these figures the dis-

counts of banks. On Oct. 1, 1878, the national banks
had under discount $830,000,000 of bills. We have no
means of knowing accurately the amount of discounts of
state and savings banks and private bankers, and must,
therefore, make the best estimate in our power. For
this purpose, we will take the deposits of the national
banks at the above date. These were in round numbers,
$665,000,000, showing the discounts to have been about
twenty-five per cent more than the deposits. The total
deposits of state, private, and savings banks, having capital, and discounting more or less commercial paper, were
$1,242,000,000. To be safe, we will assume that the dis-
counts of these banks and bankers amounted to only
twenty per cent above their deposits. It would then appear, if there has been no change since last October, that
there are in operation the following forces acting on the
industries of the United States : —

1. Gold and silver coin	$350,000,000
2. Government notes issued to the public,	347,000,000
3. National currency loaned to banks .	323,000,000
4. National banks' discounts . . .	830,000,000
5. Discounts of other banks, say . .	1,450,000,000
	$3,300,000,000

Three thousand three hundred millions of dollars, —
about threefold the amount of similar forces in operation
in 1860, or twenty years ago. There are, besides, deposits of $800,000,000 in savings banks having no capi-
tal, but which discount more or less commercial paper
on the sly with public or state securities as collateral.
The figures representing deposits and discounts are taken
from the valuable and carefully compiled report of Comptroller Knox for 1878.

11. When it is considered that the circulation and
deposits alone of the national banks, amounting to
$1,150,000,000, are immediate liabilities against $150,-

000,000 of cash assets, the remaining assets being bills
under discount and government securities, it will be seen
on what a magazine of combustible material our industries are founded.   Private bankers and state and savings
banks, though they issue no paper currency, are in no
better position.   People are everywhere contemplating
with satisfaction the commencement of a new era of
prosperity.   The wages of labor are beginning to stiffen
up. "Tramps" are growing fewer in number. The prices
of most domestic articles are increasing.   Goods are in
demand, and bills in a year or two will greatly multiply ;
and banks, to use the phrase of an English economist,
will "discount mightily."   As trading capital is thus increased and cheapened, goods and labor will rise *pari
passu* therewith. New national banks will be started,
and old ones will increase their circulation.   Gold and
silver are added at the rate of $150,000,000 a year.
Foreign trade is largely in favor of this country.   Every
thing portends an early and rapid expansion and inflation
of business and over-production, and the approach of
"the fool's paradise."   The country will soon be in the
position of the rich man in the Bible, whose barns and
garners were well filled ; but there was the law of nature,
which, like a spectre, said, "Thou fool," etc.

12. There is nothing to compare, in importance, to
which the national Legislature of the United States can
turn its attention, with that of establishing a sound system of currency ; and, to be sound, it must be wholly
detached from government and banking finance. My
last postulate is fundamental, and a great truth.

"There is a most obvious distinction between currency and finance : the one is a tool of industry, and
the other a method of conducting the business operations of nations, states, corporations, and individuals."
Hence I have drawn the logical corollary that paper

money should never be permitted to be issued for the
creation of resources, or for financial purposes, but only
to take the place, because of its convenience in handling and circulating, of metallic money. *It must be confined to serving as a substitute for the money by which
all civilized nations estimate and differentiate the value
of labor and all its products, and all things having market value. If this can be done, we shall strip industrial
crises of nearly all their power to injure the great mass
of the industrial part of society.* The evils of these periodical cyclones will be confined chiefly to those speculative, ever greedy members of the community who have
been most instrumental in raising the whirlwind. The
tools of the workmen will remain as sound and bright,
and as efficient, as ever. The mixing up, in thought by
many eminent economists, and in practice by those who
follow the bad·teaching of great men, of the two things,
currency and finance, is at the bottom of the evils in
question. The issue of paper money is not banking, and
hence banks ought not to issue it. *But it is banking
for the Government to issue "national currency" and
lend it to the banks* at one per cent tax on circulation,
and hence should not be continued. The Government
might with equal propriety enter into any other financial
or business undertaking with private parties.

13. The late Nicholas Biddle, president of the old
United States Bank, which was a partnership concern
between the Government and a body of private capitalists, said many things so pertinent to the points I am
illustrating, that I cannot forbear to quote some of them.
In a circular which he issued to the shareholders of that
institution, in May, 1829, he used the following striking
language : "Banks are often managed by sanguine persons, anxious only to increase the profits without much
personal interest or pecuniary responsibility in the admin-

istration.   The constant tendency of bankers is to lend too much, and put too many notes in circulation.   Now, the addition of many notes, even while they are as good as gold, by being exchangeable for coin, may be injurious, because the increase of the mixed mass of money generally causes a rise in the price of all commodities." Mr. Biddle's remedy for such evils, when they have become dangerous to the stability of the banks, is equally striking, and is demonstrative of the folly of allowing banks to issue paper currency at all, no matter how much security is given to guard against loss on circulation.   It is against the principle as well as the practice of the thing that I am arguing ; and security may mitigate, but cannot guard against, the evil effects.   Such evils, and the banker's remedy, are, it will be seen by Mr. Biddle's prescription, at the very bottom of the causes which lead to industrial crises.   "When the banks of a country," says this astute and able banker, "perceive such a demand for coin for exportation as diminishes their stock on hand, they should stop the exportation ; . . . by issuing no new notes, and declining to renew the notes of your debtors, you compel them to return to you the bank notes you have lent them, or their equivalents. This makes the bank notes scarce, — this makes them more valuable, — the debtor, in his anxiety to get notes, being willing to sell his goods at a sacrifice : this brings down the prices of goods, and makes every thing cheaper," and, I will add, brings on the panic and crisis which were before impending.   And such is still, and ever will be, the remedy for the evils brought on society by banks of issue and discount ; and this is the pernicious system which a part of the press of this country labors incessantly to perpetuate.   A writer of an able article on the subject of currency, which appeared some time since in one of these journals in this city, to whom I am indebted for Mr. Biddle's views, very well observes, "They first inflate the currency by increasing its volume, in order to increase their own profits; and then contract it again, to prevent their own bankruptcy, without the slightest regard for the rights or interests of the community. Notwithstanding these confessed evils resulting from banks of issue, the journal in question and its allies persist in advocating the continuance of the causes of our greatest industrial evil, when a most favorable opportunity presents itself to get rid of them by abolishing the power of banks to emit paper money altogether. The Constitution of the United States makes no provision, express or implied, for issuing and loaning to national banks "national currency," or for granting charters to such institutions. If the currency in question were sold to banks for its full face value in gold, there could possibly be no abuse of the practice, if the Government held all the gold paid for them to secure their redemption and prevent inflation. But to lend such currency to two thousand banks, chartered expressly to be so favored, is a violation alike of the organic and the natural laws.

14. It will be seen, in the next two or three chapters, how the needful amount of metallic and paper currency may be maintained by a strictly automatic process, without any cost to the nation as such. At the time of writing this chapter, the nation holds about $150,000,000 of metallic money, purchased to maintain specie payments on $346,000,000 of greenbacks, or United States notes, issued directly to the people. If the legal-tender character of these notes were abolished, and no more were sold than the people were willing to pay for in gold bullion and coin, and the bank notes were retired, we should approximate a more correct monetary system. See Chap. XXXI. for a formulated Act of Congress.

15. I add this paragraph in December, 1879, to state

that my foreshadowing of the tendency to inflation in
values has thus far been more than verified.   In September of 1878, I placed before a committee of Congress a
communication containing substantially the same facts
and arguments respecting banks of issue and discount,
and affirming that the then existing depression in business, to investigate the causes of which and recommend
remedial measures the committee had been appointed,
had already ceased, and a period of inflation had set
in, in its incipient beginnings.   Since then the prices
of nearly all commodities and the wages of labor have
simultaneously and considerably risen.   Speculation is
rife in most leading articles usually made the subject
of speculation.   There has been an aggregate rise in
the market value of stocks of fully $150,000,000, with
scarcely any increase in actual or intrinsic value.   Cotton, wheat, iron, corn, nearly all raw and manufactured
articles, have risen in a single year from twenty to fifty
per cent.   There has been added to the volume of currency about $150,000,000 of coined money, and the bal-
loon bids fair to go on expanding till another explosion
occurs.   The national banks have only increased their
reserve a trifle, and turn their loans of "national currency" to the best account for the profit of their shareholders.   As they hold but some $40,000,000 of metallic
money, they rely on that, and their ability to draw on the
Government reserve of $155,000,000, to maintain specie
payments and meet their depositors' calls on them.   All
the other banks, and all business men likewise, have an
eye on that $155,000,000.   The importations of gold and
silver, and the production of the mines, are still at the
rate of $150,000,000 a year ; but these only add stimu-
lus to speculation and inflation.   A bad harvest, or some
great failure, is only wanting to bring about a repetition
of the events of 1837, 1847, 1857, and 1873, the last date

having been postponed by the war, and the borrowing
by the nation, States, and railway companies, in foreign
markets, of $2,500,000,000 of capital, which was expended
in the United States. By the circumstance of the immense
crops of corn, cotton, wheat, and nearly every thing else,
for four successive years, and the failure of crops for two
years in Europe, the balance of trade has been turned
strongly in favor of this country, and a most favorable
time exists for establishing a sound currency. Will it be
done? I fear not.

CHAPTER XXV.

GENERAL SUMMARY OF THE ARGUMENT. — THE MONEY
PROBLEM TO BE SOLVED BY A UNIVERSAL MONETARY
SYSTEM. — PLAN FOR SUCH A SYSTEM SUGGESTED, GREAT
BRITAIN AND AMERICA TO COMBINE WITH THE LATIN
NATIONS AS THE INITIATION OF THE SYSTEM.

1. THE reader who has followed my reasoning, and
carefully considered my postulates, will probably agree
with me that the money question must be taken out of
the region of dogmatic and empirical teaching. Statesmen must treat it strictly as a science, and the issue of
coin and paper money must be confined to scientific
methods. In Great Britain and the Latin-union countries the coin issue approximates that position, but is still
imperfect, as will be seen by comparison with the more
perfect system I am advocating.

2. In respect to the issue of paper money, there is but
a slight approximation towards a strictly scientific method
in any country. The consideration of the question, as
well as the methods, is still under the control of those who
seek to make a profit out of paper money, either for the

State or for classes, notwithstanding that the results of nearly two centuries of experience condemn the practice. Instead of treating paper money simply as a more convenient tool of industry than metallic money, it has been, and still is, wholly subordinated to financial considerations and private or public profit.

3. When this proposition is accepted as fundamental, as it certainly is, the whole theory of delegating the prerogative of the State to banks or individuals, to be exercised in the issue of paper money to trade on, and for profit and gain to a favored class, falls to the ground. The question then presents itself, Can a state department, as a method of meeting the more theoretically perfect issue and management of paper money, be organized? I have endeavored to show in Chap. XVIII. that it can, by making the issue of coin and paper both automatic, to be entirely governed by the natural laws of industry. The issue of notes wholly on metal, on the original plan of the banks of Amsterdam, Venice, Sweden, and Hamburg, it has been pointed out, was founded on this theory, which worked, so long as it was adhered to, with precision, and great advantage to the public, who preferred their notes to gold; and that the evil effects of a deviation from these principles by the Bank of England was the beginning of all the evils of paper money.

4. I have pointed out that the suppression of all banks of issue in and within fifty miles of London, and the limitation set on the issues of all other banks in the United Kingdom, were steps in the right direction; though the law of 1849, imposing these limitations, failed in establishing a really sound monetary system. I have also shown, that, though the national bank system of the United States was an improvement on the old American system, it is fatally deficient in elements of science, and, if perpetuated, must control the Government, and prove

a powerful and dangerous despotism. Furthermore, I have alluded to the growth and development of a party in the United States that proposes to cut loose from the stability of a metallic currency, and to issue paper stamps for the whole amount of the national debt, which they propose to pay off in these worthless stamps of the nation.

5. On the other hand, I have kept steadily in view certain great fundamental principles, and prominent among them the distinction between money and trading power, or floating capital, and the evil effects on the minds of the people, and on the course of legislation on monetary and financial matters, of confounding the two things, and have directed attention to the important fact, that only a certain limited amount of money is needed to perform the special services for which it was invented, and that the people refuse to buy more, because it is a costly commodity, and only useful for what it will buy.

6. I have also shown, and shall presently more clearly demonstrate, how the exact amount of money needed for industrial and other purposes may be meted out, and automatically supplied through state issue departments, and how the same may be made universal, without disturbing the present circulation ; or, rather, how the one system may be substituted for the other without any industrial disturbance. I would here observe, that, having a clear and vivid perception of these important fundamental truths and principles, I have been greatly pained to witness the obstructions to the introduction of improved and readily applied methods for supplying the metallic and paper money strenuously opposed and resisted by "the practical men " and the banks of issue, who, as a rule, fancy their interests will be impaired by changes indicated by science as desirable.

7. It has been likewise shown, beyond controversy,

that the issue of paper money forms no part of modern
banking, the business of which is more than half conducted by non-issuing banks, and that the entire abolition of the word "bank-note" alone will eradicate that
delusion from the public mind.   Furthermore, I have
incidentally pointed out that the issuing of national currency to banks by the Government on public securities
held by the Government, and, in the case of the Bank
of England, by the Issue Department, being in the nature
of loans from the nation to bankers, was and is banking,
in which Governments cannot properly engage.

8. Finally, I have shown how readily a state issue
department may be created in Great Britain and America
by consolidating the respective mints in each country,
with the issue department in former with the Issue Department of the Bank of England in a new office at
Whitehall; and, in the United States, with the Treasury
issue department, in a building wholly separated from the
financial department of the Treasury.   Having, as I
hope, made these positions clear, I repeat, the true scientific method of issuing metallic and paper money is for
such departments to purchase for gold coin and notes, as
required, all the gold bullion that is offered, and as much
silver bullion and other metal for subsidiary coin as may
be asked in exchange for gold coin and notes convertible
into gold only, — the two kinds of coin and notes being
made interconvertible, in sums not lower than the lowest
gold coin.   I may again repeat, this method will give
the utmost freedom to the law of supply and demand
in its action on all kinds of money.   When gold coin is
more valuable than metal, to an extent to afford a profit
or a motive, it will be taken to the issue office and sold
for coin or notes; and when the bullion is worth the
most, the coin will be melted into ingots, or, what will
generally happen, the mints will be stopped until equi-

librium is restored.   In like manner, when there are not notes or subsidiary coin enough to serve the conveniences of the people, they will buy more with gold coin or bullion ; and when there are too many, they will sell them back to the automaton.

9. SUGGESTIONS FOR A SCIENTIFIC MONETARY SYSTEM, INTENDED ULTIMATELY TO EMBRACE ALL CIVILIZED COUNTRIES. — The efforts hitherto made to introduce a universal monetary system among the chief civilized, industrial nations of the world, have been wholly confined to coined money.   The plan I am submitting embraces also the fabrication, issue, and management of paper money, based on metal.   Without including the entire money of a country, metallic and paper, the universality of a system, it is submitted, will be shorn of half its advantages.   Hence it seems to me that such a system should be perfected in some one or more countries, and be presented, so completed, for consideration or acceptance to others, where its introduction will be most easily effected without disturbance of established systems, or undue prejudices.

10. The theory of a universal coinage system has been very ably discussed in a work by Mr. J. Meyer of Berlin (translated by Mrs. C. P. Culver, whose husband is Clerk of the Committee on Coinage, Weights, and Measures, of the present Congress), and also in another work by Mr. Aug. Eggers of Bremen, also translated by Mrs. Culver, which have been published together by that committee on account of their great value.   I desire here to express my thanks to Mrs. Culver for her able and well-rendered translation of these works, which so strongly support the theories I have reasoned out in this treatise, nearly all of which was written three years and a half ago, and nearly that length of time before I had seen those essays on monetary science.   Those who desire to con-

salt Mrs. Culver's translations will find them in the public libraries, or at the Treasury Department by inquiring for No. 8 Miscellaneous Documents of the 45th Congress, published in 1879. In many particulars the plan I had elaborated is identical with that of Mr. Meyer, except that I propose at first to confine its operations to the " Latin Union," comprising France, Italy, Switzerland, and Belgium, and the English-speaking countries, embracing Great Britain and her forty colonies, and the United States, containing forty odd States and Territories. I had proposed to make the British sovereign the initiatory unit of value, because the United States had given in to such a suggestion, or expressed its willingness to minimize the fine metal in the half-eagle so as to equalize it with the sovereign. I have, however, since reading Mr. Meyer's essay, altered my suggestion so as to accept his proposal in its entirety, as will be seen hereafter.

11. As a preface to the plan I have to suggest, I quote the following from the report of the Committee of Congress on Coinage, etc., just referred to, which is an extract from a former report of 1866 (p. 13).

" At the International Congress of Berlin, the transactions of which were reported by the United States Commissioner, and submitted to Congress, it was resolved as follows : —

" *First*, That the Congress recommends that the existing units may be reduced to a small number ; that each unit should be, as far as possible, decimally sub-divided ; that coins in use shall be expressed in weights of the metrical system, and should be of the same degree of fineness, — namely, nine-tenths fine, and one-tenth alloy.

" *Second*, That the different Governments be invited to send delegates authorized to consider and report what should be the relative weights in the metrical system of gold and silver coins, and to arrange the details by which the monetary systems of different countries may be fixed according to the terms of the preceding proposition."

The report of 1866, quoted further, very correctly remarks (p. 14 of Report of 1878), —

"The only indispensable condition of this uniformity of value is, that, in the standing unit with its divisions and multiples used in commerce, there shall be in all countries an equal amount of gold (or silver) with a fixed proportion of alloy. Each nation will retain its own devices and legends, and other peculiarity of mintage. A common name for the standard unit would be desirable, but not essential. The presence of a given amount of precious metal, mixed with a given amount of alloy, is the only absolute prerequisite for the establishment of international uniformity of coinage. The dollar of the United States, the four shillings of England, and five francs of France, are of approximate value. Several nations" (known as the Latin Union) "have adopted, under other names, the coinage of France, making it of equal value."

At the time these favorable views were expressed by the Committee of Congress (1866), indorsing also and quoting the recommendations of the late Chief Justice Chase made in 1862, while Secretary of the Treasury, gold was demonetized and dealt in as a commodity, by reason of the excessive issues of inconvertible legal-tender paper money, which state of things Mr. Chase considered favorable to the initiation of a general monetary arrangement with other nations. A small reduction in the weight of gold in the coinage, when coin was not used as money, it was thought would not be noticeable when it came back as money, by the appreciation of legal tenders, to par. But we now have an overvalued silver dollar coin which, in time, will again demonetize the gold coins; that is, so soon as the channels of circulation are fully occupied by such coin added to the large volume of paper now afloat (postulates 23, 24). This circumstance deserves serious consideration on the part of those who are laboring on that committee, as well as others, to promote a more extended coinage system in connection with the Latin Union. On the plan I propose, it will be seen the distribution of the series of coins, as well as the paper money, being left to the action of supply and demand, by a purely automatic machine, the amount of each series of coins and paper will be perfectly regulated. The plan itself is so simple, and so easily put in operation, that any man of ordinary capacity can comprehend it in a very short time. The extracts from reports of Congressional Committees and National Commissioners will pave the way for a more complete understanding of it.

12. PROPOSED PLAN.

First, Make gold the universal standard of the measure of value.

Second, Make the gold coins nine-tenths fine and one-tenth alloy.

Third, Abolish all note issues by banks and the Treasury.

Fourth, Establish in each country an independent issue department.

Fifth, Transfer the mints to these departments in the several countries.

Sixth, Agree on a unit of value, say, one and a half grains gold.

Seventh, Preserve on one side of each coin the present national devices.

Eighth, Agree on a common device for the obverse sides of the coins.

Ninth, Each department to issue certain specified denominations of notes, not lower in amount than the lowest gold coin.

Tenth, Each department to gradually call in the outstanding coin and paper money, filling their places, *pari passu,* with new coins, which can be effected by limitation in the volume of money.

Eleventh, The method of the issue will be to exchange coin and paper money for gold bullion at its market value, less a small *agio,* or seigniorage, to cover cost of management.

Twelfth, Each department to issue such denominations of silver and other subsidiary coins as may be agreed on, and of one degree of fineness.

Thirteenth, These subsidiary coins to be treated the same as paper money ; that is, to be sold for their face value in gold coin, and both paper and subsidiary coin to be redeemable by the several departments issuing them, at par in gold coin, when presented at the chief office or any agency, in sums not lower than the lowest gold coin.

Fourteenth, Each department to establish branches, or agencies, to suit the convenience of the public.

Fifteenth, The question, whether a limited amount of the accumulation of gold coin and bullion, that will accumulate, may be disposed of to purchase national securities, and reduce the public debts of the several countries, to be considered.

Sixteenth, Each department to publish weekly statements of its operations.

Seventeenth, All national taxes to be paid in national notes and coin, and be deposited for safe keeping and re-issue in the chief office, or its agencies, subject to the draft of the duly authorized Government authorities.

Eighteenth, All other necessary details to secure efficiency to be agreed on, and be subject to joint revision of the several departments after being established.

Nineteenth, Provision to be made for receiving into the union, or league, other countries.

13. The introduction of this comprehensive reform in monetary administration presents, in itself, no practical difficulties. The objections to it, like that to all reforms, comes wholly from those parties interested in perpetuating old abuses, or unchallenged errors in administration. Issuing banks and exchange brokers, who derive many millions annually from the present imperfect systems, will oppose any reform in the methods of supplying paper

money, and trading on exchanges. They claim that they hold vested rights in the premises, and hence use all their power to defeat reform measures.

14. If we accept Mr. Meyer's proposition to make one and a half grams of fine gold the unit, or initial coin of the system, which I think the best of any of the various propositions I have examined, the following comparative table will exhibit the result.

ENGLISH MONEY.			FRENCH MONEY.		AMERICAN MONEY.	
1½ grams = 4 s.	1.16 d.	= ½ £	= 5 fr. 16.6 c. =	5 fr.	= $ 99.7	= $ 1 00
3 " = 8	2.32	= ⅗ "	= 10 33.3 =	10 "	= 1 99.4	= 2 00
3¾ " = 10	2.9	= ¼ "	= 12 63 =	12 "	= 2 49.25	= 2 50
7½ " = 20	5.3	= 1 "	= 25 83.3 =	25 "	= 4 98.5	= 5 00
15 " = 40	11.64	= 2 "	= 51 66.6 =	50 "	= 9 96.92	= 10 00
30 " = 81	11.28	= 4 "	= 103 33.2 =	100 "	= 19 93.84	= 20 00

15. In comparison with the proposed new standard measure, it will be seen, by the above table, the English and French coins are at present overvalued the amounts set down in the left-hand columns, and the American coins are slightly undervalued. The former contains so much too little gold, and the latter too much. For instance, the English sovereign would have to have added five pence and three-tenths in value of metal in order to make it up to seven and a half grams of the new pound; the French twenty-five franc piece would require an increase of 83.3 centimes of metal; and the American half-eagle would have to be reduced 1.5 cents in order to bring the three coins to the equal weight of seven and a half grams. The change in the American gold coin would be so small as to be of no practical account. The percentage of deficit on the English and French coins of the present would be respectively 2.21 and 3.31 per

cent. On the present gold circulation of these countries this would entail a considerable loss on these Governments, which might be made good by a seigniorage charge on the new issues. The question of seigniorage will be briefly considered in Chap. XXVII. By this method the present gold coins might at once be made to legally represent the new standard by contraction of their volume sufficient to raise their money value above their bullion value, to prevent the new coins being melted. Of course this would cause a slight fall in the prices of things measured by the new standard, which would necessarily ensue under any plan whatever. I need hardly say, such a change must be made gradually, so as not to be perceptible to those engaged in any of the industrial pursuits. To enable those who care to verify the foregoing calculations, I would say that one gram is equal to 15.432 grains, and one grain to 0.0648 gram. We may call the gram in ordinary estimates 15.5 grains.

16. Mr. Meyer has also shown how readily the subsidiary coins — silver, nickel, and copper — may be harmonized in most countries, and I refer to his work on that subject. By being made convertible into gold standard coin, at the will of the holder, in sums not less than the lowest gold coin, and being sold for gold, or paper. convertible into gold by the several departments, the automatic process, operated by the force of the natural laws, will always regulate the issue and conversion according to the exigencies of industry, both as to the denominations and the amount of money. Hence, the question of the amount of alloy or overvaluation of silver coins would be of little consequence. We treat them as promissory notes engraved on a valuable metal. Mr. Meyer proposes to make silver coins six of fine silver and one of alloy of copper, counting the copper as silver. The profit on silver then would compensate for the loss

on gold in countries where the standard weight shall be raised. The American 412½ grain silver dollar is just now about 11 per cent overvalued. Under the metric system proposed, they could not circulate in the United States so long as one and two dollar notes are issued, because the people prefer the notes to silver dollars, on account of their lightness and greater convenience.

17. The amount of one and two dollar notes in circulation in the United States on the first of November, 1878, was $47,567,816. In order, therefore, to make the silver dollars circulate before the Government shall be compelled to pay them out by the withdrawal of all the gold reserve, it will be necessary to call in all the small notes, and give the silver dollars a forced circulation. But if the new plan of interconvertibility between silver and other subsidiary coins and gold coins and paper convertible into gold should be adopted, and no notes under the lowest gold coin are issued, there will be room for probably twenty million silver dollars, in addition to the lower denominations of that and other metallic coins, in the United States.

18. With silver coins made on a scale of one-seventh overvaluation, and convertible into gold as so many metallic notes, it would scarcely be needful to provide for the possible contingency of such a change in the relative value of the two metals as would lead to the hoarding or melting down of silver coin. In other words, it would hardly be necessary to guard against the bullion value of silver rising above the coin value, measured by gold.

19. As for the new names to be given to the new international coins, Mr. Meyer has suggested the adoption of the term "dollar," and the various coins to be specified by the multiples and divisions of the dollar. While we see foreigners agreeing on the desirability of using the term known and universally used in America,

it is surprising to find Americans desirous of inventing new and before unknown names. I indorse Mr. Meyer's proposal, with this suggestion, that the gold coins shall be called eagles, half-eagles, quarter-eagles; and so on the ascending scale, — double and quadruple eagles. The eagle, as well as the dollar, is known all over the European continent; but the term "stella," as suggested by some, is unknown and "unknowable."

VIEWS OF HON. JOHN SHERMAN, SECRETARY OF THE TREAS-
URY, FORMERLY UNITED STATES SENATOR FROM OHIO, ON
FREE TRADE AND A UNIVERSAL SYSTEM OF COINAGE.

20. The following extract from the report made by Senator Sherman (now Secretary of the Treasury) in 1868 very forcibly expresses some of the advantages to be derived from a universal system of coinage. I am indebted to the very valuable work of the late Dr. Linderman, Director of the United States Mint, 1877, for it, as well as for much other useful information on the subject of the coinage of money.

"Every advance toward a free exchange of commodities is an advance in civilization. . . . Every obstruction to commerce is a tax upon consumption; every facility to a free exchange cheapens commodities, increases trade and production, and promotes civilization. . . . No single measure will tend in this direction more than the adoption of a fixed international standard of value, by which all products may be measured, and in conformity with which the coin of a country may go with its flag into every sea and buy the products of every nation without being discounted by the money-changers.

"Gold with us is, like cotton, a raw product. . . . Every obstruction to its free use, such as the necessity of its recoinage when passing from nation to nation, diminishes its value; and that loss falls on the United States, the country of production.

. . . .

"The United States is a new nation, and therefore a debtor nation. By placing ourselves in harmony with the money units of creditor nations, we promote the easy borrowing of money and pay-ment of debts without the loss of recoinage or exchange, always paid by the debtor. The technical rate of exchange between the United States and Great Britain, growing out of the deficient nom-inal values of coin, is a standing reproach, which can only be got rid of by unifying the coinage of the two countries when both the real and technical rates of exchange will be at par, etc."

This difficulty, as stated in the last paragraph quoted, was in part obviated in the United States by an Act of Congress, which went into effect Jan. 1, 1874, that re-quires the Secretary of the Treasury annually to publish the values of the standard coins in circulation of the vari-ous nations of the world, as estimated by the Director of the Mint.

CHAPTER XXVI.

THE PROPOSED UNIVERSAL MONETARY SYSTEM FURTHER CONSIDERED. — SUBSIDIARY COINS TO BE CONVERTIBLE.

1. THE plan I have reasoned out for the establishment of national or state issue departments having sole power to issue and manage both metallic and paper money, whether confined to one country, or extended to several or all countries in the civilized world, I claim to be the only one yet devised which proposes a complete, practical, and scientific separation of the issue and man-agement of currency from the financial operations of individuals and communities. It seems to me to be the only one that will successfully and permanently preserve the currency — metallic and paper — of a country from those periodic derangements growing out of periodic panics and crises, often lasting many years, or half a life-time as in the case of the suspension of the Bank of England from 1797 to 1821, and in America for about

one-half of the time since the existence of national government. I regard the adoption of the plan, whenever it shall take place, as the first step towards checking the incipient causes of panics leading to those long and frequent derangements of industrial affairs which have become chronic in Great Britain. A sound currency, incapable of derangement itself, most certainly will prove a great blessing to mankind, even though it may not wholly exterminate the evils and consequences of over-trading. It will also most certainly preserve the great and indispensable measure of values from being so often forced out of circulation, and avert the evils of a depreciated, fluctuating, and uncertain measure taking its place.

2. I propose briefly to discuss the question of subsidiary coin, which has so often, and, as I conceive, very unnecessarily, been left in an unsatisfactory condition in most countries. No system of currency can be regarded as sound or safe which does not provide a method that shall exactly mete out to the public the necessary quantity of subsidiary coin. To create such a system, it is needful to devise a self-acting regulator. The system must be based on the theory that supply and demand, or the great predominating equation in human industries, shall determine the method of providing such coin. The laws of industry alone can regulate the volume of this portion, as they will do of the rest of the currency. Under the proposed system, all kinds of subsidiary coin must, like paper money, be made convertible into the standard gold coin at par.

3. Now, if such subsidiary coins are made convertible, at the pleasure of the holder, into standard gold coin, and are sold for the latter at par, it is obvious that their position in the monetary system will be the same as that of paper, except that they will have in themselves a

market value equal to the amount of raw material of which they are made. But the same principles will govern the quantity needed by the community for industrial purposes as in the case of paper. Being an indispensable as well as a costly tool, the public will purchase only so many subsidiary coins as are needed. Like paper, if too many are taken out, the surplus of supply above legitimate demand will presently be returned and exchanged for gold, for home or foreign use, as the case may be. There will be nothing left to the judgment or will of the managers of the issue department. It will be an automatic machine regulating itself. Can any one gainsay this reasoning, or doubt its amounting to demonstration as clear as mathematics?

4. In respect to the proposed universal monetary system, one of the results of no little importance would be the establishment of a method by which the equilibrium of the exchanges between the countries entering the league would be perpetually maintained, precisely in the same manner as the exchanges between domestic traders. Though human ingenuity has not, for obvious reasons, been able to construct a perpetual self-moving machine, the laws of nature everywhere develop perpetual action. A system, therefore, founded on these laws, and which is operated and kept in motion by them through human agencies bound to obey them, is quite another affair from those systems which are operated by personal and artificial impulses and considerations, and for the private gain of corporations, and to satisfy the greed of individuals.

5. Furthermore, under the system I propose, the *motive* for using *coin* as merchandise for settling foreign and domestic indebtedness, and for purchasing other commodities, would be minimized in its force so as to place its position in these respects at the bottom of the list

of commodities. But if, under a universal system, the
coin of one country found its way, through the medium
of travellers or any other cause, into other countries, no
inconvenience would arise, inasmuch as the perpetual
tendency to equilibrium imparted by the free action of
supply and demand would lead to an equable distribution through all the countries which have entered into the
league. There being the smallest motive, in comparison
with other things, for exporting coin, for the reasons
stated, the coin of each country would, as a rule, remain
at home, where the national stamp on one side would be
better understood, and the uses of letters of credit, circular notes, and bills of exchange, would always be preferred by travellers as well as merchants. The international coinage should, however, know no national bounds.
Its object is universality.

6. In order to invoke an unprejudiced and candid
consideration of the arguments presented, I wish to
observe, that I have endeavored, in this chapter and
throughout the entire work, to subject the principles I
have postulated to the closest logical reasoning, both by
induction and deduction, as well as by the citation of
generally admitted facts. We are as much bound to
accept truths thus established as we are such as are
demonstrated by the (so-called) *exact sciences*. It is a
mistake to draw a distinction between the two methods
of logic or reasoning. Both have equal force ; and only
those who are ignorant of both, set up what is called
"practice" against "theory." No practice not founded
on demonstrated theory is reliable, or assured to be the
best for even those who follow it. Men who manage
banks or ships, or deal in goods of any kind, are the
least to be trusted, unless they have mastered the complicated principles of political economy. Hence it is, that
the theorizing of what are called "practical men" is so

generally at fault. Their theories are simple dogmas, and no better than the opinions of the two knights who quarrelled and fought because each had seen only one side of the shield, where they had chanced to meet, and had in consequence perceived but half the truth (see chapter on Value).

7. It will now be seen, that, in order to reach a perfectly scientific solution of the money question, it is very desirable to establish the proposed monetary league of nations, and leave the currency to distribute itself under supply and demand. Though such a system as I have shown in my reasoning is perfectly applicable and necessary to nations like Great Britain and the United States, it would receive its highest development and efficacy under a widely or universally extended international league. Some other great advantages of such a system, not explicitly stated before, will be, that there can never be either too much or too little money, metallic or paper, in any country belonging to the league. There will never be "over-issues" of paper money. The great overruling law of nature, supply and demand, will maintain an equilibrium of value and of distribution. If financial or industrial crises occur in one country, or in all, their effects will be minimized by having a solid, unchangeable measure of values *always assured.*

8. The formulation of an Act of Parliament or of Congress, and of a treaty to extend the system to other countries, will not be difficult for legislators, statesmen, or diplomats, when they have come to master the subject itself. As to the establishment of a league amongst the English-speaking and the (so-called) Latin nations, there does not, as shown in the last chapter, seem to be any serious difficulties. We are already making some progress towards the adoption of a universal system of weights and measures, which is surrounded with very much greater obstacles.

9. All empirical, statistical, and philosophical or scientific reasoners, alike admit the long-continuing abuses of not properly guarded or restricted issues of bank and government notes, and deplore the vast losses and injury to society directly traceable to this cause. But nearly all hug the delusive system so subject to abuse. Few may at first agree with me in the necessity of adopting the heroic method of a surgical operation of cutting loose from banks of issue, and in the creation of a sound and healthy system. But the time will surely come when correct principles will prevail. At present the enemies of such a system are prejudice, ignorance, and a mistaken notion that bank notes are a source of profit to banks; though it has been shown, that, on the whole, banks, as well as the public, have been the losers by their issue : in a word, by acting on a mistaken view of self-interest. These lions must be got out of the path or crushed before sound theories can be reduced to practice.

10. Referring once more to the uncertain deductions drawn from statistical and actuarial lore, I cannot help regarding the attempts of professional economists to use such methods, instead of relying on logical reasoning to found theories for legislation and the conduct of industrial affairs, as most unfortunate. When we leave the field of scientific deduction and induction to mere empiricism, and reason from such masses of crude statistics of prices as have been collected by Mr. Tooke, Mr. Newmarch, and others, we place ourselves in the position of a ship in a boundless ocean, without rudder, compass, or instrument of any kind. Such tables of statistics of average values, or approximations of value, are of no real use to science ; and, so far as they seem to contradict or do not coincide with scientific principles, may be discarded as incorrect. There are cases, such as the statistics of life, where close accuracy can be attained, and where valuable

results to an important branch of business have followed. Statistics or approximations of the products of labor, prices, etc., are of doubtful value to traders, and are often misleading, as in the case of crops, merchandise, etc. But they are of no more value to the science of political economy than to that of geometry. The economist has to deal with principles ; and, if he wants to use figures, he can assume such as he desires, just as a mathematician starts from certain assumed facts for the purpose of demonstrating his problems. To attempt to build up a system of political economy, wholly, or even in part, on statistics of prices or trade, is hardly wiser than to endeavor to build a pyramid with its apex downwards, or begin building a house at the top. Statistics of bank issues and discounts, being ascertainable facts, may, however, be used for illustration, and to show the consequences of erroneous systems of economy established by legislation granting monopolies and privileges to private parties. We may show, in this way, the folly of delegating to banks and private individuals the prerogative of issuing paper money, or the exclusive privilege of conducting given industries of any kind. We may show the vast losses sustained by society, in consequence of violating correct principles, established by logic and reasoning.

11. But when we come to reason out and determine how certain phenomena are due to certain causes ; how, for instance, money, the standard of value, measures and differentiates the values of other things, we gain nothing, and only confuse ourselves, by trying to lug in the statistics of production, labor and capital, or machinery. What appear to be exceptions to scientific principles are really only unascertained laws of nature ; and that branch of inquiry is to a large extent, as yet, a *terra incognita*, where statistics are only confusing. I leave this field for others to cultivate. How the market values of products

in the course of production, manufacture, and distribution are acted on by supply and demand and by each other, is a question still affording scope for thought and reasoning. We have economists who have attempted by statistics to show how much paper money is needed *per capita;* whereas population has little or nothing to do with the matter, it being one wholly governed by the industry of a people and their productions.

12. I have several times, in the course of this work, urged the desirability of issuing one pound, and even lower notes, to occupy the place of gold coin. Some recent writers, particularly in the United States since specie payments have been resumed, are arguing against the uses of small notes. They say, "small notes should not be issued, because they almost invariably drive out of circulation all coin of the same denominations to the full extent of their issue." This is very bad logic. The ability to circulate paper money, convertible into coin, no odds of what denominations, depends on the preference which the people have for the paper as a tool of industry. It is wholly a question of convenience ; and the denominations of paper money should be determined by that great natural law of industry, so often quoted, but so little regarded in theory and practice, supply and demand. Those who think that an arbitrary and artificial method of doling out to the public what the public itself ought to be left free to determine, do violence to sound principles and good logic. The very purpose of a one pound or a one dollar note is to meet the public demand for such notes ; and, if the result is "to drive out of circulation," or, more correctly speaking, keep the coins representing the denominations in question in *reserve,* it is only what large notes do. This argument admits of no rejoinder.

CHAPTER XXVII.

SOME MORE ECONOMIC FALLACIES. — SEIGNIORAGE A TAX ON MONEY. — GREAT ADVANTAGES OF COIN OVER PAPER MONEY.

1. Professor Francis A. Walker, in his treatise on "Money," takes exception to the use of the term "common measure of value" as applied to money, because "value is a relation," or a relative expression. At best this objection is hardly more than technical. Everybody is agreed on the offices performed by money, which the term in question is intended to express. It is, in fact, no more "a relation," than any measure of length, capacity, or weight. They are all relative terms, separating a part from the whole. But there is a stronger motive for retaining the term "common measure of value" in respect to money. *It is that money itself has been so made by law of Parliament,* which has set a *scale of denominations,* as pounds and dollars, and defines the weight of pure metal assigned to each. The definition is not only according to Webster, but its appropriateness is sustained by universal usage. Besides, "measure," according to our best dictionaries, is defined to be "a rule by which any thing is adjusted or proportioned ; proportion ; quantity settled ; portion allotted." We might substitute the word "common valuator." The pounds, shillings, and pence, and the dollars and cents, constitute the scales on the several measures, referring to certain fixed quantities of metal by which we measure all values, or the value of all things. Hence the term "common measure." In Chap. V., I have shown how money measures such things, and metes out trading power in the loan market, as well as between buyers and sellers generally. It not only measures values by comparison with its own market value, but

it measures amount or quantity, so that we shall know
how much of one thing to give for a given quantity of
another thing ; and how much trading power is loaned
or paid for commodities, or other things measured or
weighed by the scale of weights and measures. " Differ-
entiator " is a better term than denominator, because that
word accurately defines what money does in determining
relative values.   Money can only be compared to the
yardstick or measure, in so far as, by its scale of denominations expressed in coins, it specifies the proportion and
amount of the money itself to be given for specified portions of the thing bargained for.   In other words, the
yard-measure, for instance, measures the quantity of cloth
demanded ; and money measures the weight of metal to
be given therefor, or its equivalent in something else.   At
this point the comparison stops.

2. It is by attaching the scale of denominations to
metal, and making the coined money and the uncoined
metal readily interconvertible, that we secure a measure
the least variable.   If our money consisted of paper
denominations held as nearly as possible to the value of
gold or other metal by limitation of their volumes, we
shall have a purely artificial method of regulating such
value, by hand, so to speak.   I, therefore, discard this
theory in favor of one that works automatically, which is
the only true and scientific method of supplying money.
By, however, combining the standard and the measure of
value in the same coin, and making bullion always convertible into coin on presentation at the issue office or
its agencies, there can never be wide divergencies between
the market value of money and bullion.   The coin may
be compared to the stem, or rod, of the " compound pen-
dulum," which is made of several metals welded or brazed
together at the two ends, so that the expansibility of the
metals, being different under the influence of heat and

cold, may counteract the tendency to variation of length. The two values being tied together in one coin, and the two things, money and coin, being readily interchangeable by coinage and melting, the superiority of the coin system at once appears.

3. All economists treat money as a medium of exchange, — indeed, as the only medium for the exchange of goods. This is clearly a misconception. Money, as money, performs a very insignificant part in what is improperly called " exchanging commodities," which are *distributed, and not exchanged*. The true and scientific view is, that " trading power," or floating capital, through bankers, as stated in postulates 35 and 36, constitutes the " medium " of distribution of labor and commodities. It is, therefore, an error to attribute to one commodity, either in the raw state of bullion or its manufactured condition of money, the sole office of distributing other things, whose market value in the aggregate, being turned into trading power in manner specified, exceeds that of money as thirty to one. *The circulating medium is, therefore, trading power, or capital, made available by bankers. I repeat, it is free trade in metal, and free trade in money, and paper based on money, coupled with interconvertibility, that determine the whole question, and strip it of all mystery.* Mr. J. Stuart Mill, quoted by Mr. Walker, saw this dimly, when he said, "it is not with money that things are really purchased." This concedes the whole question. But in the next sentence Mr. Mill goes on to say, " pounds, shillings, and pence are a sort of tickets or orders for goods." This expression only muddles the question he came so near clearing of its obscurities. These denominations do not constitute trading power, or capital, but are only the scale for measuring it. Bullion and money are capital, and, as such, trading power. The figures or numeral expressions on a yard-measure or a weighing ma-

chine do not constitute the yardstick or the machine, but indicate the length or weight of the things these "scaled" instruments are applied to.

4. The theory, so persistently and almost universally put forward by economists, and quoted by Mr. Walker, that "that which measures value must itself have value," or, as they sometimes erroneously say, "intrinsic value," the same as "*measures* of length, capacity, and weight, must have length, capacity, and weight," is another fundamental error resulting from pushing the comparison too far. The measure of the *value of money*, like the value of commodities, is set by supply and demand, or production and consumption; while supply and demand have nothing to do with *other measures*. With regard to "intrinsic value," I have stated its definition in the introduction to this work; and I here repeat, this sort of value is not what we are dealing with when we are considering money. Intrinsic value is a *quality;* market value is the *worth of a thing in the market, as measured and differentiated by money*. The intrinsic value of a spade is its fitness to the purpose of digging or turning over the ground. The *intrinsic value* of gold consists in its peculiar adaptation to coinage and all other uses of money, and works of ornamentation and utility. But the *market values* of the spade and of gold are alike determined by supply and demand. Paper is intrinsically valuable for purposes of writing, printing, and for "paper money," but is comparatively of little market value.

5. It must not, from these or any other observations I have made, be supposed that I discard or depreciate the intrinsic value of gold, or exalt the uses, or *intrinsic* value, of paper for purposes of money. I am treating all kinds of money and commodities from an economic, or scientific, stand-point. Referring again to the two essential offices of metallic money, namely, the establishing a

standard and a common measure of value, it will be seen, that by combining them in coin, and making coin or money value and the metal value easily interconvertible, we reach scientific accuracy, as far as is practicable, unless we can discover some more stable material than gold. The standard and the measure, though separable in principle, as I have shown them to be in practice, being so yoked together, interconvertibility causes their respective market values to more nearly coincide, and prevents wide oscillations in opposite directions, or the market value of the one from oscillating more violently than that of the other, in the same direction, under the action of supply and demand.

6. Professor Jevons and others have pointed out other functions or purposes served by money, but they are more fanciful than real. One of these Professor Walker has successfully disposed of. Mr. Jevons fancies that money is peculiarly adapted to "storing" or hoarding. Now, *money* is not stored or hoarded because it *is money*, but because of the metal it contains. It may be that bank notes or greenbacks are sometimes hoarded; but it is because the owner feels assured that he can get the metal for them when he wants it, or considers them "as good as gold." It is the trading power that underlies the motive of the act. He does not bury the money because it is a measure, but because the metal in it is the standard of value.

7. There has been much written and said about the "costliness of metallic money," and in favor of the superior cheapness of paper money. Mr. Aug. Eggers of Bremen, whose work, "Money Reform," has been translated by Mrs. C. P. Culver, and printed by the committee of the House of Representatives at Washington, along with Mr. Meyer's "International Coinage," has written well on this subject, and has pointed out some errors

into which Adam Smith has fallen in considering paper
money, and which nearly all economists have blindly followed.   One of these is the great economy there is in
substituting bank notes as far as possible for coin.   When
I wrote my chapters on that subject, and others, three
years ago, I had not seen Mr. Eggers's or Mr. Meyer's
works; but I have gone much farther in controverting
many hitherto generally received erroneous conclusions
of distinguished authorities.   There is one point I have
made which I again state; namely, that the public at
large pay full gold value for all the paper money they
use, and it is only the issuers who get the advantage of
any profit there may be in the substitution of paper for
metal.   I entirely agree with these authors, that the cost
of metallic money is utterly insignificant in comparison
with the market value of the products it is used to measure and distribute.   The gold in a sovereign or an eagle
will last at least a hundred years, and serve to transfer
from producer to consumer *over ten thousand* times its
value in goods, supposing it to serve such purpose only
one hundred times a year.   Besides this simple example, we may give another illustration.   The metallic circulation of Great Britain one hundred years ago was
about £20,000,000; and it has now risen, as estimated
by some, to £120,000,000, or at the average rate of
£1,000,000 a year.   The loss from abrasion, or wear,
and otherwise, of gold coin is very small, and for our
present purposes may be excluded altogether from this
calculation.   This tool, gold coin, has therefore been
increased in volume and cost at the average rate of
£1,000,000 a year in the United Kingdom.   My own
investigations have led me to believe that this estimate,
which I have accepted as the circulation of gold coin in
Great Britain and Ireland, is largely in excess of the
actual amount.   It is more than double the sum esti-

mated to be in circulation and in all the banks in 1868 by Mr. J. B. McCulloch. But I am pointing out how little it costs the people in comparison with the services it renders, and the amount of the value of all the products of capital, labor, and machinery in the United Kingdom, and hence accept the largest estimates.

8. If we assume the population of the kingdom at 30,000,000, and the increase of gold coin at £1,000,000 a year, we find that there is paid, on an average for each inhabitant, eight pence per annum to maintain the necessary supply. Again, if we accept the estimated annual value of all the products and income from past accumulations of labor and capital at, in round numbers, £3,000,000,000, the annual increase of gold coin is only as £1 to £3,000 of the gross annual products of labor and capital. If we compute the interest on the whole capital invested in the estimated coin at four per cent, the annual interest will be £5,000,000, which is as £1 to £600 of the annual yield of labor, machinery, and capital. Compared with the population, the annual interest on the capital invested in gold coin is one-sixth of a pound, or three shillings and four pence, a head; and, as this falls mostly on capital, the cost of money to the laboring classes is almost " nil."

9. Now, when we consider the services which this gold coin renders, it will be found to be the cheapest of all the tools of industry. Is it not all but, if not altogether, indispensable to the successful and easy production and distribution of this vast annual income of Great Britain, and equally so of other industrial countries? Is it not the solid rock on which the nation's industries are based? A civilized nation can no more do without money than it can without weights and measures, or spades, ploughs, and other tools. Whatever fluctuations the value of labor and its products and the market value of capital may

undergo, the gold coin remains almost unchanged in its value. Like a great rock in the ocean, it remains, in its market value, unshaken and unchanged by storms or by tides and currents. In this respect no product of industry, which is suitable for money, can compare with it for stability and durability.

10. These just and logical facts and deductions, to the mind capable of sound reasoning, demonstrate the greatest of all truths in monetary science, namely, that gold coin is not only the best, but the cheapest, money the people can have. If we compare this really inexpensive tool with inconvertible paper, or even a silver circulation, which continually varies in its trading power almost infinitely, as compared with gold, we shall at once see the advantages of the gold standard over that of any other. This is more especially the case as to the laboring man or woman; for the simple self-evident reason that the employer or capitalist always possesses, and generally exercises, the advantage of being able to provide against loss by making a charge or deduction for the risk of such fluctuations as an unstable currency is subject to. This inevitable result of such a measure of values throws the whole loss — and it often constitutes a large percentage, reaching ten to twenty per cent of the wages of the laboring classes — on those classes.

11. Furthermore, if we are going to do what so many clamor for, namely, make "money cheap" by making "cheap money" abundant, we fall into the palpable error I have so often referred to, of confounding money with capital. "Cheap money" does not make "cheap capital." On the contrary, such "cheap money" as is clamored for makes capital dear to the people, who pay full price both for money and capital. Who, then, is benefited by the issue of inconvertible money, — that is, money, paper or metallic, not convertible into the money

made of the most stable known material suited to coinage and convenient circulation and use? The answer is
at hand, and is self-evident and indisputably true. It is
only the bankers, exchange and other brokers dealing in
capital, who number even in a great nation only one in
a thousand, and a handful of skilful gamblers and speculators besides. These, then, are the chief movers in the
agitation for inconvertible paper and overvalued silver
money.

12. It will be seen, by a careful consideration of these
transcendently great truths, that, if the nation delegates
the power to banks and private parties to issue paper
money, it is done solely with the view to enable such to
make a profit, while the public at large derive no advantage whatever by the result. What, then, becomes of the
theory of Adam Smith and others, that the issue of bank
notes cheapens the cost of money to the nation? By
this method of cheapening money, as I have many times
shown, you are only giving a dangerous monopoly to a
very limited class, who have always been led by motives
of gain, or downright greed, to abuse it.

13. The question of seigniorage has occupied the attention of most writers on monetary science, and, like many
other things connected with the fabrication and supply
of money, has very often been the subject of much bad
logic. Mr. Ricardo was an advocate of a heavy seigniorage charge for supplying coin for bullion, — even as high
as fifty per cent of the market value of the bullion. Let
us inquire what is seigniorage, and then determine its
effects on the currency. As defined by Mr. Ricardo
and others, it is a charge made to the owners of bullion
for coining the same into money, or, what is the same
thing, for giving out by the state, at the mint, coined
for uncoined metal, — the manufactured for the unmanu-
factured article. It is, therefore, in the nature of a tax

imposed on one of the most necessary, if not indispensable, tools of industry, or which nobody can do without.
Now, as all taxes imposed by the state on the products
of labor are direct and artificial interferences with the
natural order of things, it becomes the special duty of
the statesman to select, as far as possible, such articles
for taxation as are either luxuries, or tend to engender
vice and idle or bad habits. When Mr. Ricardo argued in
favor of a high tax on bullion when offered in exchange
for money, he was simply adding so much to the cost
of coined or manufactured money. If fifty per cent is
admissible, as contended for by him, its effect on the
offices of money would be to diminish the quantity of
money demanded in exchange for bullion, and thus increase its trading power *pro tanto*, or, in other words, to
lessen the value of labor and its products, and of all
things possessing market value, in a like degree.

14. According to the principles I have endeavored to
demonstrate, money, of all the tools of industry, is the
one that ought to be left free from state or bank influences.   It is, *par excellence*, the one article to be left to
the free and undisturbed action and regulation, as to its
volume and circulation, of the natural laws of industry.
I have contended that its supply should be automatic, so
that those who have bullion to sell may exchange it for
coin, when such exchange will afford a sufficient profit;
and, on the other hand, if the price of bullion is such in
the open markets as to yield a profit, the owners of the
coined or manufactured money may melt it into bullion.
A heavy tax would, it must be seen, interfere seriously
with the scientific supply of this indispensable tool.   Better
far to tax spades, ploughs, and spinning-jennies, than
money.

15. I have not discussed the effect which the consumption of the precious metals, for purposes other than

currency, has on the ebb and flow of money under the influence of supply and demand. Probably the consumption in the arts and manufactures is quite as equable as for purposes of currency. Though the methods of obtaining the precious metals are continually undergoing improvement, and being cheapened thereby, the increased demand for them for currency, and works of utility and art, as well as mere ornament, probably keeps pace with the supplies. The increase of wealth in modern times has been immense, and this has led to an equal increase in the demand for the precious metals. The statistics of consumption of the precious metals, both for currency and in the arts, like most such statistics, are only guesswork after all, and cannot add much to the science of money; and the founding of a *per capita* theory of circulation is no better than to found it on the number of codfish taken annually from the sea.

CHAPTER XXVIII.

INDUSTRIAL CRISES. — THEIR CAUSES AND EFFECTS.

1. In considering this subject, we have *first*, To define what is meant by a crisis in industrial pursuits; *second*, What are the causes; *third*, What their effects on society; and *fourth*, To ascertain whether the science of political economy has yet discovered a remedy for the predisposing causes, or a method for arresting them. They are very generally called "commercial" or "financial crises;" but, as all industries conspire in some degree to bring them about and all suffer from them, I prefer the more comprehensive term of "industrial."

2. The first thing, then, is to define accurately and philosophically what an industrial crisis is. We know the

meaning assigned to crises in diseases of the body or of
the mind.   It then means that the patient has reached a
point in his malady when he will recover or die ; or, in
case of mental disorder, where the mind is restored to
a healthy condition, or is overthrown and dementia sets in
So far, then, as a comparison can be made between the
bodily and mental diseases and the maladies of society,
we may define a crisis in the latter to be, when a long-
continued condition of things, subversive of the laws of
nature, reaches a point when these laws intervene and
assert their ascendency.   Industrial pursuits do not, like
the body, die ; but they become paralyzed, and for a time
weakened and demoralized.   In some countries, such as
Great Britain, the United States, Canada, and some of the
German States, they occur more frequently, last longer,
and are more destructive than in others, such as the
" Latin Union" of countries, comprising France, Switzerland, Italy, and Belgium.   Perhaps here we may find a
clew to their most stimulating causes and aggravating
characteristics.

3. Some economic writers, and the public very generally, impute their cause to what is "unreasoning panic"
among commercial men and managers of corporations.
Thus, Professor Bonamy Price, in addressing the Cham-
ber of Commerce of New York, in the autumn of 1874,
selected the crisis of 1866, in Great Britain, as an example.
He was speaking of crises in general as a subject.   He
said, —

> "The cause of this crisis was simply alarm.   Simply that those
> vast bodies of people who had intrusted funds to this institution "
> (the London and Westminster Bank) "got into what may be called
> a panic, to use a common word.   In that state of wild alarm, all
> rushed for their money, every man catching the contagion, which
> became more catching because it was unreasonable."

The Professor then went on to show what a bank was,

what it did, and finally reached the, no doubt, correct conclusion, that crises always came forth from "the regions of the banks," to use his own words.

4. But to stop here, and say panics produce crises, would be a complete begging of the question. It would be more correct to say that crises produce panics. But that explains nothing. I have defined a commercial panic to be the culmination of a long-continued violation, on the part of the industrial members of a community, of the natural laws of industry itself, and crisis as the result. We must, then, set about finding out wherein society has done violence to, or deviated from the paths prescribed by, the laws of industry, and thus subjected itself to the inevitable penalties of prostration, and injury to public and private interests. It is clear that something must have happened, — some condition of things, of an abnormal character, must have previously existed to superinduce the panic. There must have been a predisposing cause. Panic is only an effect. We must look farther back. We must examine the methods of industry, and especially that "region" of it forming the domain of banks, where Professor Price correctly located the origin of crises, and see what we shall find there bearing on the case. A large number of the diseases "which flesh is heir to" are imputed, and no doubt correctly, to causes over which most people have more or less power or control. A certain condition of the body, the doctors tell us, "predisposes to disease." The cholera comes along occasionally; and those whose habits and bodily conditions have been irregular, or not properly cared for, are said to be "predisposed" for taking the malady. Now, this is exactly what we want to find out in respect to crises. If they "originate in the region of banks," we must see to it that the "little foxes" concealed in those regions are unearthed and made to show themselves.

5. But though industrial crises issue forth from the
region of the banks, like the evils from Pandora's box,
and carry destruction and desolation with them, we must
inquire into more remote influences: we must ascertain
how banks, which are only instruments of industry, are
enabled to so interfere with and derange the natural order
of things in society, as to bring about distrust and loss
of confidence among "vast bodies of people." Panics
do not come without cause : and there is, notwithstanding
Professor Price's *dictum*, generally, if not always, some
good reason for them ; and we must go beyond the banks
in search of it. If we only just examine how trading
power, or what is generally called floating capital, is created, and made available in conducting the industries
of a country, we shall reach a point from which we can
reason with some degree of accuracy. The main object
I have had in view in writing this work has been to eliminate fundamental errors from economic principles and
practices; and not to be able to point out, with some
degree of precision, the causes and consequences of
crises, would be a tacit admission of failure. I must,
therefore, appeal to what I have laid down as self-evident
or demonstrated, for what we are in search of; that is,
the remote causes of crises, and point out wherein business men and banks violate natural laws.

6. Let us refer once more to postulate 35, which lays
down the proposition that the bulk of trading power, or
trading capital, dealt in, in the loan, improperly called
the money market, results from the discount by banks of
bills given for goods. It has been ascertained in London,
that only three per cent of the receipts and disbursements
of banks consists of money, of which but the half of one
per cent is metallic money. The other ninety-seven per
cent, then, consists of something else than money. A part
of it is what may be called cash capital, or the savings of

industry, — the surplus of income over outgo, — or net profit. This is mostly held by bankers; and monetary science would be advanced, if a few bankers in London and New York, or elsewhere, would analyze their business for a year or so, and ascertain how much of their deposits are thus made up, and how much of discounts placed to the credit of customers. We should then know very accurately how to trace "inflation." I have estimated that four-fifths of the capital, or trading power, loaned by banks, is derived from bills and other securities, and devices for the transferrence of debts and credits, growing out of the sales of goods in course of preparation and distribution, from the hands of laborers to those of consumers.

7. Bankers use the balances of customers; but it is evident that such balances as are the results of saving, or are not the proceeds of discounted bills, which they also trade on, are not susceptible of expansion, except by the addition of the profits of new investments. It will therefore follow, that the field of inquiry is narrowed down to one or two classes of customers; namely, men engaged in active production and distribution of commodities, and speculators. In order to make the subject clear and demonstrated, we must trace the operations of a community through a cycle of years embracing a crisis, which I shall treat as a chronic industrial malady, and not as a mere momentary occurrence. We will start with what may be called a normal state of things, or, after labor and production have recovered from long depression resulting from a crisis. Laborers, producers, manufacturers, and distributors (the latter class includes bankers and merchants) are working together on sound economic principles (except so far as legal restrictions, such as protection, and erroneous dogmas about bullion and foreign trade interfere). "The outlook of the future," as it is said, is

favorable. There are no commercial or financial clouds visible, and people generally set to work. Everybody "makes haste to grow rich." Goods are cheap, and so is labor; but everybody is busy. Men willing to work can find employment. There is an equilibrium between supply and demand. This equation is indicative of a healthy condition in a country. Goods are bought and consumed as fast as produced. Bank dividends which have ruled low for several years begin "to look up." Bank stocks rise; and new banks are, in consequence, formed, and old ones grow careless about the bills that come to them. They have no means but customers' respectability whereby to determine whether a bill is the result of a sale of goods, or of a resale for speculation. Prices of goods necessarily answer to the rise in stocks of banks on an increased demand. When people are well off and "making money," they consume more. With rising prices, speculation sets in. Everybody wants "to take a turn out of the market." Each new purchaser gives his bill; and each seller takes his bill to the bank, and has it turned into trading power. The same goods are "discounted" over and over again. The disease of which I am treating "grows on what it feeds on."

8. The number of banks, especially in the United States, where there is a standing bonus of eighty or ninety per cent of paper money offering for capital to embark in that business, increases; and all banks of issue vie with each other in keeping out as large an amount of "circulation" as practicable. The increase of the volume of money adds to the inflation of goods, and labor and production are greatly stimulated and greatly increased. Everybody fancies he is growing rich, and enlarges the sphere of his operations. The importer of foreign goods, as well as the maker of domestic goods, exerts himself to the utmost; and the demand for labor raises the price

of wages. Blasting-furnaces, rolling-mills, car-builders, railway-projectors, cotton-growers, speculators, and manufacturers, and so of workers, producers, and manufacturers of woollen and nearly all the great "staples," including "breadstuffs," work "with a will," and of course their products increase in demand, both for consumption and speculation. Bills are greatly multiplied in number, and are increased in amount; and the banks "discount" (to use an expression of an eminent British economist) "mightily." [1]

9. This "fool's paradise" goes on generally for some years, say four or five, after the commencement of the "good times" when supply and demand were "at par" with each other. Excessive demand for consumption is accompanied by excessive demand for speculation. The two kinds have gone together; and the banks have promptly turned the trading power of goods into capital, to sustain the inflation of values. These institutions, now, acting on the wise advice of the eminent banker, Nicholas Biddle, already quoted in Chap. XXIV., are the first to take alarm. They first catch the panic, and promptly curtail their discounts. Is this "unreasoning panic"? or is it the return of reason and sober judgment after a period of partial insanity? They only think now of themselves and of the moment. The first thing the banks do, and which, if it does not precipitate the panic, certainly intensifies it, is to force their customers to sell their goods at a loss; and thus, in an effort to save themselves, there is an indiscriminate slaughter of traders. This causes what Mr. Biddle points out, "the return of the notes in circulation, or their equivalent," by those who owe them; and the banks, looking only to their own immediate necessities, have not stopped to ascertain who

---

[1] Bonamy Price on the error of the Bank of England in curtailing discounts in times of crises.

are sound and judicious traders, or who are mere speculators for a "turn in the market." Thus they, too, must suffer from their own acts.

10. We have now reached the point in the industrial cycle when "great bodies of people" who have deposits in banks catch the contagion, and those who have bills maturing become distracted about the wherewith to meet them. They all rush to their bank to draw their balances in cash; but the banks owe three, four, or five times the amount of cash in hand, and have no alternative but to stop specie payments. This, of course, stops the "run" on the banks; but it does not help the traders materially. The Bank of England has played that *rôle* three times since its present organization in 1844: viz., in 1847, 1857, and 1866; and the banks of the United States as often. Thus it appears that the banks first lead their customers "into temptation," and then "deliver" them over to "evil." They reverse the Lord's prayer. The effect of these causes leading to panics, and followed by what I have termed chronic crises, will be more fully stated in the next chapter. Here we may pause to inquire what laws of industry have been violated to bring about such a revulsion? who are the criminals? and are they the results of bad methods supported by bad laws? But, before answering these pregnant questions, I will, in the next chapter, illustrate by examples from history the pertinency of the foregoing description of a part of an industrial cycle.

11. Enough has now been said to show, beyond dispute, that the panic of 1866, like all others, followed by a collapse of credit, or a crisis in industrial affairs, was not the cause, but the effect, of an unsound and long-existing condition in most if not all kinds of industrial workers engaged in the growth, production, manufacture, and distribution of goods. The motive power, so to

speak, which sets the wheels of the industrial machine
in motion, is the desire of the members of the community to benefit themselves, or perhaps, strictly speaking,
the necessity that mankind is under to produce food,
clothing, and dwellings in the first instance, and then to
procure luxuries, and lay up something for old age and
for their offspring. If this end could be accomplished
through natural processes, and be strictly held to the
action of natural laws, there could be no such things as
crises. We have seen that artificial methods form a large
part of the causes leading to the point in the cycle of
years when distrust, and finally entire loss of confidence,
take place among the members of a community in each
other. It is not, therefore, "unreasoning panic" that
precipitates the break-down of credit, but the too sudden
return to reason on the part of the whole industrial community. The failure of one or two hitherto trusted
commercial houses fires the magazine or pricks the
bubble.

12. In considering the great influence of the Bank of
England on public financial opinion, and its pernicious
policy of first leading on to inflation by countenancing
an artificially low rate of interest, and, when symptoms
of unsound trade have set in, rapidly "running up the
rate," I pointed out the fact that the natural result of such
policy was to sow the seeds of the disease, and then precipitate a crisis. The directors have taken the trouble
to deny the correctness of this charge made against
them. But they might as well deny that they are responsible for changing the rate at all. Mr. Seyd, in his
work quoted in one of those chapters on the bank, has
pointed out that these changes of the "rate," from two to
as high as six, eight, or ten per cent, have occurred over a
period of years about eight times to a similar change on
the part of the Bank of France once. Hence I have

ѕоme reason to assert that the Bank of England is the head and front of crises in Great Britain. She has well earned the epithet of "panic-maker." I have also shown that this mischievous policy is the result of having all its own capital invested in government securities, which it ought to hold in cash as a margin of security. It is idle nonsense to talk of the British monetary system being sound and scientific, while this policy is pursued.

CHAPTER XXIX.

INDUSTRIAL CRISES CONTINUED. — THEIR EFFECTS AND REMEDIES.

1. IN my last chapter I defined industrial crises, and traced their causes back to original principles having their "seeds and weak beginnings" in motives of gain. I would here remark, that I have accepted the common practice of using the term crisis as a continuing condition of derangement and depression in the industries of a country succeeding a "panic." Strictly speaking, the term is one defining a turning-point, and momentary as to time. But, by general consent and practice, it is used to define the period of depression until a return to a healthy condition of industry. It will also be seen that I am not writing a history of crises, which would of itself make a volume, and one which ought to be written.

2. I propose to describe one or two to illustrate more particularly how they come about, in order to see if we can get at a scientific remedy. Like skilled physicians, economic writers must first make up a diagnosis of industrial and social maladies, and prescribe such remedies as seem best calculated to mitigate or wholly cure the evils in question.

3. Professor Price truly said, "the origins of crises are somehow connected with banks." Mr. E. G. Spaulding, formerly a member of Congress, and father of the "greenback" currency which President Grant once thought "the best the world ever saw," shall testify as to the causes of the crises of 1837 and 1857. In his "Centennial Address" to the Bankers' Association in 1876, entitled "One Hundred Years of Banking in America," Mr. Spaulding says, speaking of the banks of the United States, "On Jan. 1, 1837, the bank circulation of the country, according to the treasury reports, was $149,000,000. By Jan. 1, 1843, it was reduced to $58,000,000: a ruinous fall of prices ensued, and wide-spread distress and many failures was the consequence." Going back, Mr. Spaulding tells us, "in the seven years, from 1830 to 1837, no less than three hundred and four new banks sprung into existence, with a nominal capital of $145,000,000, and $59,000,000 of circulation. . . . The loans increased from $200,000,000 to $525,000,000."

4. Those who have carefully read the last chapter will see, that such an increase of bank loans could by *no possibility* have taken place, except by the increase of bills. This increase of bills could *by no possibility* have occurred throughout a whole country, except by resales of goods in a rising market for speculative purposes. In fact, the goods must have come to be, in their entire aggregate, represented not less than two or three times in the loan market. As bills are averaged at two months, they would aggregate in the discount ledgers of the banks for the first year (1830), $200,000,000; and in the last year (1837), $525,000,000. Thus, supposing these bills to have been all founded on sales and resales of goods, we find they have increased, in the seven years, considerably over two and a half fold. Such an increase of circulation would have been impossible, but for the large increase of paper

money. This will give some idea of the enormous amount of inflation effected wholly through the banks of issue and discount of that period.

5. Still speaking of the same crisis, Mr. Spaulding says, referring to the outbreak of it in 1837, —

"Each day developed some new case of insolvency on the part of the banks and individuals. Finally the distress extended to all classes of business; credit was destroyed; the panic became general, when, in May, 1837, all of the banks of the country suspended specie payments."

6. He next comes down to the great crisis of 1857, of which he says, —

"This crisis, like the revulsion of 1837, was caused by too great an expansion of credit. Debts in all forms became excessive. The railway system had been largely extended on borrowed capital," etc.

These extracts from Mr. Spaulding's account of American banking will serve the purpose of illustration; and I shall only briefly refer to British experience, where equal disasters were brought on by exactly similar causes. Mr. Spaulding's address is very valuable evidence of the impolicy of tolerating banks of issue, or the issue of bank notes at all, in any form or manner. It would have been more appropriate to have called his address, " A History of the Disasters arising from the Issue and Use of Bank Notes in America for One Hundred Years," or it might have been entitled, " One Hundred Years of Banking in America, demonstrating the Erroneous Policy of Delegating to Banks the Prerogative of the Nation to Issue Paper Money for Private Gain." The last title would have been very appropriate, as well as very impressive.

7. I will only add, in reference to the greatest and most disastrous of all crises through which American industry has ever passed, — namely, that of September, 1873, from which the country has only just emerged after five years

of severe depression, — that it was due to the same description of causes as those stated by Mr. Spaulding as
having superinduced the crises of 1837 and 1857. It
may be observed, that, although the paper currency of
the United States is now at par of gold, there exists an
immense inflation of credit, as shown in Chap. XXIV.
Nevertheless, the wages of labor, and the market value
of goods, are still low.[1] But let not those who are clamor-
ing for " more money " suppose that this condition will
long continue. The business and wealth of the country
have quadrupled since 1840 ; and we must, therefore, take
that into the account in considering the crisis of 1873.

8. The experiences in Great Britain in the matter of
crises, both before and since the re-organization of the
Bank of England in 1844, have been similar to those in
America, and are ably described by numerous economic
writers. That of 1825 may be taken as a fair sample.
Mr. Courtney, M.P., and Mr. Henry Dunning McLeod,
have given short but graphic descriptions of this crisis
which set in in December of that year. In the latter part
of the year 1824, there prevailed a large amount of inflation in paper money and bank discounts. Labor and
goods had been steadily rising in market value from the
bank resumption in 1820, and were already excessive.
This condition, I have shown, begets numerous bills,
which the banks freely turned into trading power by discounting. Capital, of course, was abundant and cheap.
Just at this time the Government recognized the independence of the Spanish-American colonies, and a new
field of speculation suddenly spread itself before the peo-

[1] This was written in March, 1879. It is now March, 1880; and the progress
of the cycle has made rapid advance. Wages have everywhere risen. Prices have
gone up in even a greater ratio, and men are everywhere striking for still higher
wages. How long will it be before the inevitable crash will come? Who will answer
his question? Paper money — bank notes wholly — has increased $40,000,000 in
a year, and goes on increasing.

ple. A large number of new banks of issue were started,
each with from four to a dozen branches which acted as if
they were independent banks. The shares of these new
banks were nominally £100, and, with only £5 paid, often
sold for £40, so anxious were the people to rush into banking. The volume of paper money was raised a hundred
and twenty per cent in a little over a year. The Bank of
England competed with the mushroom banks for its share
of the circulation and discount business, which was swelled
ratably with the volume of notes. This state of things
went on increasing in intensity for a year. We are told,
" Princes of the blood, nobles, members of Parliament,
bishops, clergymen, lawyers, doctors, merchants, clerks,
and mechanics joined in the universal saturnalia of speculation." Such a scramble to get rich existed once in
France, over a hundred years before, in the palmy days
of John Law. In December, 1825, the inevitable crash
came ; and nearly everybody was pauperized. Maiden
spinsters, governesses, clergymen, lawyers, doctors, and
the thousands of usually prudent people, who had ven-
tured all they had in bank stocks, and South American
and Mexican schemes, lost all ; and a universal cry of
distress went up throughout the land. But though the
losses of this period, directly traceable to the banks of
issue and discount, amounted to or were estimated at
£150,000,000 sterling, the country went through another
almost similar experience during the next ten years ; and
the crisis of 1837 was the result. New losses and fresh
distress were thus superinduced ; and a period of six or
seven years of depression led to the passage, in 1844, of
Sir Robert Peel's Bank Act, limiting the issue of bank
notes to those then in circulation, and abolishing all other
than those of the Bank of England within fifty miles of
London. But this did not cure the evil. Three more
crises have since occurred ; viz., in 1847, 1857, and

1866, to which the one of the current year, 1879, may be added.

9. Here we have presented, in a brief but authentic form, evidences on an immense scale of the correctness of the principles I have stated. We have irresistible testimony of the logical formula of "like causes produce like effects." We find logical reasoning and practical facts conspiring to show that the place where crises are "hatched" and panics are started is "in the regions of banks" of issue and discount. The excessive issue of notes renders possible the excessive discount of bills founded on sales or resales of goods, and must, therefore, be held to be the incipient causes. The first stimulate the latter. An increase in the volume of currency and discounts reduces the market value of money and trading power, and exactly, and *pari passu* therewith, a rise in the market value of labor and goods. Convertibility, it will be seen, is no remedy for the evil. The remedy, so far as currency is concerned, is to be found in the plan I have laid down in this work, and more particularly in Chaps. XXIV. and XXVI., for the issue of money of all kinds, and in the draft bill for an Act of Congress following.

10. This exposition of principles will not be complete without pointing out how so much evil results to industry by crises. To reach a clear logical conclusion, we must consider the basis on which a large proportion of industry is conducted. It falls to but few to start in life with what is called "cash capital." The farmer either rents his farm, or buys it by paying down a certain amount. The merchant, with rare exceptions, is possessed of no more than ten to twenty-five per cent of cash capital, and not unfrequently begins wholly on credit. The banks do business on a very moderate margin. They trade largely on "other folks' capital" deposited with them for

convenience and safe keeping, for more or less of which they pay interest. The Bank of England and the national banks of America invest their capital, in part or in whole, in public securities, and rely mostly or wholly on borrowed capital to trade on. The specie they hold is merely borrowed. It belongs to depositors. The Bank of England, as I have shown, holds about one pound in thirty of specie against the latter amount of instant liabilities, and maintains itself by its prestige and great facilities for borrowing out of the cash held in the Issue Department to cover notes. Hence the intense sensitiveness of the managers in respect to the trade in bullion.

11. This is the normal condition of these great and greatly predominating institutions in Great Britain and the United States. Every person of the most ordinary powers of ratiocination must now perceive how these oft-recurring heavy depreciations in the value of goods, lands, etc., wipe out, as with a sponge, these margins on which nearly all classes conduct their industries. There has been a gradual rise in prices, and a corresponding increase in the means for manufacturing trading capital through a period of some years. All kinds of industrial business have responded to this all-pervading influence. Industry has, in fact, steadily adapted itself or yielded to the causes stated. Then comes the period in the cycle when sober reason re-asserts itself, and panic is the result. The whole system topples down ; values shrink, thirty, forty, fifty, and sometimes more, per cent. Those who felt strong with thirty per cent margin, now find themselves beggared. The banks have compelled them to sell their property at a loss, in order "to return their notes or their equivalents." Many banks are in straits, and large numbers fail.

12. We have now examined the whole period of an industrial cycle in the two most conspicuous countries

where banks of issue most predominate. We find these cycles continually recurring in greater or lesser degrees of similarity. I remarked, in passing, in paragraph 9, that the remedy, so far as paper money was concerned, had already been pointed out in previous chapters. That remedy can only be found, as I have shown, in abolishing bank notes and supplying paper money by the state, through a department wholly separated from the exigencies of finance, national and private, and selling it, pound for pound, dollar for dollar, for gold or silver coin.

13. But what inferences are we to draw from the almost entire freedom from panics and crises which exists in France, where there is only one bank of issue, and where the Bank of France notes are sold for gold? This bank, unlike the Bank of England and the two thousand banks of issue in the United States, has not all, or nearly all, its capital derived from shares, invested in public securities. Unlike the Bank of England, it discounts commercial paper "mightily." It is not, like the British bank, a dealer to a preponderating extent in foreign and railway loans. Mr. Seyd has shown this in his work on the "Error of the Note Issue of the Bank of England." When the English National Bank gets into a strait, it finds all its share capital, and half of other folks' capital which it trades on, invested in government and other securities, including railway debentures and foreign government stock, which have fallen in market value, and cannot be sold to relieve itself without a heavy loss. There is nothing, then, left for it but to "pray to Hercules" to come to its relief.

14. I now ask British and American statesmen to ponder over these facts, and see if they cannot find a remedy in the suggestions I have made, and in assimilating the banking systems to a condition similar to that which has given to France freedom from crises, and in conformity

with the natural laws of industry. The first step is, unquestionably, to get rid of bank notes. Furthermore, I
say emphatically, if banks are to be allowed to suspend
payment on occasions of great panics, let the principle be
extended to all classes, temporarily. This is what the
Bank of France did to all its customers, in 1872, by an
Act of the National Assembly, which granted an extension
of time for payment of bills (*vide* chapter on Bank of
France). Such a law would prevent the banks destroy-
ing their customers to save themselves, and would serve
to stop panic, and enable prudent men to liquidate their
own indebtedness, instead of being forced into insolvency.
But I predict, that, with a sound monetary system, panics
and crises will cease, as in France. "Like causes produce like effects." Q. E. D.

CHAPTER XXX.

INDUSTRIAL CRISES CONTINUED. — HOW "PROTECTION TO
DOMESTIC INDUSTRY" COUNTERACTS THE NATURAL ORDER
OF THINGS, — FIRST CAUSING EXTREMELY HIGH PRICES
AND OVER-SUPPLY ; THEN, BY RE-ACTION, EXTREMELY LOW
PRICES : THUS SUPERINDUCING AND INTENSIFYING CRISES.

1. A SIMPLE statement and analysis of the protective
system will serve to show the fundamental error on which
the system rests. Its object is to build up or enlarge the
scope of certain classes of industries by the imposition
of taxes sufficiently high to exclude, to an adequate degree, the like productions of foreign countries. The public
at large, who are the consumers, are thus compelled to
buy the goods of the home producers and manufacturers
at a materially enhanced price. The immediate result is,
not merely the addition of the amount of the tax to the

price before set on the protected goods, but also a profit on the duty paid. For instance, where an importing merchant was before content to sell for twenty-five per cent profit, and a protective duty of forty per cent is enforced (and the conscience of the protectionist is often not satisfied with less than sixty, eighty, or even one hundred per cent), he adds the forty per cent, and a twenty-five per cent profit on that, making the whole fifty per cent; and all this in addition to the cost of transport, insurance, agency, etc.

2. This is a brief but true statement of the purpose and desired effect of protection. Let us inquire who are benefited and who are injured by the plan. When industrial pursuits are left entirely to the natural laws, or to the distribution of natural causes and forces, it is obvious that a just equilibrium will be maintained by the action of supply and demand. If one country, or *the people of one country* (which is the more correct way of expressing it), purchase the productions of the people of other countries, they must pay for them with the productions of their own labor, or with articles — such, for instance, as gold and silver — which they obtain or produce by such labor; and, as stated in postulate 44, "all trade continually tends to balance itself, or to equilibrium." Hence it logically follows, that all interferences with this natural tendency to equilibrium, on the part of governments, is injurious to the general interests, just to the extent to which their power and influence can be made effective.

3. But the economist, who seeks to establish true principles, has to analyze the general effect of these artificial methods of building up home industries. Discarding entirely from view the higher sense of eternal justice and fitness of things, or what might be supposed to be the sentiment and purpose of the Creator of all things, in regard to the whole human family, we shall find enough

in the demoralizing effect of protection on the people who it is claimed are benefited by it, to utterly overthrow the theory on which it is founded. In other words, the practical effects at home demonstrate the fundamental error of the system. The fact is, the capital and the labor which are thus artificially attracted into the protected industries, are not, to any material extent, drawn from foreign countries. Let us, then, see where it comes from in the United States. No one will pretend to assert that the capital and labor employed in countries like France and Germany, where protection still rules, were drawn from Great Britain, Russia, China, or the United States. Why, then, should the protectionists of America claim that such has been the case in respect to the latter country? It is absurd to claim that such has been the case. Experience, as I shall clearly demonstrate, shows that both the capital and the labor employed under the hot-house system of establishing manufactures in the United States, as in all other countries where the system still lingers, *are diverted or attracted from other home callings and industries into those which the State seeks to build up by imposing on all consumers protective duties or taxes. It is a tax on all for the advantage of a few.*

4. The argument set up by protective philosophers, that in time protection brings about such an amount of home competition as to cheapen the protected articles, and make them more abundant, than if the law did not offer a premium for the diversion to them of capital and labor, is a mere begging of the question. It is an assumption which overthrows the system itself. To appeal to the facts, let us take the leading protected industries of the United States as examples. These consist of the productions and manufactures of iron, steel, and every thing connected with the construction and operation of railways, iron ships, and cotton and woollen goods. The manu-

factures in question existed in a very healthy and growing
condition prior to the great civil war, the exigencies of
which afforded both the excuse and the opportunity to
those who are ever ready to avail themselves of such
catastrophes to get their hands into other people's pockets, to establish the present vast system of public plunder.
Congress and the nation became demoralized by that great
struggle ; and a system worse than that of Spain in the
palmy days of Ferdinand and Isabella, from which that
country has not yet recovered, became firmly fixed on the
United States.

5. These are simple historical facts. We have now to
trace out the results. It may fairly be claimed, that had
"a revenue tariff" been established, — that is, a tariff
that would have yielded the largest amount of revenue,
if you like, — instead of the one that was passed, and
remains still in force (the proceeds of which, so far as
"protection" was effected, have gone into the pockets
of a small number of individuals who monopolized those
privileged productions), it would have inured to the nation, and have been applied in liquidation of the public
debt and reduction of taxation. It is not claiming too
much to say, that such a revenue tax would have paid
off the entire debt by this time ; and the burden would
have fallen lighter on the general public than it has
during the fifteen years which have elapsed since the
close of the war. In making this very obvious claim, it
is simply saying that the protective system has benefited
certain limited classes of individuals who embarked and
continue in these industries, say to the aggregate extent
of one hundred millions a year. This will become apparent when we analyze the effects on other industries, and
will hardly be denied by any.

6. Take the conspicuous case of iron and steel rails,
on which a duty equal to about $28 a ton was imposed.

This, together with the cost of transport, agencies, and
other incidental expenses, raised iron rails to $80 and
steel $120 a ton in 1872.   Engines, cars, and other rail-
way supplies, went up accordingly. These enormous taxes
built up a limited number of great capitalists, and ruined
thousands and thousands who invested their means in
providing the much-needed highways of civilization. The
laborers employed in these stimulated industries were not
benefited. They were drawn from other, and in many
instances more congenial, occupations. An inflated currency, also, tended to increase all prices, as measured by
it, still more : so that, after all, the increase in the wages
of labor did not benefit the working classes ; as the cost
of their living rose in proportion. This is always the
effect of a protective system. By drawing both labor and
capital from other industries, which do not come within
the category of protection, the prices of the productions
of the latter sympathize with those of the general mass
of commodities, and rising prices engender speculation ;
and so "the disease grows on what it feeds on," till the
inevitable day of disaster bursts like a thunderbolt on the
whole community, and universal crisis sets in. Now, had
the tax on foreign rails not been made prohibitive, but,
say, $10 a ton, there would have been a large revenue
therefrom, and the price of rails would never have ruled
higher than $60 for iron and $90 for steel descriptions.
Such a diminution in cost would have greatly increased
the consumption ; and the country would have been supplied with thousands of miles more railways, at less cost,
than it now possesses ; hundreds of millions of additional
wealth would have been created by such means ; and the
increased revenue would have gone, as I have shown, to
the liquidation of the public debt, instead of into the
pockets of a small class of capitalists, who alone have
been profited.

7. Looking a little below the surface of things, we shall find that these protected industries, prior to the crisis of 1873, drew both capital and labor away from farming, — that is, from the production of cotton, wheat, corn, and other farm products, which engage three-fourths of the entire population of the United States. Farming is by far the most important industry of the United States, which possesses an almost boundless extent of rich and cheap wild lands. The products of agriculture far exceed in value all others put together, and the sop of protection held out to the farmers is wholly a delusion. Canada is the only competing country; and the market price of the leading farm productions of both countries — such as wheat, corn, butter, pork, and beef, as well as cotton — is determined by the foreign demand. Therefore, the farmers of the United States are humbugged into the belief that a duty of thirty or forty per cent on most of those products benefits them ; when in fact their admission into the United States free would produce no appreciable effect on their market values, because the surplus of both Canada and the United States is exported to transatlantic countries, which set their selling prices at home. But this is a digression from the purpose of this chapter, which, however, I could not resist making.

8. To return to the argument. The effect of the American protective system has been, as I have pointed out, to draw labor and capital from agricultural pursuits, or which would have gone into such pursuits, and drive them, by means of the bounty offered by the Government, into the classes of manufactures I have mentioned. An immense stimulus was thus given to all the manufactures of iron, railway supplies, and woollen and cotton goods. Everybody became anxious "to make hay while the sun shone," and the business was largely "overdone." The wages of labor rose so high that farmers were unable

to compete with those engaged in manufactures, and the surplus of their productions diminished or remained stationary ; and the lines of steamships had to be reduced in numbers and tonnage. This helped to maintain the price of farm products at home. But in 1873 this condition of things rose to such a point of inflation that all that was needed was a spark to set off the combustible mass. The failure of the banking firm of Jay Cook & Co. supplied the spark of fire, and precipitated the explosion, perhaps by a few months ; for it was inevitable.

9. It will now be seen how important a part protection played in the vast system of American industries, thus suddenly wrecked in September, 1873. Hundreds of millions of capital had been diverted or abstracted from investments into which it had grown up, and then formed a part of the prior industrial system. Though agriculture had been depleted of a portion of its means and labor, it was for a time sustained by the enhanced demand for its productions, and consequent increase in price ; but, when the general paralysis came on the country, it, too, suffered severely. As it was the last to feel the stimulus of the inflation mania, so was it the first to recover. It will not be disputed that the class of industries which suffered most severely and were longest depressed by the crisis of 1873 was essentially that which had been, and still is, most heavily taxed for "protection to domestic industry." The demand for these "protected" articles was greatly diminished by the panic; and the pressure to sell, to meet liabilities to banks and others, caused a heavy fall in prices. A vast army of laborers were turned loose, without employment, and were compelled to beg, or work for a bare subsistence. The country was overrun with "tramps." Farmers were able once more to employ labor at a low rate, and then followed a yearly increase in the quantity of all kinds of farm products.

If it had not been for the failure of crops during the last two years in several European countries, "breadstuffs" would have been a drug in the American market. The abundance in America came most opportunely for the needs of Europe.

10. Thus it appears that the impediments imposed by governments on the natural order of the industries of the people continually tend to disturb those industries, and superinduce, intensify, and prolong industrial crises. Even if we were to admit that certain great industries have been fostered to the extent claimed by the illogical reasoning of the protectionist, if reasoning it can properly be called, the destruction of capital and the injury to labor must far exceed those doubtful advantages. A single year has sufficed (I am now writing in March, 1880) to tide Great Britain over the "hard times," caused partly by the failure of two harvests, and partly by overproduction in former years.

11. I have said nothing of over-consumption. It must, however, be taken into account. "Over-consumption" relates chiefly to capital, but in a lesser degree to goods. It is when large amounts of capital are drawn from productive and paying business, and becomes irretrievably sunk in unproductive undertakings. Thus, vast sums were drawn from the general industries during the first eight years of the cycle I have described, and were either wholly sunk, or the time of payment became so uncertain and long deferred as to materially enhance the inciting causes of the crisis of 1873, as well as in all preceding ones. There is, no doubt, a considerable degree of extravagance engendered by the inflation of values and the consequent high prices of labor, as well as goods. Men spend more on their personal comforts, embark in wilder speculations, and squander more on luxuries, in such times. The thoughtless do not take cognizance

of the "rainy days,"—of the changes in fortunes, or the periodic recurrence of crises. This heedlessness of economic principles leads to more or less "over-consumption." There is no great warehouse in which this class store the superabundance of to-day to supply the pressing needs of days to come.

12. If the principles of economic science were better understood by public men, and a knowledge of them could be more widely diffused among the people, the evils of over-production and over-consumption would gradually be reduced to a minimum. When the evils I have pointed out as largely resulting from protection in the United States shall become so great, and of such frequent recurrence, as to bring forward a new class of public men, and a purer system of public administration results therefrom, the country will assuredly throw off the baneful trammels of protection and monopolies fostered by the States and federal governments. The great Union of States has prospered in spite of these unnatural interferences with industry. Not protection, but free trade, among forty States and Territories has been the mainspring to this prosperity.

13. We have now seen how protection first checked the development of agriculture, stimulated manufactures, by attracting capital and labor in an unnatural manner from other callings, and then, causing a plethora of such unnaturally fostered products, utterly broke down, inflicting immense and long-continued suffering on the whole community, but more particularly on the laboring classes ; and then, by an equally logical result, unduly drove an excessive amount of capital and labor back into agriculture. It first produces very high prices, and then, by its break-down, creates very low prices ; while true economic science teaches that steady employment in all pursuits, and equability in prices of goods and labor, are

most conducive to general prosperity, and the happiness and advancement of society.

14. France, like the United States, has been in the main a prosperous country, not by reason of shutting out foreign productions, but because of a wide expanse of well-cultivated country, cheap communication, and a well-organized system of general industry. Much, too, is due to the saving and industrious habits and characteristics of the people. But, had her statesmen emulated Great Britain in the breaking down the absurd and altogether useless barriers of protection, France would to-day out-rival all nations in her home industries and her foreign commerce. She now has a fairly good system of government, and only needs a commercial system founded on the laws of nature, or the true principles of industry, which permit men to buy and sell where they please, and not where a few interested members of society determine for them, to greatly expand her industrial energies. Her first consideration, as viewed by the economist, should be a moderate revenue tariff, and a treaty of alliance with Great Britain and the Latin nations, which would enable her to disband half her armies.

CHAPTER XXXI.

INDUSTRIAL CRISES. — THEIR CAUSES AND REMEDIES FUR-
THER CONSIDERED. -— THE CONCLUSION.

1. IT appears from the facts stated in the last two chapters, and the logical deductions drawn therefrom, that industrial crises revolve in nearly equal cycles of time in those countries to which they are peculiarly indigenous. It was also pointed out as an historical fact, that those countries having scientific systems of banking and

currency, governed by the natural laws of industry, have
for a long period been almost wholly exempt from these
periodic disturbances.   There are still other considerations, to which I invite the attention of economists and
statesmen, relating to causes, as well as effects and remedies, which have not yet had sufficient discussion.   I
have shown how those causes, leading to distrust, panic,
and crisis, had their beginnings in the great facilities
afforded by banks of issue and discount for expanding
their circulation of notes, and, concurrently therewith,
the volume of trading capital, by discounting commercial
paper.   It will be recollected that I estimated that eighty
per cent of the entire trading capital dealt in in the loan
market consisted of the proceeds of bills given chiefly
for goods in course of production and distribution, and
pointed out that the chief source of inflation was to be
found in the multiplication of these bills.   The reader
will please keep these facts in mind.

2. I now propose to inquire what part is played by the
remaining twenty per cent of capital, which expands only
by the slow process of the savings of industry, and the
general surplus of production over consumption.   The statistics on this subject are hardly better than guess-work ;
though by a careful analysis of bankers' accounts for a
considerable time, and in numbers sufficient to give close
approximations, it might be possible to reach a tolerably
accurate estimate.   The late Lord Overstone estimated the
net annual savings of the whole of Great Britain to have
been, some thirty years ago, about £150,000,000 ; and we
may accept that as the best we have.   We may now claim
it to have risen to £200,000,000, — say $1,000,000,000.
In the United States it will be larger, owing to a greater
industrial population, and to the rapid development in
the value of new lands continually brought into cultiva-
tion, which is as solid a source of wealth as any other,
and is as permanent and reliable.

3. Here is a question of the very gravest description for economists, and especially statesmen, to weigh. If we only pause, and grasp the subject, we shall see that the continual tendency to a plethora of this kind of capital is a matter which forces itself on our consideration. The effects of a crisis destroy a certain amount of this kind of capital, or actually acquired wealth; but there is a great fund, so to speak, placed by members of all industrial communities beyond the reach of destruction by crises. The owners of this wealth become more conservative, as well as those who hold it in trust, in consequence of these disasters and losses; and hence the accumulation goes steadily on, even in times of depression. Hence, also, the rate of interest becomes very low for loans of such capital, and it is sought by all to lend or invest it on the highest order of securities. It has thus happened in Great Britain, and now lately in the United States, that these governments have been able to fund their debts at very low rates. The secret of Mr. Sherman's funding $500,000,000 of 6 per cent debt at 4 per cent is due to this circumstance; and, had he understood the economic question better, he could have effected it at 3.6 or 3.5 per cent just as readily. The crisis of 1873, and the destruction of confidence in other more permanent investments, taken in connection with the fact I have stated about the accumulation of wealth, are still in active operation (May, 1879); and unless new fields for investments of a more permanent character are opened, or a new mania for speculation in goods and railways sets in speedily, the balance of the debt of the United States can readily be funded in 1881 at 3 per cent. Mr. Sherman is only, after all, "the fly on the coach-wheel," which fancied he had "kicked up all the dust."

4. It was wholly due to this tendency to a plethora of

acquired wealth that enabled England to fund her debt at 3 per cent; and a time may come when it can be reduced by the sale of terminable annuities, or otherwise, to 2 per cent. The rate in the public markets just now for loans on government securities, in London (May, 1879), is 1.5 and 3 per cent. Consols may soon be at a premium; and United States fours may go to 10 premium under a long-continued distrust of other securities of a permanent character. I have pointed out, however, that the main cause of crises is the discount of paper given for goods, and multiplied by resales for speculation. But the matter of accumulated capital is a problem of vast proportions. If men cannot find fields for safe and paying investments, there will be a tendency to spend more, or, more correctly speaking, *there will be a diminished motive to save, and an increased and stimulated over-consumption.*

5. This brings us directly to the point demanding the attention of economists and public men, — What can be done to enlarge the sphere of profitable investments in permanent undertakings? We shall understand the breadth and length of the subject by asking a few questions. *First,* Is there a limit to the productive enterprises of the world? *Second,* Are we near that limit? To which I am ready to answer, there is a limit, with our present methods of conducting the industries of the people, though very far from being as yet reached. This is my answer to both these questions. Then comes the pertinent and really perplexing question, What can be done to improve our methods of production and distribution, and provide an abundant field for investments of a permanent character, available and easily reached?

6. I have now broached the greatest problem of modern society, and the greatest ever considered by the economist. The tendency to the accumulation of wealth in a

few hands has often been considered before. This result of modern society has been regarded by many as setting a limit on the equitable distribution of the results of labor, and, in consequence, of the productive capacity of the people. It certainly must be acknowledged, that the motive to individual effort is diminished when men see great monopolies fostered by legislation and encouraged by laws made almost wholly with the view of promoting the interests of those who have acquired in any way the control of vast properties, and especially of the improved methods of distributing goods and transporting passengers.

7. Paine proposed, a hundred years ago, to limit the accumulation of capital by taxation. Various plans have been discussed ever since the days of Aristotle, who was, in a sense, a communist. He advocated public tables, to be supplied at the public expense, where all might assemble, and live alike. It is not my purpose to enter upon a long disquisition on this subject, which is daily becoming more and more a topic of agitation. The method of co-operation seems to be a success, and in that direction the solution of the problem may be found. It has gained an extensive footing in Great Britain, though little in the United States. It is as yet almost unknown in America, which fosters by legislation monopolies in all forms. The legislatures of States as well as of the Union have become the instruments to do the bidding of those who control railways and conduct the chief manufactures of the entire country. In these bodies men are "bought and sold like sheep in the shambles."

8. The subject I am considering opens up the whole question of taxation, in which sounder and more equitable principles are yearly gaining ground in Great Britain, where the whole income of the state is derived from a few articles, and these mostly belonging to the class known

as luxuries, and an income tax, which to the largest extent falls on those enjoying the accumulations of past industries and such as have drawn the higher prizes of life, which is the most equitable method of taxation.

9. In the United States, there has not been force, knowledge, or virtue enough to reach even a stepping-stone towards an equitable system of taxation. Legislation is more or less controlled by a system of "lobbyism," organized and backed by combinations of capitalists who find their advantage in protective duties and the issue of paper money. The Federal Government is deficient in the matter of leadership in Congress. Forty committees in the House of Representatives, and thirty in the Senate of the United States, whose presiding officers are appointed by barter and bargaining, divide the legislative duties, and are the judges of what measures are appropriate for Congress to pass. Thus, Congress has become a sort of "impossible body," as some eminent public man once characterized it. Those who administer the government are often without influence in the Legislature, in which they have no seats. It has become a system of cabals devoid of unity of purpose or action, and is totally at variance with any possible theory of parliamentary government. The members of both Houses concern themselves chiefly about the patronage to public offices ; and hence spend a large part of their time in " President making," as it is, no doubt, very properly called, or in subsidizing out of the national treasury various industries.

10. The American system was, perhaps, well enough suited to a sparse or wide-spread population possessed of state administrations, when the whole did not exceed four millions. But now, with a population twelvefold that number, and a vast accumulation of wealth, it does not fulfil the ends of a free and still rapidly expanding people. The " spread-eagleism " and vague " stump oratory " of

fifty, or even twenty, years ago, begin to pall on the tastes
of the people.   Universal suffrage, as in France in the
days of the second empire, has become the key to monopolies.   The conventions of parties form an *imperium
in imperio*, and name the deputies they wish to have
voted for at the elections by those who stand in the
light of constituents.   These nominations are all but
universally sold to those who can pay most in cash, or in
promises of official positions.   Even the presidency, as
well as the senatorial honors, is in this way sold, like the
Roman Empire at one period, to the highest bidder.   Civil
Service Reform, so successful in other constitutional countries, is at this hour "a snare, a mockery, and a delusion"
in the United States.   Neither party has presented a well-
digested measure in Congress, to settle definitively the
manner of appointing competent men to fill the offices
of federal or state administrations, which a President is
vainly trying to introduce in one or two departments.

11. These considerations are pertinent to the subject
I am discussing, because they are the stepping-stones to
a more perfect system of industry, having its foundations
laid wide and deep on those principles which are termed
"fundamental," or which are deduced from the action of
the natural laws.   If we are ever going to erect a solid
and durable industrial structure, we must begin at the
bottom, and remove all the rottenness engendered by
generations of class legislation and interference with the
natural order of things, and with the tendency which every
thing has to obey and become the subject of those natural
laws, when let alone.

12. The duty of all well-organized governments is
clearly to protect the weak against the strong, the encroachments of the avaricious rich on the rights of the
poorer millions.   In that respect much has to be done,
both in Great Britain and her colonies, and more espe-

cially in the United States. The methods of gathering up the small savings of industry by rich or professional speculators, for the purpose of carrying out costly undertakings whereby a few reap the "lion's share," are surely such as should be brought under state or national supervision. The granting of franchises of an exclusive nature, or which, within certain territorial limits, are by the nature of things exclusive, — such as the right to use streets in cities for railway lines, or through the country, where competition cannot set a limit to charges for the use of railways, — has become an evil of vast proportions, and in the United States is steadily on the increase. These seem to be cases where some supervisory power, outside of the Legislature, like the courts of judicature, should be established.

13. Finally, the providing of more extended methods for absorbing the continually accumulating savings from labor and income of all kinds must be regarded as "a safety-valve" to industrial pursuits. It would be a most important gain to society if there could be some plan devised to effect this object in conformity with those laws of industry which free labor, or labor free from the baneful trammels of protection imposed by legislatures, always develops. It is to promote this end that I have written this work ; and I hope the labor and thought I have bestowed on it may lead others to follow up the subject in all its branches, and aid in perfecting the economic edifice, so as to give to it the sanction of science and sound logic, in which it is as yet deficient.

NOTES.

I. — Postulates 10–16.

THERE is no better established principle in monetary and industrial science, than that the market value, or trading power, of inconvertible *legal-tender* paper money is in the inverse ratio of its volume. If supply is in excess of demand for industrial uses, it will manifest itself by a rise in the foreign exchanges, and in a premium on the metallic money used as a standard of value. Another circumstance connected with inconvertible paper is worth noticing. If it be not legal tender, it will be quoted at a discount on metal, instead of the reverse, just as the United States legal-tender notes are quoted in Canada, and other places where they are not legal tender. It will therefore be seen, that, under a single issue department, like the Bank of France, it is perfectly practicable to hold legal-tender paper at par with gold, or, as Mr. J. B. McCulloch has it, to raise it above par of gold simply by a limitation of its quantity. But I have elsewhere very clearly shown, that there would, in such case, be wanting the elasticity of metallic money, which, like the waters of the ocean, the lakes, and the rivers, continually tends towards equilibrium.

Although the proposition is self-evident and logically true, it is very little regarded by public men. An analysis of the circulation of the Bank of England, during its twenty-one years' suspension, shows very conclusively, that the market value of the bank note fluctuated in conformity with the overruling law of supply and demand. And, in March (1878), we see the effects of contraction, both by the surrender of over $40,000,000 of national bank circulation in the United States, and of some $15,000,000 of legal-tender notes retired under the so-called Resumption Act. Both kinds of paper money have risen to within three-fourths of one per cent of gold par. What effect the overvalued silver coinage, just now being set afloat, may have on the future value of paper money will require a little time to determine; but it is as certain as that the earth revolves on its axis, if the Silver Law remains in force long enough to produce a circulation anywhere from $100,000,000 to $200,000,000, both silver and paper will fall to the level of the market value of the metal; and furthermore, if the paper inflationists succeed in getting out more paper, silver in its turn will be driven out of circulation, and will be at a premium, as measured by the paper standard. The laws of nature are immutable; and there will then be three measures of value, and traders can take their choice.

The Bank of France is now (March, 1878) in the seventh year of suspension, but its notes have been held at par with gold by the limitation placed on their issue. So also has the value of silver coin been, in like manner, maintained by the cessation of its coinage the moment depreciation set in. Every schoolboy ought to learn this self-evident fundamental principle : that every thing having market value is subject to the great governor of values.

II. — POSTULATES 35, 36.

THE distinction between the two kinds of capital, or trading power, dealt in, in the loan market, is very obvious. As before stated, it is so clear that bankers and loan brokers might readily separate them in their accounts. A general statement of the proceeds of all bills discounted, which supply the chief trading fund of a banker, separated from other deposits, would very accurately determine the comparative amounts of the two kinds.

It may sound a little paradoxical to say so, but it is absolutely true, as a matter of fact, the borrowing customer of a banker is a lender to the banker of the value which he lends back again to the borrower. It is the check that does the work, — the check that very seldom is converted into actual money. In effect, the banker simply lends a man back his own property made into trading power by means of the check.

True it is, there is another class who lend to the banker balances of accumulated capital, — the savings of industry, and of income over outlay, — who are seldom borrowers; and the contributions of this class to a banker's stock of trading power he can trust to as a trading margin, though such deposits go into the common pool from which all draw their supplies. This pool, I have elsewhere shown, is also increased in volume, by the usual balances of all sound traders held by them at their bankers to meet promptly any and all emergencies, — such as unpaid bills of customers, returned drafts, etc.

III. — POSTULATE 38.

INASMUCH as the true and natural regulator of the rate of interest, which is the price paid for the use of capital, is the law of supply and demand, all artificial methods of controlling such rate are clearly and fundamentally wrong, and injurious to the industries of the people. In my chapters on the Bank of England, I have pointed out the fact, that the practice of the bank of raising and lowering the rate was justified, on the plea that it was necessary to "act on the exchanges" in order to regulate the trade in bullion. I wish to make the case quite clear, as to the effect of the practice on the business affairs of the country. The rationale is, that the raising of the rate makes *dear capital*, and *dear capital makes dear goods*. Consequently it prevents the shipment of *all kinds of goods* as well as bullion, and thus acts injuriously on the general trade. This amounts to logical demonstration, and shows the bad effects of the practice of the bank of meddling with the natural regulator of the loan market.

This fundamental truth will become still more striking, when we consider that the sales of goods create the bills discounted in the loan market, where they constitute a preponderating proportion of the trading power loaned. There can be no pretext set up that the trade in bullion, which the bank seeks to control, *is, in any respect whatever*, different

in principle from that of the trade in any other commodity.
The prominence, therefore, given to the bullion trade by
newspaper writers, merchants, and bankers, is wholly without justification, and simply misleads the public. There is
no mysterious relation, as implied in Mr. Seyd's plan of "establishing a more equitable working system between bullion
and interest." The idea is an offshoot of the old "mercantile theory." Mr. Seyd might, with equal propriety, set up a
claim in favor of cheese or any other commodity that is the
subject of foreign trade, as "all things dealt in, in domestic
and foreign trade, exert an influence on the .price of capital
in the ratios of their respective gross values." The bullion
theory is an absurdity.

IV. — CHAP. XI.

THE following excellent exposition of the errors respecting the *balance of trade* is from the pen of a practical business man in New York, — Mr. Charles H. Marshall: —

[From "The New York Herald," Jan. 23, 1878.]

THE BALANCE OF TRADE. — ABSURDITY OF THE THEORY THAT
WE ARE RICHER BECAUSE WE EXPORT MORE THAN WE IM-
PORT. — AN ELUCIDATION BY CHARLES H. MARSHALL.

To the Editor of the Herald.

IN the excellent report of the committee of bank officers, submitted to the meeting at the Clearing-House, occurs a reference to
the improving condition of the country as shown by the so-called
"balance of trade," which is said to be at present in our favor
instead of against us, as in previous years; and the writer of the
report would lead one to infer, that, in his opinion, this is a desirable condition for a nation to occupy permanently in respect to
its commercial transactions. Now, I have no disposition to criticise a document so faithfully and ably written as this report, and
which it is hoped will produce the best results in averting the passage of the silver swindle; but it seems to me that this "balance
of trade" theory is a delusion which ought to be dispelled, as facts
show that what we are accustomed to call "a favorable balance"
is in reality an unfavorable one, and that, instead of regarding the
existence of the former as a subject of congratulation, it is in
reality an indication of national poverty.

Now, what are the facts in regard to the "balance of trade," so termed? They are these : Creditor nations — nations which draw largely of the world's wealth, consequently rich nations — generally show what we would call an unfavorable balance of trade. A single example will suffice. In 1842 the exports of Great Britain exceeded her imports by some £38,000,000. But was she then in a prosperous condition? Far from it. On the contrary, poverty and starvation were everywhere rife. The wages of the best laborers averaged but six to seven shillings a week, while in the manufacturing districts it seemed as if ruin must overtake both employer and employed. From 1854 to 1876 the imports of Great Britain were largely in excess of the exports. In no year has this excess fallen much below £24,000,000 (exclusive of bullion and specie), and in 1876 the preponderance of imports over exports (not estimating specie) was £118,378,111. From 1854 to 1874 — a period of twenty years — the excess is estimated at £1,107,855,114. This includes both specie and bullion.

Clearly, then, England has been growing poorer during this period, according to the "balance of trade" theorists. But has she in fact? A morning paper published a long article, a few days since, to prove that she is becoming gradually impoverished, — spending her capital and savings, so to speak ; but, somehow or other, she does not seem to show it. Pauperism has decreased within her borders ; taxes have been diminished (notably the custom duty on sugar, which yielded £5,000,000 per annum, and which has been done away with altogether) ; her commerce has steadily increased ; her fleets cover every sea ; she raised last year, by a purely revenue tariff, £19,994,882. Is her poverty so very serious, after all?

Now, take our own case. From 1855 to 1875 the "balance of trade" was in our "favor" (so termed) but three times, and always in times of panic and commercial disaster ; while during the periods of our greatest prosperity and most rapid growth the "balance of trade" has been against us. In other words, we have in seasons of prosperity ostensibly bought from, more than we have sold to, foreign countries. In 1858, after the panic of 1857, the conditions were reversed, and we had a "favorable" balance of $8,672,000. In 1862 it was $1,315,000 ; and in 1874, after the panic of 1873, it rose to $18,876,000. All these three periods were certainly not prosperous episodes in our history.

With the exception of the above period, the "balance of trade" was invariably against us, and from 1855 to 1875 amounted to

$2,410,721,000. Will any one contend that this showing indicated poverty, while the present indicates wealth? I should hardly think so, if facts be consulted. But consider if it is not absolutely essential that a country which does a profitable business with other nations should show a "balance of trade" against it? I, for instance, ship 1,000 barrels of flour to the Liverpool market, which cost me, say, $5,000. I expect to sell them at a profit; and as a matter of fact I do realize on my venture, say, $1,000. I thus have a sum amounting to £1,200, or thereabouts, the total result of my shipment. I buy with this sum £1,200 of Manchester cottons, which I import into the United States. The custom-house returns show here an excess of imports over exports, on this one transaction, of $1,000. But am I poorer? Am I not richer to the extent of this sum, and is not the country of which I am a citizen richer as well?

The late Mr. Horace Greeley used to consider that a Utopian prosperity consisted in a condition of society where all should sell and none should buy. This is what "protection" in vain seeks to accomplish. But when Mr. Evarts said, on a late occasion, that, if we would sell to foreign nations, we must buy from them, he uttered a truth which annihilated the "balance of trade" theory at a blow. And I will add, that, if we sell at a profit to foreign nations, we must buy from them, as expressed in money values, more than we give; else we are trading at a loss. True it is that our present exports are gradually liquidating our debts abroad; and, so far as we are doing this, we may congratulate ourselves: but we cannot point to it otherwise than a proof that we are not rich. When real prosperity comes to us, and our debts are cancelled, it will be found that we will return (as all should wish we may return) to a condition of trade when, our capacity to consume being increased, we shall take largely of foreign products; and if our imports then exceed our exports, according to custom-house valuations, there will be nothing in this to create apprehension. On the contrary, it should inspire confidence and hope.

I am, etc.,

CHARLES H. MARSHALL.

APPENDIX I.

I.

VIEWS OF M. MICHEL CHEVALIER ON THE PREROGATIVE OF THE
STATE TO ISSUE PAPER MONEY.

THE first of the following letters, which the writer had the honor to receive from the above-named eminent French economist, was published in a pamphlet which he issued in London, in 1874, on the erroneous policy of the Bank of England in the matter of its efforts to regulate the price of capital by raising and lowering the "rate," in order to control the trade in bullion: —

[Translation.]

27 AVENUE DE L'IMPÉRATRICE,
PARIS, 7th March, 1872.

DEAR SIR, — I must apologize for the delay in answering your letter of the 26th December. The reason of this delay is the attention which this letter merits. It is perfectly logical, and based on the correct principles of the science of political economy in relation to currency. Unfortunately, most governments ignore or depreciate these principles, and too readily trample them under foot. If the American Government had conformed to them during the war of secession, their enormous debt would have been smaller by hundreds of millions. If the Government of France had even a faint knowledge of these principles, it would not have issued such a dangerous amount as 2,800,000,000 of francs ($560,000,000) of paper money, with the possibility of internal trouble.

It might be well to quote the words addressed by the Swedish Chancellor Oxenstiern to his son, when the young man was about to visit the courts of Europe : "Go, my son, and see with how little wisdom the world is governed."

I am therefore much impressed by your letter, and the pamphlet which accompanied it, — "A Plea for Uncle Sam's Money," — and have been waiting to find time to reply at some length. But I fear I may do wrong to defer longer, as this might lead you to believe that your communication is indifferent to me, when the contrary is the case. And, besides, why should I write you a long letter? I have not to convert you, since on the whole we are of the same opinion.

The fundamental principle on which you base your arguments [theory] is, that the power of issuing paper currency belongs to the state, and is one of the essential attributes of the state for the same reason as the coining of specie, or metallic money. This principle being conceded, the granting of the power, without compensation, to a company of private stockholders, is in the nature of a feudal monopoly. Perhaps, if it were sold to such companies for its value, and the proceeds paid into the national treasury for the benefit of the public at large, no grave inconvenience would result to the nation. (This is a delicate question to examine and determine.) But the giving it without an equivalent is an unjustifiable sacrifice of public interests.

In the years 1833 and 1844 this subject was under consideration in the British Parliament, and resulted in a remarkable exposition of principles, entirely in accordance with your ideas. The two most considerable personages who took part in these discussions were, first, in 1833, Lord Althorp, then Chancellor of the Exchequer in the Liberal ministry of Earl Grey; and in 1844, Sir Robert Peel, then First Lord of the Treasury. Lord Althorp, not having a clear idea of what was done afterwards, — the division of the Bank of England into two departments, the one for the issue of notes, and the other for banking, — and fearing the confounding of the two in the hands of the Government, became excessively cautious; but he thought the profit of the issue should belong to the Government.

Sir Robert Peel supported the same views in more decided language in a passage of his speech in the House of Commons on the 6th of May, 1844. The reason which led the Parliament of Great Britain, in that year, to agree to the proposition of that statesman, and abandon the idea of reserving to the Government the benefit of the issue, administered directly by the Government itself, was the prejudice of the English nation for customs consecrated by time and tradition. He presses in this speech that sentiment in the following striking words: —

"The true policy in this country is to work as far as possible with the instruments you have ready at hand; to avail yourselves of the advantages which they possess from having been in use —

from being familiar — from constituting a part of the habits and usages of society. They will probably work more smoothly than perfectly novel instruments of greater theoretical perfection. If we disturb that which is established, let us have some good practical reason for the change."

I shall feel obliged, my dear sir, to be informed of the progress of this discussion in America ; and I beg you to accept my distinguished consideration.

MICHEL CHEVALIER.

H. Bowlby Willson, Esq., New York.

The following is the passage in Sir Robert Peel's speech, first referred to by M. Chevalier, which he kindly furnished with his letter above given : —

"Some have contended, and I am not one to deny the position, that, if we had a new state of society to deal with, the wisest plan would be to claim for the state the exclusive issue of promissory notes, as we have claimed for it the exclusive privilege of coinage. They consider that the state is entitled to the whole profits derived from that which is the representative of coin ; and that, if the state had the exclusive power of issuing paper, there would be established a controlling power which would insure, as far as possible, an equilibrium in the currency."

II.

[Translation.]

27 Avenue de l'Impératrice,
Paris, June 17, 1876.

Dear Sir, — I received a long time ago your pamphlet, " The Money Question," in which you did me the honor to insert one of my letters. I have delayed, from day to day, to thank you, and now, when I write, incur the risk of my letter no longer finding you in London. This would vex me much. I shall therefore be greatly obliged if you will write me a few lines on the receipt of this.

I have to observe the sound doctrine, — the privilege of issuing bank notes (paper money) ought to be reserved to the state which should derive the advantages and profits. You are right in maintaining this opinion, and it is what must finally prevail in America. But, besides this which I have already communicated to you by letter, I have something else to say. It is, that ten years ago I advocated this opinion in a series of articles bearing my name that appeared in the " Journal des Débats." This newspaper, being

highly esteemed, you will probably find in some of the Paris Clubs.
The numbers in which these articles appeared were the 4th, 11th,
and 16th February, 2d March, and one in May, 1864. I do not
recollect the exact date of the last, — it may be the 6th, 7th, or
8th. If you find them, I should like you to read the observations
on banking generally. But the point on which I have mainly insisted is, that in future the right to make and issue bank notes
payable to bearer should be reserved to the state; that is, to whoever directs the United States Government.

I remain, dear sir,

Faithfully yours,

MICHEL CHEVALIER.

H. Bowlby Willson, Esq.,
30 Montague Place, Russell Square, London.

III.

THE STATE ISSUE DEPARTMENT FOR INDIA.

The following information respecting the introduction
of paper money into India was kindly furnished the writer
by direction of the Marquis of Salisbury, Chief Secretary
for India, and will be interesting, especially to American
readers: —

India Office, S.W., 8th April, 1876.

Sir, — I am directed by the Secretary of State for India, in
council, to acknowledge the receipt of your letter, dated 24th
March last, requesting information regarding the metallic and paper
circulation in India, for publication in a work you are preparing on
this subject with reference to the principal commercial countries of
the world ; and I have now to reply to your questions in the order
in which they appear : —

1. The denominations of silver coins in India will be found on
reference to sect. 6 of the accompanying Act relating to Indian
coinage, with which I am directed to furnish you.

2. The total amount of silver coined and issued during the last
twenty years (1856 to 1874-5 inclusive) is stated to have been
£142,190,605 ; but there is no means of stating the amount in circulation in India.

3. The amount of paper circulation in India, as it stood on the
1st January, 1876, was, rupees, 112,158,630 (about £11,110,000).
The denomination of notes so circulated were for 5, 10, 20, 50, 100,
500, 1,000, and 10,000 rupees, each.

4. These notes circulate, not only in towns, but commonly throughout India; and, though at first not generally understood, appear now to be highly appreciated by the people.

5. This question (which related to the economizing of metal by the issue of one or two lower denominations of notes so as to meet the wants of the vast number of small dealers and laborers) is clearly a matter of conjecture, and the Secretary of State must decline to express an opinion on the subject.

6. Gold is not a legal tender in India; but you will find at sect. 4 of the Act which accompanies this letter, the denominations which may legally be coined. It can, however, be considered in the light of bullion only, and fluctuates as such. The coinage (gold) is very limited in India, amounting to £1,178,363 during the years 1855 to 1873-4 inclusive.

I am instructed by Lord Salisbury, to add in conclusion, that information is being collected by the Committee of the House of Commons appointed to consider the important question of the present depreciation of silver, which will be accessible to the public on the issue of their report.

I am, sir, your obedient servant,

GEORGE HAMILTON.

H, Bowlby Willson, Esq.

IV.

The Act referred to in the above letter of Lord George Hamilton, Under Secretary of State for India, went into force in 1861; and below will be found tables showing the denominations of notes issued, and their value in sterling, and the progress and fluctuations in the volume of notes.

DENOMINATIONS OF NOTES.			
10,000 rupees, or £1,000 sterling.			
1,000	" "	100	"
500	" "	50	"
100	" "	10	"
50	" "	5	"
20	" "	2	"
10	" "	1	"

The law authorizing the issue of state notes went into force on Jan. 1, 1861, as above stated; and the following table, made up in each year to the 30th March, shows the result of its operation in pounds, and is taken from "The Statesman's Year Book" for 1876: —

1862 . . . . £3,690,000	1869 . . . . . £9,959,296
1863 4,926,000	1870 10,470,883
1864 5,350,000	1871 10,437,291
1865 7,427,327	1872 13,167,917
1866 6,898,481	1873 12,864,037
1867 8,090,868	1874 11,145,191
1868 9,069,569	

V.

VIEWS OF GENERAL SPINNER, LATE UNITED STATES TREASURER, ON PAPER MONEY.

TREASURY OF THE UNITED STATES,
WASHINGTON, Feb. 8, 1873.

DEAR SIR, — Your letter of the 6th inst. has been received.

It is of little consequence, in a practical point of view, whether paper money can be accepted as money in a scientific point of view, or not. It seems to be settled now that it answers, under certain conditions, all the purposes as a circulating medium for which a metallic currency is used in our country. This is an accepted fact, whether it can be demonstrated on scientific principles or not. It will therefore be necessary to accept the fact that paper money can be used as money.

That there can be too much, as well as too little, money is true to a degree, even with an exclusively metallic currency.

I have been drifting to the opinion, that, inasmuch as more circulation is required in most industrial and commercial communities at certain seasons of the year than at other times, the question is, how to give the currency such an elastic quality that it will adjust and accommodate itself to the real business wants of a community at all seasons and times.

Against preconceived opinions, I have come to the conclusion, that, of all the devices that have as yet been proposed, the one to authorize a limited amount of United States stocks, bearing an interest of 3.65 per cent per annum, that would be exchangeable for legal-tender notes, and redeemable with legal-tender notes at all times, at the option of the holder of either, these securities would more nearly satisfy the desired object than any other plan. I mention 3.65 as the rate of interest, because this sum is just one cent a day on one hundred dollars, and would be easily computed; besides, being too low for a permanent investment, and high enough to attract temporary investments when money is abundant.

I hope you will publish your well-digested opinions. The question of finance is the absorbing one now, and will continue to be until it is finally settled. The views of all thinkers on the subject should be drawn out, so that those whose business it will be to settle the question may have the opportunity to examine, compare, and digest them. In this way they will more surely arrive at correct conclusions.

Very respectfully yours,

F. E. SPINNER.

H. B. WILLSON, Esq., NEW YORK.

VI.

TREASURY OF THE UNITED STATES,
WASHINGTON, May 17, 1874.

DEAR SIR, — Your letter of the 15th inst. has been received.

I also received, several days since, your instructive pamphlet on " The Money Question; " and I read it with much satisfaction.

Your criticisms on my plan to prevent the annual alternate superabundance, and, after, painful stringency, in the money marts of the country, is made in a manner so frank and fair that I have no reason to find fault with it or with you.

With you, I agree "in the propriety of preserving the greenbacks, and abolishing the bank paper money." But this is now impracticable. The banks are strong enough to rule both the Government and the people.

The whole tendency of things is altogether in the other direction from what we would have it; and we, and those who think with us, can't help it.

The policy now is, to increase the number of banks and their circulation, and to restrict the treasury issues. So matters will have to drift for a while longer.

I doubt whether any Washington newspaper would publish the letter of M. Chevalier.[1]

[1] This paragraph refers to the refusal of the leading journals of New York to publish M. Chevalier's views in favor of the right of the nation to issue and possess

The whole of your pamphlet ought to have an extensive circulation. It would do much good.

Very respectfully yours,

F. E. SPINNER,
Treas. of the U. S.

H. BOWLBY WILLSON, Esq., NEW YORK.

VII.

Gen. Spinner has lived long enough to see his fears about the power of the national banks to "rule both the Government and the people " of the United States on the currency question, severely shaken, if not wholly dissipated, at least for a time. The danger now is, that the advocates of a national currency, of all shades, having united, and passed a law to issue a silver dollar, overvalued nearly ten per cent, will lose their power to control the public sentiment in favor of a sound specie-paying national currency. There being no need for a silver dollar when the people are satisfied with a greenback dollar equal to and payable in gold, the silver coin will drag the greenback down to its own level of ninety-two cents, *just so soon as enough are got in circulation to rule the market.* It is one of those notable illustrations of the moral of the fable of the dog that lost the substance (of the piece of meat) by dropping it in the stream, to catch at the shadow he saw on the surface of the water.

VIII.

The following remarks or criticisms on the money question in America, including a plan suggested for transferring the national bank issue of notes to the nation, are reproduced from the pamphlet issued by me in London, in 1874, referred to by M. Chevalier in his second, and also by Gen. Spinner in his second letter, already given in this Appendix. The letter, addressed to Gen. Spinner for President Grant, the general had copied and laid before the President, then an ardent "greenbacker," just before his sudden conversion to the pro-bank party.

the profits of paper money. All the pro-bank journals have long closed their columns against the arguments of even the most eminent economists who advocate a State issue of paper money.

APPENDIX II.

VIEWS OF EMINENT AMERICAN STATESMEN AND ECONOMISTS OF PAST GENERATIONS ON THE RIGHTS OF THE NATION TO ISSUE PAPER MONEY, AND POSSESS ITS PROFITS.

1. *Mr. Jefferson's Views.*

The views of Mr. Jefferson are all the more valuable, inasmuch as he took a prominent part in framing the Constitution of the United States.

In vol. vi. of his "Letters to Mr. Eppes," Mr. Jefferson says, —

"In the Revolutionary War of the old Congress, the States issued bills without interest and without taxes. They occupied the channels of circulation very freely, till those channels were overflowed by an excess beyond all calls of circulation. But though we have so improvidently suffered the field of circulating medium to be filched from us by private individuals, yet I think we may regain it."

At p. 140 he expresses himself very decidedly: —

"Bank paper must be suppressed, and the circulation restored to the nation, to whom it belongs."

Mr. Jefferson, in using the words, "the States issued bills," etc., meant the "Congress of the States," and not individual States. The last quoted paragraph is perfectly explicit in saying, "the circulation" must be "restored to the nation." His idea was, that " Treasury bills bottomed on taxes, bearing or not bearing interest, as may be found necessary, thrown into circulation, will take the place of so much gold and silver, which last, when crowded, will find an efflux in other countries, and thus keep the quantity of medium at its salutary level."

At p. 199 he says of this government paper money, —

"If their credit falter" (that is, the national notes), "open public loans, of which the bills alone shall be received as specie. Let banks continue, if they please ; but let them discount for cash alone in every other country on earth, except Great Britain and her too often unfortunate copyist, the United States."

2. *Mr. Calhoun's Views*

are well expressed in the following extracts from several of his speeches. It is proper to explain that Mr. Calhoun was chairman of a select committee of the House of Representatives which reported the first bill for incorporating the Bank of the United States during the session of 1816, when the paper currency was in a very unsatisfactory condition. He favored the plan of a national bank then, as he many times afterwards explained, not because he considered it the best method of supplying "a sound paper currency of uniform value throughout the Union," but because at the time "it was the only one that was possible" to get through Congress. His speech in support of this bill, delivered Feb. 26, 1816, is a very excellent exposition of the true principles of monetary science ; and he strongly insisted on the necessity of making paper money convertible, under all circumstances, into metallic money, and, at the same time, graphically pointed out the evils of a depreciated and fluctuating "medium of exchange." At p. 157, vol. ii. of his works, he says, —

"We have in lieu of gold and silver a paper medium, unequally, but generally, depreciated, which affects the trade and industry of the country; which paralyzes the national arm ; which sullies the faith, both public and private, of the United States, — a medium no longer resting on gold and silver as its basis."

He mentions the significant fact that the banks and banking capital had increased from the one State bank of " North America," at the period when the Constitution was framed, with its $400,000 of capital, to 260 similar banks, with a gross capital of $80,000,000, and a circulation of about a like amount, when there was barely $15,000,000 of specie in the country, and the bulk of that held on government account. It seems a pity that Mr. Calhoun, with such clear perceptions of sound principles, felt compelled to yield to expediency.

Mr. Webster, then a member of the House of Representatives, strenuously opposed the bill reported by Mr. Calhoun, which, eighteen years later, he moved to extend, when the Act was about to expire by effluxion of time. By this time (1834) the two life-long opponents had changed positions on this measure; and we find Mr. Calhoun and Mr. Webster face to face in the Senate of the United States, the former arguing against the Webster bill for the extension of the bank charter. I will quote one illustration given by Mr. Calhoun of the scientific principles of paper money, as applicable to the discussions of the present day as it was then.

"If," said Mr. Calhoun, "we take the aggregate property of a community, that which forms the currency constitutes in value a very small proportion of the whole. What this proportion is in our country, and other commercial and trading communities, is somewhat uncertain. I speak conjecturally in fixing it at one to twenty-five or thirty, though I presume this is not far from the truth; and yet this very small proportion of the property of the community regulates the value of all the rest, and forms the medium of circulation by which all its exchanges are effected." This was a pretty good *guess* at the amount of money of all kinds used in comparison with the gross amount of capital, or trading power, actually employed in conducting the industries of the people, which we now know from actual analysis (*vide* postulate 32). In a subsequent speech (1838) he raises his estimate to thirty to thirty-five per cent. This proportion has no doubt materially diminished since 1834, when Mr. Calhoun made his speech, caused by the more rapid transit and distribution of the products of labor, and the improved methods of banking and clearing houses. I quote another example given by Mr. Calhoun, at p. 347 of the same volume, as illustrative of the principles of money.

"If we turn our attention," he says, "to the laws which

govern the circulation, we shall find one of the most important to be, that, as the circulation is decreased or increased,
the rest of the property will, all other circumstances remaining the same, be decreased or increased in value exactly in
the same proportion. To illustrate: if a community have
an aggregate amount of property of $31,000,000, of which
$1,000,000 constitutes its currency, and that $1,000,000
should be reduced one-tenth part, that is to say, $100,000,
the value of the rest will be reduced in like manner, one-
tenth part, that is, $3,000,000."

In other words, " the trading power of currency is in the
inverse ratio of its volume, all other things being equal " (*vide*
postulate 4). If the volume of money be increased, its
trading power diminishes; and the prices of commodities
and labor will appear to have risen. If, from any cause, the
volume is diminished, the price of goods and labor will
appear to have fallen.

All those who quote Mr. Calhoun's arguments in favor
of a national issue of paper money, — which are sound and
unanswerable, — and attempt to apply them in support of
an inconvertible paper currency, will do well to give heed
to what he said on that subject. Here it is: —

"With these convictions, and entertaining a deep conviction
that an *unfixed*, *unstable*, and *fluctuating* currency is to be ranked
among the most fruitful sources of evil, whether viewed politically
or in reference to the business transactions of the country, I cannot give my consent to any measure that does not place the currency on a sound foundation."

This speech of 1834 discloses the fact that the banks
had increased, from 260, in 1816, with a capital of about
$80,000,000, to 450, in eighteen years, with a gross capital
of $145,000,000, and a corresponding increase of circulation,
but no increase of metal behind the notes, and nearly all of
which was then held by the Bank of the United States.

In another speech, vol. iii. p. 111, referring to the state
of things at the close of the war with Great Britain, he remarks, —

"Specie payments were coerced, with us, by the establishment of the Bank of the United States, and a few years afterwards in Great Britain by an Act of Parliament. In both countries the restoration was followed by wide-spread distress, as it always must be when effected by coercion; for the simple reason that banks cannot pay unless their debtors first pay, and that to coerce the banks compels them to coerce their debtors before they have the means to pay. Their failure must be the consequence; and this involves the failure of the banks themselves, carrying with it universal distress. *Hence I am opposed to all kinds of coercion, and am in favor of leaving the disease to time, and the action of public sentiment and the States, to whom banks are alone responsible.*"

Mr. Calhoun did not perceive the primary cause for the distress produced by contraction, but mistook what is in reality an effect for such cause. The "distress" in such cases results from the circumstance that trade to a large degree is conducted on mere "margins," or capitals, of only ten or fifteen per cent of the credit involved, and hence the shrinkage in value of a currency of ten or fifteen per cent brings ruin on a large class. I could quote much more from Mr. Calhoun's numerous speeches on the currency, to show how strongly he argued in favor of a convertible currency, but must refer to his speeches for such arguments. There are other good arguments relating to the principles of currency in his works, that are too valuable to omit. At p. 240, vol. iii. of his works (speech, Feb. 15, 1838), he very forcibly remarks, —

"I hold sound, stable currency to be among the greatest encouragements to industry and business generally; and an unsound and fluctuating — now expanding and now contracting, so that no honest man can tell what to do — as among the greatest discouragements. The dollar and the eagle are the measure of value, as the yard and the bushel are of quantity; and what would we think of the incorporation of companies to regulate the latter, — to expand, or contract, or shorten, or lengthen them at pleasure, with the privilege to sell by the contracted, or shortened, and buy by the expanded, or lengthened? . . . But I go farther, and assert confidently *that the excess of paper*, as *well as* of its unsteadiness, is unfavorable to the business and industry of the country."

In his speech of March 22, 1838, he declares, —

"I now undertake to affirm positively, and without the least fear

that I can be answered, what heretofore I have but suggested, —
that a paper issued by Government with the simple promise to
receive it in all its dues, leaving its creditors to take it or gold and
silver, at their option, would, to the extent that it would circulate,
form a perfect circulation, *which could not be abused by the Government*, and would be as steady and uniform in value as the metals
themselves."

Again he says (vol. iii. pp. 123, 124), on the same page
(vol. iii. p. 306), —

" If I were to go into the legality of such a currency, I would be
able to prove that it is within the constitutional power of Congress
to use such a paper in the management of its finances, according
to the most rigid rule of construing the Constitution ; and that
those, at least, who think that Congress can authorize the notes
of State corporations to be received in public dues, are estopped
from denying its right to receive its own paper."

I shall close these extracts from Mr. Calhoun's speeches
with a few selected indiscriminately, which seem to have
merit, and a bearing on the currency question, now under
agitation in America.

Of the advantages of a national over a bank currency, he
said, —

" It is a striking advantage over bank circulation in its superior cheapness as well as greater stability and safety. Bank paper
is cheap to those who make it, but dear — very dear — to those
who use it, — fully as much so as gold and silver. It is the little
cost of its manufacture, and the dear rates at which it is furnished
to the community, which give the great profit to those who have
a monopoly of the article. . . . On the other hand, the credit of
the Government, while it would greatly facilitate its financial operations, would cost nothing, or next to nothing, both to it and the
people, and of course would add nothing to the cost of production,
which would give every branch of our industry, — agriculture, commerce, and manufactures, — as far as its circulation might extend,
great advantages both at home and abroad."

" It appears to me, after bestowing the best reflection I can
give the subject, that no convertible paper — that is, no paper
whose credit rests on a promise to pay — is suitable for currency.
It is the form of credit proper in private transactions between man
and man, but not for a standard of value to perform exchanges

generally, which constitutes the appropriate functions of money or currency."

"No one can doubt but that the Government credit is better than that of any bank, — more stable, more safe. Why, then, should it mix up with the less perfect credit of those institutions? Why not use its own credit to the amount of its own transactions? . . . *And why should the community be compelled to give six per cent discount for the Government credit blended with that of the banks, when the superior credit of the Government could be furnished separately, without discount, to the mutual advantage of the Government and the community ?*"

3. *Views and Opinions of Daniel Webster.*

Mr. Webster's utterances on the right of the nation to issue paper currency are particularly noteworthy, as coming from America's greatest statesman and lawyer, and from the circumstance that he belonged to an opposite school of politicians from that of Messrs. Jefferson and Calhoun. The point of difference between the two schools of his time on the currency related to the question of the right of Congress to make treasury notes " *legal tender,*" to which he took exceptions.

In his speech on " The Specie Circular " issued by President Jackson's government, delivered Dec. 21, 1836 (see his " Speeches," vol. iv. p. 271), he says, —

"Most unquestionably there is no legal tender; and there can be no legal tender in this country under the authority of this Government or any other, but gold and silver, either the coinage of our own mints, or foreign coins at rates regulated by Congress. This is a constitutional principle, perfectly plain, and of the very highest importance. The States are expressly prohibited from making any thing but gold and silver a tender in payment of debts ; and although no such express prohibition is applied to Congress, yet as Congress has no power granted to it in this respect, but to coin money and regulate the value of foreign coins, it clearly has no power to substitute paper, or any thing else but coin, as a tender in payment of debts and in discharge of contracts."

On the other hand, Mr. Webster insisted with great force on the right of Congress to issue treasury notes, and make them legal tender in payment of all national taxes. Whether equally logical reasoners may not think that Mr. Webster did not, after all, do a little hair-splitting for party ends, in drawing this nice distinction between making national notes legal tender for debts due the nation, and denying the right of Congress to extend that quality in dealings between man and man, is a question open for consideration. But if the notes issued by the nation are guaranteed convertibility into legal-tender coin, and are not legal tender as between the Government and the public, it is of no real consequence whether they can or can not be made by Congress legal tender in payment of debts generally. He says in the same speech, —

"But when Congress lays duties and taxes, or disposes of the public lands, it may direct payment to be made in whatever medium it pleases. The power to lay taxes includes the power of deciding how they shall be paid; and the power granted by the Constitution to dispose of the territory belonging to the United States carries with it, of course, the power of fixing, not only the price and the conditions and time of payment, but also the *medium* of payment."

At p. 281 (same vol.), he says, —

"I admit that a currency composed partly of bank notes has always a liability, and often a tendency, to excess, and that it requires the constant care and oversight of government.

"I am of the opinion that even convertibility of bank notes into gold and silver, although it be a necessary guard, is not an absolute security against occasional excess of paper issues."

The following extract (p. 284) shows that Mr. Webster was not always careful to distinguish between money, the tool and measure of values, and capital, of which it is only an insignificant part : —

"With great general prosperity, good crops generally speaking, an abundance of the precious metals, and a favorable state of the foreign exchanges, men of business have yet felt for some months an unprecedented scarcity of money."

Most clearly Mr. Webster meant that capital, or loans, were then scarce, otherwise his language is nonsense. Only a few months later the great financial and business collapse took place, followed by the long-continuing crises lasting

over five years. The fatal year 1837 was then "casting its
shadows before it;" and the time was near, when, as Dickens
expressed it, "there was no money, absolutely no money."
Then it was the nation should have stepped boldly in, and
issued currency notes in moderate amounts, to fill the place
of the exploded and trashy bank issues. Mr. Webster
pointed out that the Government, having a surplus revenue,
had locked up all the specie in its various depositories. What
the Government *could have done*, was to have suspended the
collection of taxes, which would have been an immense relief
to the commerce and industries of the country, and issued
paper money convertible on demand for all its requirements.
Thus the opportunity would have been given to set such
money afloat. But it might have done more. It might
have undertaken some large public improvements, — such as
canals, railways, just then coming prominently into vogue,
or even common "post roads," — and thus to have got out
$100,000,000 of paper money to in part recoup the $140,000
of those beautifully engraved, but valueless, notes of exploded
banks. It will be borne in mind, that there was at this time
a large accumulation of public funds, and the question had
been what to do with it.

But let me quote Mr. Webster's reasons for the condition
of things he describes: —

"The agricultural State of Indiana, for example" (p. 285), "is
full of specie: the highly commercial State of Massachusetts is
nearly drained. In the mean time the money in Indiana *cannot be
used*. It is waiting for the new year. The moment the Treasury
grasp is let loose from it, it will tend again to the great centres
of business; that is to say, the restoration of the natural state
of things will begin to correct the evil of arbitrary and artificial
financial arrangements."

Mr. Webster did not clearly perceive that the great financial operations of the world were no longer carried on with
either metallic or paper money, however important a *rôle*
they have to perform, but by bills and other securities given
in payment of goods, which are turned by bankers into trading power. He did, however, great justice to his knowledge
of the fundamental principles of monetary science, when

he laid down in his speech delivered in the United States Senate on the 28th September, 1837, four months after the great crisis had set in, the following broad proposition, which I have set down amongst the postulates (34) : —

" It is the constitutional duty of Government to see that a proper currency, suitable to the circumstances of the times and the wants of trade and business, as well as to the payment of the debts due to the Government, be maintained and preserved, — a currency of general credit, and capable of aiding the operations, *so far as these operations may be conducted by means of the circulating medium ;* and that these are duties, therefore, devolving on Congress in relation to currency *beyond the mere regulation of the gold and silver coins.*"

The Italics in this proposition are mine, as the language is very expressive and explicit. All other Italicized passages are Mr. Webster's own. In another sentence he says, —

" I admit at once, that, if the currency is not to be preserved by the Government of the United States, I know not how it is to be guarded against constantly occurring disorders and derangements."

Again he says, —

" I wish it to be observed, that I am now contending only for the general principle, and not insisting on the constitutionality or expediency of any particular means or any particular agent."

In support of his views, Mr. Webster refers to President Madison's recommendation to Congress, in his message of Dec. 5, 1815, to issue treasury notes. I therefore quote what Mr. Madison then said : —

4. *Views of Mr. Madison on the Right of the Nation to issue Paper Money.*

" The absence of the precious metals will, it is believed, be a temporary evil ; but, until they can again be rendered as a general medium of exchange, it devolves on the wisdom of Congress to provide a substitute, which shall equally engage the confidence, and accommodate the wants, of the citizens throughout the Union. If the operations of the state banks cannot produce this result, the probable operations of a national bank will merit consideration ; and, if neither of these expedients be deemed effectual, it may be necessary to ascertain the terms upon which the notes of the Government (no longer required as an instrument of credit) shall be issued on motives of general policy, or as a common medium of circulation."

On this express recognition by President Madison, Mr. Webster remarks, —

"Here, sir, is the express recommendation to Congress to provide a NATIONAL CURRENCY" (these words are emphasized by Mr. Webster himself), "a paper currency, a uniform currency, for the use of the community, as a substitute for the precious metals, and as a medium of exchange."

At p. 350 Mr. Webster spoke almost prophetically of the times in which we live. He says, "I was beside the Ohio River on a journey, when I heard of the suspension of the banks, and had occasion frequently to express the opinion I am now maintaining : "—

"That a new era had commenced; that a question of principle, and a question of the highest importance, had arisen, or would immediately arise; that hereafter the dispute would not be so much about means as about ends; *that the extent of the constitutional obligations of the Government would be controverted ; in short, that the question whether it was the duty of Congress to concern itself with the national currency* MUST INEVITABLY BECOME THE LEADING OBJECT OF THE TIMES."

The last words were emphasized by Mr. Webster himself, and the "times" he referred to seem to have arrived. The apprehension of the author is, that the inflationists may ruin the efforts of those who desire to have the currency question settled on a sound and durable basis. The pro-bank partisans are using it to great advantage to frighten men of property — the great mass of whom are either interested in banks or ignorant of the principles of money — into exerting their influence against a national paper circulation.

Statistics of the United States (Hand-Book of). A record of the Administrations and Events from the organization of the United States Government to the present time. Comprising brief biographical data of the Presidents, Cabinet Officers, the Signers of the Declaration of Independence, and Members of the Continental Congress ; Statements of Finances under each Administration, and other valuable material. 12mo, cloth 1 00

"The book is of so comprehensive a character and so compact a form that it is especially valuable to the journalist or student."—*N. Y. World.*

What is Free Trade? An adaptation for the American reader of Bastiat's "Sophismes Economiques." By EMILE WALTER. 12mo. 75

* * * "The most telling statements of the leading principles of the free-trade theory ever published, and is, perhaps, unsurpassed in the happiness of its illustrations."—*The Nation.*

LATEST PUBLICATIONS.

Mongredien (Augustus) **The History of the Free-Trade Movement in England.** (Library of Popular Information.) 16mo, cloth 50

"It is a small book, but it contains a great story. It ought to be read by every citizen who can read at all."—*N. Y. Observer.*

Coöperation as a Business. By CHARLES BARNARD. A volume containing a summary of the results of coöperative work in the United States and in Europe, in manufacturing, trade, house-building, etc. 16mo 1 00

SUMMARY OF CONTENTS.—A Hundred Thousand Homes—Fustian and Paisley Shawls—Insuring the Baby's Life—The People's Banks—Interest and dividends— My Lady Shops—Provident Dispensaries—Conclusion.

"A little book of much interest and usefulness, which contains more exact information concerning the practical application of the coöperative principle than any other volume with which we are acquainted."—*N. Y. Evening Post.*

Economic Tracts. (Published for the Society for Political Education).

II. **A Priced and Classified Bibliography of English and American Works** on Political Economy and Political and Social Science, recommended for general reading and as an introduction to special study. Prepared by W. G. SUMNER, DAVID A. WELLS, W. E. FOSTER, and G. H. PUTNAM. 8vo, paper 25

III. **Subjects and Questions** pertaining to Political Economy, Constitutional Law, the Theory and Administration of Government, and Current Politics. 8vo, paper 10

IN PRESS.

The American Citizen's Manual. A practical treatise on the relations of the citizen to government, City, State, and National, and on his duties, responsibilities, and privileges. Edited by WORTHINGTON C. FORD. The volume, while issued in compact form convenient for reference, is planned to give a comprehensive summary of the nature of American administration, local and national, and to supply full information on all the details of the work of a citizen.

Economic Monographs:

A Series of Essays by representative writers, on subjects connected with Trade, Finance, and Political Economy.

The titles of those that can no longer be supplied are omitted.

I. **Why We Trade, and How We Trade;** or an Enquiry into the Extent to which the existing Commercial and Fiscal Policy of the United States Restricts the Material Prosperity and Development of the Country. By DAVID A. WELLS. 8vo, paper, ... 25 cents.

III. **The Tariff Question** and its relation to the Present Commercial Crisis. By HORACE WHITE. 8vo, paper, ... 25 cents.

IV. **Friendly Sermons to Protectionist Manufacturers.** By J. S. MOORE. 8vo, paper, ... 25 cents.

V. **Our Revenue System and the Civil Service: Shall They be Reformed ?** By ABRAHAM L. EARLE. 8vo, paper, . . 25 cents.

VI. **Free Ships.** By Capt. JOHN CODMAN. 2d edition. With a review of the plan of Senator BLAINE and Secretary SHERMAN, for the restoration of the American carrying trade. . . . . . 25 cents.

VII. **Suffrage in Cities.** By SIMON STERNE. 8vo, . 25 cents.

VIII. **Protection and Revenue in 1877.** By Prof. W. G. SUMNER, author of " History of Protection in the United States." 8vo, paper, 25 cents.

X. **An Essay on Free Trade.** By RICHARD HAWLEY. 8vo, paper, ... 25 cents.

XI. **Honest Money and Labor.** By the Hon. CARL SCHURZ, Secretary of the Interior, ... 25 cents.

XII. **National Banking.** By M. L. SCUDDER, Jr., Chairman of the Honest Money League, ... 25 cents.

XIII. **Hindrances to Prosperity:** or, the Causes which retard the adoption in this Country of Financial and Political Measures of Reform. By SIMON STERNE, 8vo, sewed, ... 25 cents.

XIV. **Adulterations in Food and Medicine.** By E. R. SQUIBB, M.D. 8vo, sewed, ... 25 cents.

XV. **International Copyright;** An Historical Sketch, and a Consideration of some of its Relations to Ethics and Political Economy. By GEORGE HAVEN PUTNAM. 8vo, sewed, ... 25 cents.

XVI. **Free Trade,** as promoting peace and good will among men. By CHARLES L. BRACE. . . . . 25 cents.

XVII. **Bi-Metallism.** By the Hon. HUGH McCULLOCH. 8vo, sewed, ... 25 cents.

XVIII. **Labor-Making Machinery.** By FRED. PERRY POWERS. 25 cents.

XIX. **Andrew Jackson and the Bank of the United States.** By WILLIAM L. ROYALL. . . . . . . 25 cents.

G. P. PUTNAM'S SONS,   NEW YORK.